▢ ▢ ▢ POLITICS

ON THE FRINGE

The People, Policies, and Organization

of the French National Front

▢ ▢ ▢ EDWARD G. DECLAIR

Duke University Press

Durham & London

1999

© 1999 Duke University Press

All rights reserved

Printed in the United States of America on acid-free paper ⊚

Typeset in Stone by Tseng Information Systems, Inc.

Library of Congress Cataloging-in-Publication Data appear
on the last printed page of this book.

❏   ❏   ❏   *For my parents, Ed and Betty Lou*

CONTENTS

ix   List of Figures

xi   List of Tables

xiii   Acknowledgments

1   Introduction

11   ONE   The French Far Right: The Legacy of History

32   TWO   The Far Right Reappears: The Creation of the National Front

59   THREE   Initial Success: Election Victories in 1984 and 1986

79   FOUR   Legislative Losses and Beyond

115   FIVE   The Political Agenda of the National Front

138   SIX   The Leadership and Organization of the National Front

172   SEVEN   Voting for the National Front

193   EIGHT   The Far Right in Comparative Perspective

212   Conclusion

225   Afterword

235   Appendix 1: Elected and Party Positions Held by Respondents in 1988

237   Appendix 2: Evolution of the National Front's Political Bureau

239   Notes

247   Bibliography

257   Index

FIGURES

12   1.1 The Families of the French Far Right

49   2.1 Creation of a New Political Party

50   2.2 A Model for the Study of New Parties at Three Stages of Development

70   3.1 National Front Vote, 1984–1988

91   4.1 National Front Vote, 1989–1997

159   6.1 Internal Organization of the National Front

165   6.2 The National Secretariat and the National Delegation

168   6.3 The Circles and Associations of the National Front

177   7.1 1965 Tixier-Vignancour Presidential Vote, by Region

178   7.2 National Front First-Round Score in the 1993 Legislative Elections, by Region

180   7.3 National Front First-Round Score in the 1997 Legislative Elections, by Region

191   7.4 Actual and Potential Universe of National Front Supporters

❑ ❑ ❑ TABLES

43   2.1 The National Front's Share of the Vote in National Elections, 1972–1981

51   2.2 Facilitators of Party Creation

55   2.3 Obstacles to Party Creation

62   3.1 1984 European Parliament Election

68   3.2 1986 Legislative Elections

69   3.3 1988 Presidential Election

72   3.4 Facilitators of Electoral Breakthrough

75   3.5 Obstacles to Electoral Breakthrough

83   4.1 1988 Legislative Elections

86   4.2 Percentage of Votes for National Front Presidential and Legislative Candidates, 1988

87   4.3 First-Round Total Right Compared with Second-Round Front Performance, 1988

100   4.4 1995 Presidential Election, First-Round Results

107   4.5 Facilitators of Party Durability

112   4.6 Obstacles to Party Durability

119   5.1 Issue Correspondence between National Front Elite and French Public

123   5.2 Issues Priorities of National Front Elite

135   5.3 Issues Priorities of Front Elite Compared to Front Supporters and Total French Population, 1988, 1993, and 1995

141   6.1 Composition of National Front Political Bureau, as of 1998

149   6.2 Comparison of Front's Three Leadership Groups

149   6.3 Previous Party and Organizational Affiliations of
           National Front Elite

186   7.1 Evolution of the Vote for French National Front,
           in Percentages

188   7.2 Evolution of the Vote for French National Front
           in Legislative Elections, in Percentages

❏   ❏   ❏   ACKNOWLEDGMENTS

Many people provided support and encouragement throughout the long process of writing this book. I first need to thank Stella Cohen-Scali and Patrick Campistron for helping me translate my original questionnaire into French. Michael Ansaldi, a true polyglot, deserves special mention for his tireless assistance in finding just the right word so that I would not do a disservice to the original thoughts of those I interviewed.

I also thank the twenty-nine *frontistes* who consented to be interviewed for this project. Many of those interviewed have taken on increasingly important roles within the Front's organizational framework; their continued presence at the highest levels of the party's leadership underscores the import of their voices. They were not only gracious, but given the rigors of an election campaign they were surprisingly generous with their time. What sets this work apart from other published works on the Front is that I have not substituted my voice for theirs.

The following people have cumulatively spent many hours in the library tracking down sources for me: Jeff Albright, Eric Byer, Christina Dickert, Carolyn Holmes, and Kelly Koczak. I thank them for their support and help in bringing this project to fruition. Susan Roach, interlibrary loan expert extraordinaire, deserves special recognition for always going that extra mile to uncover sources that were often difficult to obtain. Don Borock deserves special thanks for reading the manuscript when others were unwilling to find the time.

I especially want to thank James Glenn, who provided support and research assistance above and beyond the call of duty. At the French Embassy, Betrand Mercier de la Combe, was most helpful in providing documentary support. And, in France, Albert Philippe provided research support during those crucial moments when I was unable to uncover what I needed in the United States.

Russell Dalton has provided continued support over the long life of this project. His willingness to read and reread early drafts of what was once my thesis only helped to improve the final product. Vincent McHale, Andreas Sobisch, and Frank Wilson read this manuscript in an earlier draft, and provided excellent suggestions for improving the final product. Their comments and criticisms were deeply appreciated.

At Duke University Press, I found tremendous support and sage advice as I entered the world of publishing. Valerie Millholland shepherded this project through the review process, and I thank her for selflessly giving of her time, making solid suggestions, and being very patient as the French continued to go to the polls in the middle of the project. Patricia Mickelberry saw the book through the editing and production process and was very supportive of this first-time author. Her gentle urgency and continued support were significant sources of strength as I endeavored to meet production deadlines.

Le Front National est une force populaire de libération, un

instrument politique de régénération, il est le chemin par

lequel la France peut de nouveau rentrer dans l'histoire.

—Bruno Mégret, delegate-general of the French

National Front[1]

In the aftermath of the 1981 legislative elections, Simone Veil, a former Cabinet minister and European Parliament president, addressed the leaders of the dispirited and scattered forces of the French far right and stated, "You do not represent one percent. You do not exist" (Begeron and Vilgier 1985, 188). At approximately the same time, Christopher Husbands examined the far right's poor political prospects and its inability to attract votes in the country's working-class neighborhoods and surmised that "Specifically in France the working class is apparently almost totally immune to such racist political mobilization" (1981, 92). Other noted experts have sung this chorus. In 1983, Jean-Christian Petitfils concluded his survey of the French far right by stating, "It no longer exists as a political force" (124). More recently, Alain Duhamel commented that "The National Front seems to have stopped making headway and even seems unable to maintain itself at its current level" (1993, 237). Throughout French history, political observers have often underestimated the far right's talent for survival. This is a common approach taken by those who are unwilling to face the far right's incredible ability to redefine itself according to the prevailing political climate. Contrary to the experts' opinions, the French far right is ascendant. It broke into the European Parliament in 1984, became the leading party of France's working class in 1995, and received 15 percent of the vote in the 1997 legislative elections, its highest total ever.

Crafting an obituary for the French far right is clearly a dangerous proposition, given that even a cursory examination of French history reveals a constant appetite for the politics practiced by its representatives; pundits and politicians alike should be more wary of voicing such cavalier attitudes. Although electorally moribund and spiritually bankrupt throughout the 1970s and the early 1980s, the French far right, in the guise of the National Front, has emerged in the latter half of the 1990s as the dominant and most vital force in French politics. The French far right, seemingly nonexistent at the dawn of the 1980s, has successfully transformed itself into the arbiter of French elections. The political resurrection of this important partisan player serves as the central theme of this study.

After a rapid and unexpected rise to political prominence in the mid-1980s, the French National Front endured a series of significant setbacks at the close of the decade. The loss of its parliamentary group in the National Assembly following the legislative elections of 1988, the death of its secretary-general, Jean-Pierre Stirbois, in the fall of the same year, and the dramatic departure of a number of prominent leaders compounded an already difficult situation. These events made it increasingly difficult for the fledgling party to maintain its precarious position in the complex arena of French partisan politics.

According to some, the Front's political survival had become a questionable proposition. Although the National Front was weakened by this turn of events, more recent election results indicate that the party currently attracts the support of approximately 15 percent of the French public. This core electorate has also demonstrated a fierce loyalty that is unmatched by the electorates of the system's other major parties. Moreover, the declining strength of the system's more mainstream parties and the continued political frenzy over immigration has helped the Front rebound from the temporary setbacks of the late 1980s. Weakened mainstream parties and contentious immigration debates coupled with the never ending specter of double-digit unemployment and the unanticipated French hestitation about increased monetary union have contributed to the fertile ground that serves to nurture the political and electoral aspirations of the French far right.

The electoral successes and failures of the National Front in recent years provide an interesting backdrop to the party's continued but uneven development. A brief sketch of its participation in electoral politics since its creation illustrates this point more fully.

Created in 1972, the National Front languished in the electoral arena during the decade of the seventies. Jean-Marie Le Pen, the party's only president, has always insisted on participating in every electoral contest, but the party's constant campaigning failed to produce concrete results until the early eighties.

The Front first achieved national prominence during the municipal elections of 1983 in Dreux. The now infamous political alliance between the National Front and the local organizations of the more moderate and respectable, right-of-center Rally for the Republic (RPR) and the Union for French Democracy (UDF) "had the impact of a bomb in the world of French politics" (Petermann 1986, 81). But its role as a political party of national importance was not established until the 1984 European Parliamentary elections, when it received 10.95 percent of the total vote. The Front's place in the French political party system was subsequently confirmed in the 1986 legislative elections and again in the 1988 presidential contest. The growth of the National Front up to this point had been nothing short of spectacular.

The ability of Jean-Marie Le Pen to wage a national campaign was evident in the 1988 presidential election. The first round of the presidential contest was held April 25, 1988. François Mitterrand, the incumbent president, and Jacques Chirac, then the prime minister, received 34 percent and 19.9 percent of the total vote, respectively; as the top two vote recipients, Chirac and Mitterrand competed in the runoff election. Le Pen, the candidate of the National Front, garnered 14.5 percent of the total, representing well over 4 million votes. Although he did not receive enough votes to qualify for the runoff election, his performance was indeed a spectacular contrast to his aborted presidential bid in 1981. Unable to obtain the required 500 sponsorship signatures to have his name placed on the presidential ballot, a humiliated Le Pen was forced to observe the election from the sidelines.

The National Front began to experience electoral difficulties once Mitterrand began his second seven-year term as president and decided to dissolve the National Assembly. For the National Front, the euphoria of the presidential election was short-lived. The results of the 1988 legislative election provided a striking contrast to Le Pen's performance in the presidential elections. The party received 9.65 percent of the votes in the first round of the elections, but only one National Front candidate was eventually elected. The Communist Party, by comparison, with 11.32 percent in the first round, placed twenty-seven of its candidates in the National Assembly. The National Front's vote was essentially equivalent to its 1986 score, but the number of elected deputies was different because of the reversion from a proportional representation electoral system to the traditional two-round majority system in 1988.

Subsequent electoral contests continued to provide mixed signals. The Front received under 5 percent in the first round of the municipal elections held in the spring of 1989. But after the completion of the second round of balloting, the Front was able to claim a modest success. The party had placed 804 of its candidates on municipal councils throughout the country; the Front's leadership was particularly proud of its success in the important population centers of 30,000 or more inhabitants, where it had elected 237 of its candidates. Although at this point, the Front could not claim to be a major influence in French municipal elections, it had begun to anchor itself in the difficult and important arena of local French partisan politics. The Front's modest gains in the 1989 municipal elections did not mask its political vulnerability; it had a difficult time securing quality candidates to compete in the nationwide local elections.

The results of the European Parliament elections held in June 1989 were more encouraging. The Front once again demonstrated its ability to attract votes in a system of proportional representation, receiving slightly more than 11 percent, enabling it to return to the Parliament with the same number of deputies it had elected in 1984. It would have been difficult for the Front to survive another poor showing, but the attraction it continues to hold over its hardcore supporters attests to the significant role the party and its leader currently play in French politics.

Regional and cantonal elections that followed in 1992 continued to confirm the Front's increased local presence. In the regional elections, the Front received 13.6 percent of the vote. This record result for a non-presidential election enabled the party to elect 239 regional councillors. The Front's renewed electoral vigor continued in the 1993 legislative elections, but, although the party's candidates received 12.5 percent of the national vote, the two-round single-member majority system prevented it from gaining representation in the National Assembly.

Two years after his party was once again denied representation in the National Assembly, Le Pen began another quest for the ultimate prize of the French political system: the presidency. Le Pen's success carried the Front to new electoral heights; he captured 15 percent of the vote and actually improved on his record-breaking score of the 1988 elections. Municipal elections followed shortly thereafter, and the National Front performed well. Although the party's candidates attracted only 6.7 percent of the vote, this translated into 1,075 elected officials; moreover, the Front actually elected mayors to three medium-size cities. A fourth *frontiste,* Catherine Mégret, won election to the mayoralty of Vitrolles in the winter of 1997.[2]

The setbacks that the Front experienced at the end of the 1980s became distant memories as the party achieved success in regional and municipal elections and began to firmly anchor itself in the lucrative arena of local politics. The reversal of the party's fortunes and its ability to persevere are clear indications that the Front is not merely a "flash party" à la the Poujadist phenomenon of the 1950s. Nor can the party be summarily dismissed, as many scholars have done, by labeling its share of the vote a mere manifestation of the omnipresent French protest vote. Survey research evidence indicates that Front voters are not voting *against* the status quo but rather voting *for* the ideas espoused by the party's leadership. In the first round of the 1995 presidential elections, fully 60 percent of those who voted for Jean-Marie Le Pen said they did so because of the party's program. This represented the highest such total for all nine of the first-round presidential candidates; in fact, only 47 percent of Lionel Jospin's supporters said the candidate's program was the factor that most influenced their vote, and only 39 percent of Jacques Chirac's partisans cast their ballot because of his political program (Perrineau 1995). With elected officials at the municipal, regional, and European levels as well as four mayoralties in cities with populations over 30,000, the Front was well situated for the legislative elections that were to take place in 1998.

Originally, National Assembly elections were scheduled for the spring of 1998, but President Chirac, pressured by the austerity measures demanded by the advent of European monetary union, decided to gamble with his massive 80 percent majority in the legislature and called for elections in the late spring of 1997. Although most preelection polls indicated that Chirac's conservative coalition would handily win the elections, the first-round results contradicted the pollsters.

This abrupt call for elections seemed, at first, to catch the Front off guard; nevertheless, the party emerged from the first round of balloting with 15 percent of the total vote. In the context of National Assembly elections, this represents the French far right's highest vote total ever. Although the Front was unable to translate its first-round score into a large parliamentary presence, its strength at the local level has been confirmed by its record-setting score in these elections.

This brief synopsis of the National Front's electoral history provides an overview of the party's development, but it does not explain how the party has successfully entrenched itself in French partisan politics. This study will attempt to answer the how and why questions related to the Front's political evolution.

This study traces the Front's political development from a small, marginalized party to the third largest political force in France after the Socialists and the Gaullists. The party's development is detailed by examining the political experiences and attitudes of the people who helped create and nurture it—the party's primary leadership. This is accomplished by pursuing three different but related avenues of inquiry. The first method of inquiry involves a concerted effort to examine the voluminous secondary literature, both journalistic and academic, that has appeared on the National Front. The second avenue includes a consideration of party documents as well as the memoirs and books written by the leaders of the National Front. This includes works by such party stalwarts as Jean-Marie Le Pen, Bruno Mégret, and the late Jean-Pierre Stirbois. Other frontistes, individuals who are less well-known than Le Pen and Mégret, have also contributed to the party's documentary heritage; such party loyalists as Michel de Rostolan, Roger Holeindre, and Georges-Paul Wagner represent three separate traditions within the political universe of the French far right, and their published political memoirs contribute to our understanding of the party's early development. In addition, the works of former frontistes Yann Piat and François Bachelot, internal documents such as the party's constitution, the various manifestos and campaign literature promulgated during different election periods, as well as detailed ideological defenses of the party's political platform provide additional documentary resources. The final avenue of inquiry complements the first two; it includes detailed interviews with twenty-nine leading members of the Front's political elite (see Appendix 1). The journalistic and academic sources combined with the leaders' memoirs and the historical record generated by the party itself serve to corroborate the information collected during the elite interviews. In essence, the elite interviews serve as a springboard for analysis, but the information collected during the interview process is corroborated and cross-checked by what is available in the public domain.

During the summer of 1988, twenty-nine primary leaders of the French National Front were interviewed for this study. The identification of these party elites began with a positional analysis of the party's leadership, which led to the Front's 1986–88 parliamentary group; elected in 1986 with thirty-five members, the group eventually decreased to thirty-two members after the defections of Yvon Briant, Bruno Chauvierre, and Hervé Le Jouaen. Of these former National Assembly deputies, fifteen were interviewed for this study. During the interviews with the members of the Front's parliamentary group, certain people were repeatedly mentioned as important decision makers who were generally unknown to the general public; this led to interviews with an additional fourteen frontistes. The elite respondents were thus identified by a combination of positional and reputational approaches. Birenbaum (1992b) identifies fifty-two national-level leaders of the Front; twenty-two were interviewed for this study. An additional seven rising political operatives were also interviewed. The high overlap between Birenbaum's list of high-ranking Front elites and those interviewed for this study indicates that some consensus exists on the primary decision makers within the French National Front.

Although conducted in 1988, the elite interviews remain an important source of knowledge about the party's leadership cadre. The respondents' continued presence at the highest levels of the party's organizational hierarchy underscores the important roles they play as decision makers within the Front and as reservoirs of internal party knowledge.[3] Moreover, the elite interviews provide a rare insight into an organization that has so often been reduced to tabloidlike stories that describe only the flamboyant behavior of its leader.

Although the National Front currently plays a pivotal role in contemporary French partisan politics, this was not always the case. A political reality since 1972, the Front was perpetually unable to solidify its position in the French party system; election after election, whether at the local or national levels, the Front ran a slate of candidates only to fail to win representation. As noted, it finally secured its first true taste of electoral legitimacy in 1984. How it succeeded and how it plans to maintain its position are crucial questions; attempting to answer such questions requires strategic data collection. I chose a two-stage strategy. The first stage involved face-to-face interviews that lasted on average one hour and twenty minutes; the second required the respondents to complete a written questionnaire. This survey included mostly closed-ended questions; it also replicated some questions from a previous Euro-Barometer survey.

The Front's political leadership possesses the most intimate knowledge of the party's path to prominence. These individuals have detailed information about the significant strategic choices they made to compete successfully in French partisan politics. They possess firsthand knowledge of the factors that helped or hindered the party's development. They witnessed the party's development at the closest range possible, and they played crucial roles in this process. The elite respondents in this study are simultaneously informed observers of and causal influences in the development of the National Front.

Chapters 1 through 4 trace the political and electoral development of the National Front. Chapter 1 focuses on the philosophical antecedents of the National Front by placing special emphasis on the development of the far right in French politics. The major far right organizations, from Action Française to Ordre Nouveau, the parent organization of the Front, are discussed by examining the links that exist between the Front's current leadership and these other organizations. Chapters 2 through 4 continue this chronological approach but also introduce important theoretical issues about political party development. The National Front's evolution is analyzed by applying the life cycle model of political party development that serves as the focal point of this study. Chapter 2 introduces the model and undertakes an analysis of the political and institutional factors that encouraged or hindered the creation of the National Front. The elite perceptions of party development are critical to our understanding the Front's development: How did these people act? What actions did they take? What decisions were made at the party's creation? Their retrospective perceptions are always examined in juxtaposition to the historical record, thereby creating an automatic check on their version of history.

Chapter 3 details the Front's first national-level success and examines the circumstances that led to that breakthrough; the second stage of the life cycle model serves as the focus of this chapter. In chapter 4, we consider the Front's ability to endure, examining its development from the heady days of early 1988 to the present. Electoral success and failures are addressed, with special attention paid to the Front's future prospects.

A thorough examination of the Front's political agenda is presented in chapter 5. Responses from the elite interviews are compared to data from mass-level surveys, thereby examining whether the Front is in tune or out of touch with the voting public. An attempt is made to present a complete view of the Front's political agenda rather than a narrow focus on the party's most sensational anti-immigrant policies. The constant evolution of the party's political agenda is also considered by combining the elite interview data with the postinterview writings produced by prominent frontistes as well as with campaign documents and other party publications.

The party's organization and the composition of its leadership are the focus of chapter 6. The leadership is examined by introducing the three distinct recruitment paths that lead to leadership status in the Front; the party elite's previous political experiences, education, and socioeconomic background are also analyzed. Considerable attention is paid to the core leadership of the Front, the party's most powerful members, who hold seats on the powerful Executive Bureau. In addition, we introduce the organizational structure, designed to extend the Front's regime beyond the purely political arena.

Chapter 7 examines the Front's mass-level support and the shifts in that support. A combination of aggregate analysis and individual-level survey research presents a comprehensive picture of the National Front voter. Aggregate analysis of electoral data details the special political cartography of the Front's mass-level support, and individual-level survey research helps create a profile of Front voters.

The final chapter introduces far right organizations in other countries and briefly discusses the differences and similarities that exist between these other organizations and the National Front. Concluding remarks stress the omnipresence of the French far right, at the same time highlighting the distinctive character of the contemporary National Front.

As of this writing, the role the National Front plays in the contemporary arena of French partisan politics continues to expand. In the most recent legislative elections, the Front surpassed the UDF to become the second largest political party on the right of the political spectrum. Although the party ultimately elected only one National Assembly deputy, it essentially arbitrated the final results of the legislative contest.

French voters face an uncertain political future in a party system that has seen the legislative majority shift in every National Assembly election since 1981.[4] Given the long period of political stability that predated the Socialist Party's rise to power in 1981, the French voting public is naturally disconnected from its previous partisan ties. In many respects, the National Front has profited from this increased instability in the French party system. Understanding how this previously impotent and marginal political party has exploited this instability and how it evolved to become the only thriving political force in French politics today is the purpose of this study.

THE FRENCH FAR RIGHT:

THE LEGACY OF HISTORY

Le Front National a été jurdiquement créé en 1972, mais

il est en réalité l'héritier d'un certain nombre de tendances

qui sont beaucoup plus anciennes.

—Former National Assembly deputy [1]

The French National Front, relative to other political parties in advanced industrial states, is a new political actor, and its actual political viability is of an even more recent vintage. Though created in 1972, it played virtually no role in French partisan politics until 1983, when it achieved its first minimal electoral successes in municipal and by-elections. The National Front is thus a relative newcomer to the political arena, but as a representative of the French far right, the Front is also a successor to a political tradition that has woven itself in and out of the fabric of French politics for decades. The party is the most recent manifestation of "the extreme right [which] constitutes an unstable world whose structures modify themselves according to socioeconomic conditions and varying political configurations" (Chombart De Lauwe 1987, 13).

To understand the role the National Front plays in the contemporary political arena, we must examine it in the appropriate historical context. The movement was legally chartered in 1972, but much of its philosophical core mirrors a considerably older political tradition. Action Française, the Vichy government under the Occupation, *le mouvement Poujade,* l'Organisation de l'Armée Secrète (OAS), the electoral campaigns of the 1960s, and the student revolts that followed have all contributed to the party's ideological baggage. The links between these organizations and the modern-day National Front are unmistakable when one examines the rhetoric and personnel that it shares with the many far right organi-

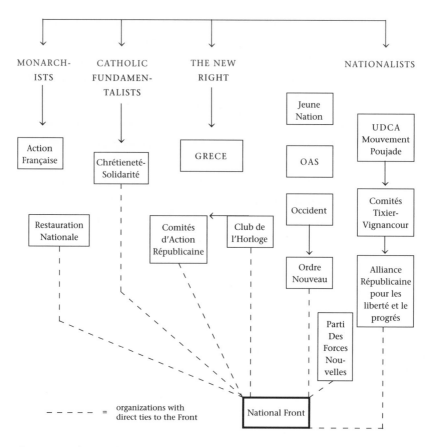

Figure 1.1 The Families of the French Far Right
Sources: Pons 1977 and Charlot 1986.

zations that antedated the Front's appearance on the national political scene. Figure 1.1 outlines, in an abbreviated form, the genealogy of the contemporary French far right.

The Heritage of the National Front

The National Front represents a natural continuation of an omnipresent political tradition in French society. This tradition is characterized by a number of themes: "the belief of a natural order, the defense of certain traditional values, suspicion of democracy—at least in its parliamentary form, xenophobia and even latent anti-Semitism" (Roussel 1985, 95). The leaders, activists, and supporters of the National Front share a political legacy dominated by the extremist movements that have inhabited the underbelly of the French far right for generations. The process whereby the many far right movements melded together to form the National Front is best described by a member of the party's Bureau Politique:

> The National Front was legally created in 1972, but in reality it has inherited a number of tendencies that are much older. Jean-Marie Le Pen's great virtue is that he has succeeded in unifying all of these tendencies, that he has brought them all together to create a coherent force. In the Front, one finds former Poujadists who joined simply because of fiscal or economic reasons, traditional Catholics who are scandalized by the Socialist influence in the church, as well as Algerian veterans disgusted with the failure of Gaullist policy in Algeria. I could list even more of them . . . even monarchists. In reality, a truly determined right has existed since before the Second World War. One needs only to call to mind the problems with the Croix de Feu and the Action Française between the two wars . . . these currents of thought existed and Jean Marie Le Pen inherited them.[2]

The ensuing discussion draws upon this historical richness and briefly discusses the Front's ideological antecedents. The party's direct links to the past are vividly outlined by carefully examining the previous political experiences of the Front's leadership cadre.

Action Française
One of the primary progenitors of the National Front is Action Française. The far right in France has often been defined by its virulent anti-Semitism, and Action Française successfully manipulated the hostility for many years. French anti-Semitism reached a fever pitch with the Dreyfus affair at the end of the nineteenth century. Captain Alfred Dreyfus, a promising young Jewish officer, was accused of spying for the Germans in 1894. His trial, conviction, and subsequent appeal became a lightning rod for all of the anti-Jewish sentiment in France; the episode became a national melodrama that divided loyalties throughout the country. The Dreyfus Affair spawned what many consider to be the first truly fascist organization on the European continent. In response, Action Française was much more than merely anti-Semitic; its leaders effectively utilized the national furor over the Dreyfus Affair to weave

together a number of other far right themes into one coherent whole. Its founders, Maurice Pujo and Henri Vaugeois, originally conceived Action Française as a "republican movement" (Soucy 1986).

Charles Maurras joined the group soon after its creation, and his influence over the organization was immediately apparent. His support and defense of the monarchy became a pillar of the group's ideology. Maurras traced the problems of French society to 1789 and blamed the "four alien nations"—Jews, Freemasons, Protestants, and foreigners—for having contributed to the political turmoil that had followed the Revolution. According to Maurras, a revived monarchy working closely with the Catholic hierarchy would restore order to a rapidly changing society. Throughout the twentieth century, subsequent far right movements repeated Maurras's eloquent justifications of his theories. Nolte contends that "Maurras was the first man . . . who drove conservatism beyond the limits dividing it from incipient fascism" (1965, 116).

The themes espoused by Maurras at the beginning of the twentieth century are today being echoed by the Front's leaders. When asked to contemplate his party's future political viability, this *membre fondateur* parrots maurrassian rhetoric as if no time has passed since the Dreyfus Affair:

> Future obstacles—the lobbies. Very difficult to know, but it may be the Jewish lobby, the Freemason lobby, the Protestant lobby, but they are only lobbies. They don't represent the majority of Jews in this county, nor the majority of Protestants of this country. The Freemasons only represent themselves. All of this nice little world is aligned against us.

Action Française quickly developed into a powerful political machine, and Maurras's break with republicanism firmly entrenched the movement among the radical right. This appealed to many beleaguered conservatives, but especially attracted the stauncher Catholics. Although the leadership of Action Française was dominated by the nobility, "the bulk of its troops . . . came from the lower middle classes and the white-collar professions" (Soucy 1986, 14). Action Française claimed it received some support from all socioeconomic sectors of Catholic France. The organization's daily newspaper was an important source of political propaganda and was required reading in all intellectual circles—left or right.

The extremist politics promoted by Action Française successfully penetrated student organizations. The National Front includes individuals who were very active in such student groups. This National Assembly candidate and Front loyalist recounts his early political experiences as student activist in Action Française:

> I started to get interested in politics when I arrived in Paris in 1934. My first political activity was as a dedicated activist of Action Française at the Law Faculty. While at the Law Faculty, I was a militant activist of Action Française. I was the person in charge at the Faculty. I propagated nationalist ideas and took an interest in most of the students who were also in this movement. And I don't regret anything, because it was in Action Française that I acquired my political culture.

Obviously proud of his prior membership in Action Française, this high-ranking member of the Front has remained committed to the far right's cause for over fifty years. The participation of such individuals in the Front, at the highest echelons, demonstrates how the party creates the perfect environment to nurture hostilities harbored for over a generation. Although integral to Maurras's philosophy, the restoration of the monarchy is not a central element of the National Front's belief system. Nevertheless, monarchists are welcomed and feel comfortable in the Front, and according to this member of the party's Bureau Politique, one can find much of Maurras in the speeches of Jean-Marie Le Pen:

> [F]or example, it's indisputable that Action Française played an important role. There are monarchists in our organization, and one could say that in certain ideas, not on the economic level, but on the level of philosophical values, Le Pen is somewhat close to Maurras. I'm saying that on the philosophical level one can find some of Maurras's ideas in Le Pen's speeches.

Action Française was not only the first such group in France, but it also proved to be one of the most enduring. Its philosophical descendants are now found in Restauration Nationale, which remains committed to a revitalized monarchy. The Front's links to this organization are direct. As this former National Assembly deputy recounts his prior political experiences, he underscores the links between his party's present and the extreme right's past:

> There is in France a royalist current, a monarchist one, let's say traditionalist, OK? And it was to this milieu that I gravitated from

about 1950 until just about 1975. The first political organization I joined, in about 1950, was Restauration Nationale. I began, at that time, by taking on some responsibilities at the local level. I was living in the fifteenth arrondissement of Paris, and from 1950 to 1958 I was one of the leaders of the fifteenth arrondissement section of Restauration Nationale. From 1958 on, I played a more active role at the heart of this movement. I became a lecturer and gave dozens and dozens of lectures over the years, and then I became the secretary-general of the National Political Institute, which is the training organ for the movement—for the young people and the university students in the movement.

Action Française was not an isolated phenomenon. The political environment in the immediate post–World War I years nurtured myriad far right political movements. A number of major and minor political organizations hovered on the extreme right of the political spectrum. One thing most of these newer groups had in common was the belief that Action Française had become somewhat complacent in actively pursuing its political goals. Ironically, Action Française, which was created to move beyond the political conservatism of the more staid Ligue des Patriotes, quickly became viewed as the symbol of the old and ineffectual far right. Maurras's tendency to overintellectualize the political situation failed to attract a steady stream of new recruits to the movement after World War I. Newer, more vital organizations began to siphon off large numbers of potential Action Française activists.

Two of the more visible and vocal organizations during the interwar period were the Faisceau and the Jeunesses Patriotes. The perceived complacency of Action Française in conjunction with the 1924 arrival to power of the Cartel des Gauches encouraged the creation of these new, more activist far right movements. Georges Valois, a protégé of Maurras, laid the foundation for the Faisceau after a trip to Italy in 1924, and Valois's organization was quickly attacked by Maurras in the rightist press. These early fratricidal divisions on the rightist fringe foreshadowed the tumultuous conflicts the contemporary far right would undergo in future years.

Croix de Feu, initially a veterans association, also played an important role during this period. Like Faisceau before it, Croix de Feu benefited greatly from the military mind-set of its membership, which surpassed 450,000 in 1936. At the time, the French left labeled it the most dangerous fascist threat (McMillan 1985). The tight relationship that developed between the far right and the military was to endure and become even more pronounced once the Algerian conflict reached crisis proportions. The links between the military and the far right continue today, the Front encourages and solicits the support of veterans and has created a national network of ancillary organizations to promote and maintain these links. The most important of these organizations is the Cercle National des Combattants (National Veterans Circle), founded by Roger Holeindre in 1985.

Economic chaos and a government scandal of immense proportions pushed the rightist organizations into the streets on February 6, 1934. It is estimated that 40,000 demonstrators, members of all the major groups—Action Française, Jeunesses Patriotes and Croix de Feu—marched on the Chamber of Deputies. This extreme antiparliamentarianism would remain a primary feature of the far right; moreover, it would be a central core of the Vichy regime. Although the revolt did not succeed in destroying the Third Republic, it did bring down the Daladier government.

Vichy

The collapse, after only six short weeks of fighting, of the French forces in World War II brought about the new regime of Marshal Philippe Pétain. Pétain, a World War I hero, quickly took control of the desperate French nation. The National Assembly voted to dismantle the Third Republic on July 10, 1940, effectively putting itself out of business. With little left to hamper him, and aided and abetted by Pierre Laval, Pétain was left to deal directly with the German occupying forces. The causes and consequences of the years under Vichy rule have been endlessly debated by historians; this brief discussion seeks only to underscore the thematic convergences that exist between the French far right and Vichy France, not to resolve longstanding historical conflicts.

Under Pétain, France broke with the liberal mind-set that had dominated the country since the Revolution (Azéma 1993). According to René Rémond, Pétain's National Revolution was nothing but a belated "counter-revolution"; "No more elections, deliberative assemblies, political parties, freedom of the press, or freedom of assembly: those who had never accepted 1789 and liberalism finally got their revenge" (1982, 235). The French far right welcomed this new National Revolution advocated by Pétain; it was finally getting its long-desired political revenge on the forces of liberalism. The establishment of the Vichy regime was in many ways a victory for the French far right. Pétain's political and moral agenda vindicated the political dinosaurs who had remained radically opposed to parliamentary democracy.

Pétain, his ministers, and much of the French polity held the politicians and institutions of the Third Republic responsible for France's quick and humiliating defeat at the hands of Nazi Germany. This was viewed as a most appropriate excuse for dismantling the Third Republic. Antiparliamentarianism was no longer a slogan of the street revolts but rather the law of the land. Pétain's attacks on parliament implied that representative government was indeed unworkable.

In addition, his conception of France under the Occupation mirrored many of the other themes of the far right. Pétain immediately reestablished ties between the state and the Church; the anticlerical sentiments of the 1789 revolution had no place in Vichy. Pétain's France was to be a moral one; he emphasized the centrality of the family in French society, while stressing the need for a higher birthrate. All of these ideas would be resurrected in the 1980s by the National Front; family, religion, and an emphasis on morality have proven to be philosophical cornerstones for the far right, and they continue to form the central core of the Front's ideological foundation. This frontiste, speaking in 1988, could just as easily have been discussing the far right's view of France at the dawn of the Vichy era: "I think that France's primary problem is the almost total absence of any moral authority. . . . There is a great deal of moral, spiritual, and ideological confusion."

The Front's rabidly pro-natalist policies are easily traced to Pétain's desire to increase the feeble French fertility rate—a constant theme of the French far right. In the contemporary scenario, policies to increase the French birthrate have taken on an increased urgency because of the arrival of millions of Islamic immigrants. The urgency of this fear is outlined in this quotation from *Passeport pour la victoire* (Passport for victory), a publication distributed by the Front during the 1988 presidential elections:

> As a point of fact, 1.65 children, on average, are born to each French mother, and more than five children are born to each foreign woman from the Maghrib. If in twenty years we still want to be French, one of our most important priorities must be to set in motion a natalist policy that favors French families (1988, 43).

The extent of Vichy's collaboration with the Germans has been a source of controversy, but its desire to appease the occupying forces is quite evident in its treatment of Jews, both French Jews and those who could be identified as foreign born. As previously noted, anti-Semitism has been a favorite theme of the far right since the Dreyfus Affair; McMillan argues that Jews "were expendable pawns in his [Laval's] power game of trying to negotiate the best possible deal for France with the Third Reich" (1985, 134). Anti-Semitism during the Vichy years was compounded by an extreme sense of xenophobia. Eastern European Jews had been immigrating to Paris for years; these people were the first to be sacrificed by the Vichy government. "Some 60,000–65,000 Jews were deported from France, mostly foreigners who had relied upon traditional French hospitality. Perhaps 6,000 French citizens also took that gruesome journey" (Paxton 1972, 183). The anti-Semitism of Action Française and the leagues of the thirties was now public policy. In the contemporary political arena, Le Pen's inability to distance himself from anti-Semitic rhetoric demonstrates once again the links the Front shares with the historical French far right.

The collapse of Nazi Germany brought with it the collapse of Vichy. For its collaborationist posture during the Occupation, the far right was essentially banished from French political life for the next decade. Its role as a viable political movement was negligible until the mid-1950s.

Le Mouvement Poujade

The decade of the 1950s proved to be an important period for far right movements in France. The electoral success of le mouvement Poujade in 1956 resurrected the major rightist themes: antiparliamentarianism, antistate, anti-Semitism, and so on.

Pierre Poujade's battle with French fiscal authorities began innocently enough when, on July 22, 1953, he was named president of a small local organization created to protest changes in tax collection policies. His rise to prominence was absolutely meteoric (Hoffmann 1956). This small *comité de défense* became the Union de Défense des Commerçants et Artisans in November 1953. The movement held its first national convention in Algiers in November 1954. Algiers proved to be a somewhat prophetic location for this meeting, given the role the far right would play in the Algerian fight for independence.

Two very important points need to be emphasized when discussing le mouvement Poujade: (1) it was originally a spontaneous reaction to new tax pressures, and (2) Poujade's eventual ties with the extreme right were not planned from the outset. Rémond, in his seminal study of the French right, stresses the first point: "At its origin, Poujadism was nothing but a movement defending a specific socioeconomic category [the petite bourgeoisie], which believed its existence to be threatened and its future in question" (1982, 251). Poujade did not originally envision his movement as the banner of the extreme right. His concerns were individualized; he verbalized and acted upon the disgust and disdain many self-employed shopkeepers and artisans felt for the bloated, monolithic French bureaucracy.

Debate has centered on the probable location of le mouvement Poujade on the left-right political scale. Rémond (1982) places Poujade's movement on the far right because of its adept combination of nationalism and antiparliamentarianism. This is a logical conclusion because of the type of mass-level support Poujade eventually acquired. Though not originally conceived as a far right movement, its voters, at least a large share of them, came from the far right. Parliamentary deputies, such as the proto-nationalists Jean Marie Le Pen and Jean Demarquet, also contributed to changing the tone of le mouvement Poujade. Le Pen participated in the movement along with friends and colleagues who years later would follow him to the National Front. This former National Assembly deputy and Front Bureau Politique member describes his first political activity in this way:

> It's been already a long time, when I was about 16 years old. I grew up in a maurrassian environment—basically, you could say a royalist one, and at a very young age I found the public sector very interesting. I participated, in a sense from a distance, in such movements as the Young Poujadists.

Antiparliamentarianism and anti-Semitism were traditional far right themes dating back to Action Française; the Poujadists quickly expanded beyond the limited political boundaries of their antitax revolt and added these components to their political agenda. Latent racism combined with other traditional far right themes eventually served to entrench the Poujadists on the extreme right.

The legislative elections of January 1956 proved a resounding success for the movement. The party received 5.2 million votes. This represented 11.6 percent of the vote and enabled le mouvement Poujade to seat fifty-two deputies in the National Assembly. However, its success was short-lived, because the parliamentary group was immediately implicated in a scandal when eleven deputies of the fifty-two-member parliamentary group were summarily expelled for illegal campaign activities. Pierre Poujade and his compatriots burst onto the French political scene with great fanfare, but they were to disappear as quickly as they appeared, thus earning the brand of quintessential flash party.

L'Algérie Française and the Extreme Right

The military generally welcomed de Gaulle's 1958 return to power. Far right circles also viewed with favor the increased responsibilities granted to de Gaulle, the first president of the newly created Fifth Republic. The military and the extreme right generally believed de Gaulle to be an ally who would be capable of solving the Algerian crisis. They were mistaken.

The fight to maintain French control of Algeria brought France to the brink of civil war. After its devastating loss at Dien Bien Phu, the military was now attempting to regain its pride; it had been humiliated in the struggle for Vietnam and did not want to repeat the experience in Algeria. For the vanquished veterans of Dien Bien Phu, the only acceptable outcome was the complete collapse of the Algerian revolutionary movement. Any further erosion of the declining French empire was not to be tolerated.

The Algerian crisis was decidedly more complex than what had transpired in Vietnam for two important reasons. Constitutionally, unlike Vietnam, Algeria was legally a part of France. Moreover, Algeria was home to approximately 1 million French settlers, known as *pieds noirs,* whose families had been calling the country home for decades. These two different groups of people formed the ideological foundation of the OAS in 1961. Like so many movements of the far right, the OAS was an ad hoc mixture of people with a number of competing goals. Perhaps the two groups with the greatest differences were the military and the pieds noirs: the military was fighting to regain its honor as well as for the greater glory of France, whereas the pieds noirs were fighting to protect their homes and their heritage.

As de Gaulle assumed the presidency, he continued to profess his desire to maintain a French Algeria, thus keeping what remained of the dwindling French empire intact. But as the situation in Algeria continued to deteriorate and it became increasingly obvious that the colony could not be held, de Gaulle changed his approach to the crisis. This new, more pragmatic approach was viewed with contempt in far right circles. A member of the Front's Comité Central comments on de Gaulle's decision to abandon his promise to maintain a French Algeria: "In 1958, after the Algerian war, General de Gaulle returned to power. He comes back to power in order to keep Algeria French, and then he just turns his back on his promise." This new, more pragmatic approach to the Algerian crisis was vehemently attacked in the more nationalistic sectors of the French polity and provoked the military and the French settlers into action. Among the pro-French Algerian factions this shift in policy became known as de Gaulle's betrayal. The general's decision provoked a schism within rightist political circles; although the French far right had been initially favorably disposed to de Gaulle and Gaullism, the decision to grant Algeria its independence irrevocably separated the far right from the Gaullist mainstream.

As de Gaulle's desire to defuse the Algerian crisis through compromise became increasingly apparent, the military and the French settlers became more desperate. The referendum of January 1961 found 75.2 percent of the electorate supporting the general's policy of independence for Algeria. De Gaulle clearly had the support of the French polity, but the quickening pace of the independence process led to open sedition on the part of the military. The first initiative, Groupement de Commandos Parachutistes de Réserve Générale (GCP), ended after only four days. The failure of the GCP carried the OAS to the center of the controversy.

Participation in the OAS was an important mobilizing event for many on the far right. The links between the National Front and the OAS are clear; many frontistes trace their political awakening to the Algerian crisis and their participation in the OAS. When asked to describe what first attracted him to politics, this former National Assembly deputy and member of the party's Bureau Politique points to the Algerian crisis:

> I got actively involved after 1962, but not strictly speaking with politics. I was concerned with the problems tied to a French Algeria and decolonization. Let me be more precise: I supported a French Algeria, and it was at that time that my military career ended. Let me be even more precise: I joined the OAS, only staying for a short time, and eventually found myself in prison for the next two years, and it was upon leaving prison that I began to participate as an activist in the usual sense of the term: being a militant, participating at meetings, etcetera.

The image of the Front as a collection of hardened, war-weary *anciens combattants* is rooted in reality. Many of the Front's leaders did participate, on the side of the extremists, in the Algerian crisis. Granted, the contemporary National Front is made up of more than just those who qualify as anciens combattants, but this is an integral part of the Front's ideological heritage that cannot be denied. Christian Baeckeroot, Roger Holiendre, Jean-Marie Le Pen, and the late Pierre Sergent, all former members of the Front's short-lived parliamentary group, are just a few of the party's leaders who can claim to have served in Algeria. The Front's links to the Algerian crisis in particular and the French military in general are direct and have not become attenuated with the passage of time. Another member of the Front's Bureau Politique began his military career in Vietnam combating the Communist threat that had taken on increased symbolic significance for the French far right as the pace of decolonization quickened:

> As soon as I could, I joined the army and left for Indochina . . . and I did three tours of duty in Indochina. We were fighting against Asian Communism, against the Vietminh, and more than half of the French soldiers who were there, let's even say 75 percent, were violently anti-Communist.

His military career eventually led him to Algeria, where he became integrally involved in the OAS crisis:

> I was wounded in hand-to-hand combat, I took a bullet to the head, and then I stayed in Algeria as a civilian, demobilized in Algeria as a civilian. And there, I worked with the Muslim youth. I ran a youth center with three hundred young people—it was not governmentally supported. Also ran a nongovernmentally supported Scout troop. It was through these organizations that I tried to make French citizens out of young Algerians. I was for the integration of Algeria and the Sahara into France, because I thought that if there were to arrive a large number of Muslim Algerians in our country it could pose a problem, which could possibly be tempered by the existence of a French Sahara.
>
> I returned finally to France to go to prison. I was a member of the OAS, a partisan of a French Algeria, and I created one of the rare underground organizations that existed; there must have

been three of them all totaled. I was transferred to France with all the other Europeans who were with me and condemned to fourteen years of hard labor. One year for the first escape attempt, three years for the first underground organization, and ten years for the second underground organization. I was incarcerated for three and a half years.

Other groups emerged and attempted to rekindle the furor over a French Algeria, but their attempts were thwarted by de Gaulle's supreme authority to outlaw, by simple decree, movements and organizations he viewed as suspicious. Jean-Marie Le Pen and a number of supporters organized le Front National des Combattants (FNC). An obscure organization that never played as influential a role as the OAS, the FNC was nevertheless an important mobilizing force on the far right. Another membre fondateur of the National Front stresses his role in the FNC:

I was the secretary-general of that organization. Our primary preoccupation was keeping Algeria French. In this movement, we especially recruited people who had participated in the different conflicts which occurred after the war. This organization was dissolved by de Gaulle in 1961. After that, I participated in the fight to keep Algeria French, but in a clandestine manner since de Gaulle had outlawed all the associations, all the movements that participated in any way with keeping Algeria French. We were ruthlessly hunted and followed. At the time all you had to do to get thrown into prison was to agitate openly for a French Algeria. . . . Most of our friends were incarcerated in camps that weren't concentration camps, but internment camps. At the time there must have been more than 5,000 people who were either in prison or in internment camps—all the handiwork of the "democrat" de Gaulle.

The clash between the OAS and de Gaulle during the early 1960s proved an important turning point for both the general and the French far right. De Gaulle's complete victory allowed him to establish his authority over other individuals and groups on the right. The far right's failure to solidify its base and effectively oppose the general caused it to lose much of its political credibility. Despite the dire predictions, the revolt of OAS and its supporters did not "lead to a French fascism born out of defeat. On the contrary, the National Opposition appeared to fall apart and abandoned a unified style" (Duprat 1972, 64). The conclusion of the Algerian crisis deprived the far right of one of its most energizing themes; moreover, it signaled one of the lowest points in the ebb and flow of the French far right. Attempts were made to revitalize the far right with the Tixier-Vignancour presidential campaign, and the student-based organizations Occident and Ordre Nouveau, but it was to take over twenty years for the far right to emerge from its isolated position.

Comité Tixier-Vignancour

The de Gaulle era, especially the years between 1963 and 1968, proved very difficult for the extreme right. The Algerian crisis had passed and the test of 1968 was yet to come. In a brilliant tactical maneuver, de Gaulle had successfully denied the far right one of its main battle cries. His astute foreign policy initiatives and pretenses of *grandeur* usurped the far right's control of the nationalism issue. During this period, although the deck was decidedly stacked against it, the far right once again made an unsuccessful attempt to coalesce its disparate elements.

The presidential election of 1965 provided the impetus for the next resurgence of the far right. De Gaulle's appeal to the populace in the referendum of October 1962 had been successful: the president would henceforth be elected by direct vote. The now ubiquitous Jean-Marie Le Pen immediately began to prepare for this new opportunity. Toward the end of 1963, Le Pen created the Comité d'Initiative pour une Candidature Nationale. He advocated running a candidate, supported by a united far right, against de Gaulle. This candidacy, whether successful or not, was to serve as the foundation for a new national party on the far right. It was to be the catalyst for the creation of a truly unified Opposition Nationale.

After a period of protracted debate, Le Pen's committee eventually agreed on Jean-Louis Tixier-Vignancour, whose political past was firmly anchored on the extreme right; he had held the post of adjunct secretary of information in the Vichy government. In addition, his public profile was high, his name inextricably linked with far right causes because of his role as defense attorney for such extreme right celebrities as General Raoul Salan and Colonel Jean-Marie Bastien-Thiry.

Le Pen and his committee correctly concluded that there existed a natural constituency for the new Opposition Nationale. The wounds of the fight for a French Algeria were far from healed. Those who felt betrayed by de Gaulle's Algerian policy, namely the military and the dispossessed pied noirs, would serve as the foot soldiers for this newly united force.

The actual campaign proved to be a high-energy undertaking. Tixier-Vignancour, well managed by Le Pen, was a dynamic campaigner: "In the months before the election he spoke in every town with a population over 50,000 and, in the summer of 1965, he took a caravan the whole length of the French coastline" (Anderson 1974, 290). But more important than Tixier-Vignancour's mass appeal was his ability to draw other far right movements into the fold. His defense of Salan and Bastien-Thiry, two far right extremists implicated in the violence surrounding the Algerian conflict, earned him the gratitude and support of their many comrades in arms. He also received the endorsements of such student-led movements as Occident and Europe-Action. This support was tested when Occident boycotted the Paris municipal elections in 1965 against the wishes of the Comité Tixier; nevertheless, the candidates of the far right were marginally successful, receiving 10 percent of the vote.

Le Pen, in his role as Tixier-Vignancour's campaign manager, played an important part in bringing together these disparate groups hovering on the far right fringe of French politics. Although the volatile combination of student activists and disaffected Algerian war veterans did not survive the aftermath of the Tixier-Vignancour campaign, it presaged the ideological melting pot that would eventually become the National Front.

Tixier-Vignancour's constant harangues against de Gaulle also enabled him to acquire the endorsements of the major pieds noirs groups. His endless criticisms of de Gaulle's Republic and his emphasis on nationalism placed him squarely on the right. It appeared that Tixier-Vignancour was going to do well; he himself predicted victory in a runoff with de Gaulle. But the loosely structured coalition on the far right never fully merged into a cohesive whole. Tixier-Vignancour received only 5.27 percent of the vote, his candidacy ending in failure. But Tixier-Vignancour was only partly to blame. During the course of the campaign, he had modified his political posturing to become less reactionary; this served to confuse and offend a part of his potential electorate without attracting the centrist vote. Other things were beyond the lawyer's control. Jean Lecanuet, a very popular right-wing politician, made a last-minute decision to enter the race and thus deprived Tixier-Vignancour of a good portion of his potential electorate. In addition, Le

Pen's brush with the law because of a scandal involving his record company also damaged the campaign.[3]

Tixier-Vignancour's failure quickly became the failure of the far right. As his organization began to self-destruct after the election, the various leaders of the far right made mad dashes for their own little groups to create and direct. Once again the far right proved incapable of maintaining a cohesive organization. Le Pen's hopes for a united national party were finished, at least for the time being.

After a serious dispute with Tixier-Vignancour, Le Pen retreated to the Club du Panthéon, a far right think tank and social club. Tixier-Vignancour, on the other hand, initially tried to hold onto his place in the spotlight by creating, in 1966, the Alliance Républicaine pour la Liberté et le Progrès. A number of competent individuals followed him to this new organization, among them Christian Baeckeroot and Jean-Pierre Stirbois, who would eventually be elected to the National Assembly under the banner of the National Front. But this second political initiative on Tixier-Vignancour's part rapidly disintegrated.

The failure of Le Pen to solidify the far right through Tixier-Vignancour's presidential campaign placed the groups and movements of this political current in a precarious position for the rest of the decade. The far right was unprepared for the events of the late 1960s, and because it was unprepared it failed to capitalize on the far-reaching changes that took place in the French political landscape during the spring and summer of 1968.

Occident and Ordre Nouveau

As if to foreshadow the student revolts of the latter part of the 1960s, the strongest organization of the dispirited and marginalized extreme right was a student group. Occident was created by Pierre Sidos during the early months of 1964. The organization's militants were quite young, with a majority of its members in high school and college. As a youth movement, it was more interested in political street theater than intellectual dogma. This lack of doctrinal strength proved to be a major handicap for the organization; moreover, it was the recognition of this fact by some on the far right, most notably Alain de Benoist, that led to the creation of an intellectually vigorous wave of far right philosophers and writers, eventually labeled la Nouvelle Droite (the New Right) by the French media.

This new right is best characterized by the writings produced by the leaders of Groupement de Recherches et d'Études pour la Civilisation Européenne (GRECE). In an effort to separate itself from the student antics of first Occident and later Ordre Nouveau, this amorphous collection of philosophers attempted to create an alternative to the historically ineffectual far right. Throughout the 1970s, GRECE and its offshoot, the Club de l'Horloge, produced high-end publications wherein they debated their proposals, always keeping a measured distance between themselves and the student activists. Delving into pseudo-scientific debates, GRECE argued that there was no such thing as equality among peoples. GRECE and the Club de l'Horloge produced a flurry of activity and interest through the 1970s, but eventually faded from view when their racism and dressed-up anti-Semitism was revealed under the microscope of public scrutiny (Eatwell 1996).

The complete debacle of the OAS experience left the extreme right in a very difficult position. Due to a pronounced lack of political options, a number of the less militant supporters eventually gravitated to Gaullism. The Tixier-Vignancour episode had once again forced the far right to question its electoral efficacy. As noted, Occident had originally supported the Tixier-Vignancour campaign but expressed reservations about participating in the Paris municipal elections. When Tixier-Vignancour began to shift to the center, the hardliners of Occident could take no more; they broke with him completely.

The years immediately after the 1965 presidential campaign passed slowly for the far right. With the OAS rapidly becoming ancient history, especially in the minds of the younger militants, and the individual efforts of Tixier-Vignancour hardly newsworthy, the mass media had little to cover on the far right fringe of French politics. Thus, the small demonstrations and antics of Occident dominated the leftist press by default. The movement's primary tactic was to disrupt the meetings of its opponents. Those opponents were no longer the supporters of de Gaulle; the new enemy of the far right was now the leftist-oriented student organizations. At this time Occident had approximately 500 active supporters; counted among their ranks were two future prominent frontistes, Michel de Rostolan and Jean-François Touzé.[4]

In the late 1960s the far right began to shift its political focus away from attacks on de Gaulle in a search for new issues. *Europe-Nation,* a far right periodical, began to publish articles about the increasing number of Algerians in France and their deleterious impact on the French way of life. This was a telling sign of things to come. The extreme right identified the student-led Communist groups as the primary enemy. Occident, as a student organization, remained more interested in street-level skirmishes with the left than in developing a coherent political program, but the elimination of Communism from France became an important rallying cry for the organization's youthful militants. In a shift from previous far right organizations, Occident began to emphasize the "recurrent theme of an endemic communism" (Chebel d'Appollonia 1988, 312).

Vehement anti-Communist sentiments mobilized many of the National Front's future militants into political action. This provided, in essence, a third generation of supporters for the French far right. The first generation had mobilized during the height of Action Française; the second's catalyst for action was the fight for l'Algérie française. The third generation took to the streets to protest what it viewed as the ever increasing influence of the far left. Many present-day National Front supporters claim to have been pulled into political action by their strong anti-Communist beliefs. This member of the Front's Bureau Politique and former National Assembly deputy traces his political awakening to the student unrest of the 1960s:

> In 1968, I was 18 years old. It was my first year at the Faculty—the University of Nanterre, which was the center of all the student agitation. I went through this revolution in complete disagreement with the movement because I wasn't a Marxist. At the time, I began to understand the importance of ideology. And it was at that moment that I acquired a political conscience that was resolutely anti-Marxist.

As the political situation became more tense in the spring of 1968, the extreme right was forced to choose between the major combatants: "to participate in the fight against the regime on the side of the left," or, "on the contrary, . . . to ally ourselves with the regime to fight against Bolshevism" (Duprat 1972, 195). Duprat, a central figure and principal theoretician on the far right, argues that the extremists on the right were forced to make such a choice. The Communist threat, believed to be the most menacing, led Occident to the streets against the left, thus tacitly supporting the regime created by and fashioned for the hated de Gaulle. But it really was no match for the superior numerical strength of the many leftist organizations.

At the beginning of the fall term in 1968, membership in Occident increased to 800. Some students of the period argue that violent protest by the leftist organizations forced right-leaning students into political activity. As a high school student, this National Front activist recalls how he first entered the political arena in reaction to the leftist influence during the 1960s:

> My first political activity was in high school, where I participated in the creation, it was after 1968, of a small group of students that we named the Organization of the Anti-Marxist Fight. Our principal activity consisted in distributing leaflets against the Communists, the leftists in the school, and getting knocked around because they often attacked us.

The governmental prohibition of Occident in November 1968 did not prevent the leaders of the extreme right from participating in politics. Its leaders and dedicated militants quickly gravitated to new organizations. They regrouped and formed a number of different organizations, indicating their total disregard for the governmental decree outlawing Occident. This is a common pattern among organizations of the far right in France: forced to disband, they rally around a new name with essentially the same personnel and political program. Although a number of organizations were created, they were too engaged in their petty personal rivalries and individualized conflicts to replace the infamous Occident. The demise of Occident, the most visible organization of its time, led to a power vacuum on the far right.

Alain Robert, formerly a member of the disbanded Occident, and Gerard Longuet founded the Groupe Union-Droit which later became the Groupe d'Union et de Défense (GUD) at the Law Faculty of Assas in early 1969. This student organization played a very important role in establishing a firm foundation for the organizations that followed. Longuet's participation in the GUD led to success in a student election at Assas; the group received 13.5 percent of the vote. This minor victory encouraged the GUD's leadership to pursue a more vigorous agenda, which included the creation of yet another organization. Thus, the leaders of the GUD in concert with a number of former Occident members founded Ordre Nouveau in November 1969.

This new organization was to be more than a mere student group confined to the university campuses of Assas, Clichy, or Clignancourt. From the outset, Ordre Nouveau established lofty goals for itself: "We want to acquire a dimension beyond that of a sect or a minor group. Action for only action's sake is ended. We want to build a large party, like the Italian MSI [Italian Socialist Movement], which we have set up as a model for ourselves" (*Pour un Ordre nouveau* 1972). Its first major rally was planned for December 12, 1969, but the night before the meeting the locale was bombed. Ordre Nouveau immediately took to the streets. The bombing proved to be but a temporary setback for the nascent organization.

The movement's importance increased rapidly during its first few years. It solidified its place on the extreme right by the summer of its first year. As Ordre Nouveau grew in importance, other extreme right groups, such as Pour Une Jeune Europe and Action Nationaliste, began to lend their support: "the movement imposed itself on rival groups and the press was talking about nothing but Ordre Nouveau. At the beginning of the 1970s, Ordre Nouveau was the extreme right. To such a point that the big shots of this political family, in semi-retirement since the end of the Algerian war, . . . start[ed] to pay attention" (Dumont, Lorien, and Criton 1985, 89).

Although not yet active in electoral politics, the extreme right was represented throughout France in the country's high schools and universities by such organizations as GUD and Ordre Nouveau. It was the latter that played the preeminent role in espousing the politically undisciplined rhetoric of the French far right. Ordre Nouveau was a group of approximately 5,000 members, consisting mostly of student activists, operating on the far right fringes of French politics. In fact, over half of the movement's active supporters were students, with approximately 40 percent coming from the universities and 17 percent from high schools (Milza 1987). Its immediate ideological predecessor, Occident, had been disbanded by governmental decree in 1968, and it was the leaders of this outlawed organization that regrouped to form Ordre Nouveau in 1969. This scenario provided the backdrop for the creation of the National Front, for it was from the cradle of Ordre Nouveau that the National Front emerged to become the most dominant electoral force on the far right since the Poujadists of the 1950s.

THE FAR RIGHT REAPPEARS:

THE CREATION OF THE

NATIONAL FRONT

En 1972, c'était la perception d'un vide politique, un vide

politique à droite . . .

—Charter member of the National Front [1]

Political parties do not just suddenly and mysteriously appear on ballots at election time. They must be not only created: they must be nurtured, developed, and strengthened. Successful political parties operate like intricate machines as they advance in the complex battle of electoral competition. The mechanisms of party development are singularly important because political parties are fundamental to the process of governing in advanced industrialized democracies.

Most political parties must navigate a difficult path before they are prepared for electoral competition. The creation and early development of the French National Front provide an excellent illustration of the difficulties a new political party faces during the initial stages of its political life. This period in the Front's history involves a complex mix of political initiatives, institutional imperatives, and personal ambition. The National Front's early years provide an illustration of what new political parties face as they attempt to anchor themselves in a mature party system.

As detailed in the previous chapter, the political tradition espoused by the extreme right has been an integral part of the French political landscape since the latter half of the nineteenth century. In discussions with the leaders of the Front, the theme of an omnipresent traditional right was essential to their understanding of the role of the extreme right in French politics. After the student revolts of 1968, they deemed the creation of a new nationalist political party an inevitability. Those who participated in the Front's creation believed it was a natural continuation of a long-established political tradition. From their perspective, a new party had to emerge to carry on the nationalist right's struggle and establish itself as a viable political contender in French partisan politics. This perceived inevitability of a new far right party is adeptly explained by this former National Assembly deputy:

> The struggle of Jean-Marie Le Pen and others of the traditional right did not begin in 1972. It was nourished by a certain number of events since the end of the war: the Gaullist problem, the war in Indochina, the loss of the former French colonies. Gaullism strangled the French right in mixing together people and problems. Gaullism is a very special phenomenon which has upset the French political landscape for a long time. A group of people who were always anti-Gaullist, who never approved of Gaullist policies in Algeria, realized the need to create this political force with a clear agenda, based on the values of the right. The National Front was created in 1972, but I don't think this is a special date. It's a movement which goes much further back than 1972.

Although many people now active in the party were confident that the far right would reemerge, the reality of the situation in the late 1960s and early 1970s was quite different. In fact, the dramatic cultural and political events of 1968 served to underscore the relative weakness of the traditional right. The views of the traditional right were conspicuously absent from the electoral arena of French partisan politics during this volatile time. In fact, the turbulent political and social period of the late 1960s proved to be a difficult time for the extreme right. It had lost the ideological initiative to the extreme left and had become electorally impotent. As one frontiste says, "In 1968 there was not a genuine political party on the right."

Although the far right was not a viable force in the late 1960s, the progress of the newly energized left and the specter of its possible dominance could have provided fertile ground for the creation of a new nationalist political party to follow in the mode of the Poujadists and the Comité Tixier-Vignancour. Many on the far right, including this member of the Front's Political Bureau, felt that the energy generated by the Tixier-Vignancour effort should have created a newly revitalized insurgency on the far right:

There were many factors, but the most important among all these was the failure, the end of the Tixier-Vignancour experience on the right. This candidacy especially registered a reaction against Gaullism, against de Gaulle and most notably against the abandonment of the European population, as well as the Algerian Muslims, for that matter. Tixier-Vignancour obtained only 5 percent of the votes, which was a small amount, but it could have served as the foundation for the development of a political party.

The politically impotent remnants of the far right were extremely critical of the governing center right's performance during the 1968 crisis. Another member of the Political Bureau argues that the center right was horribly flawed and that its leaders were incapable of representing the concerns of the traditional right, the "true" right:

> We thought that there was a void on the political front. That is to say that no person, no party, no movement represented our views, our ideas . . . or was defending the policies that we wanted to see implemented. For many years they had been nothing but a fraudulent right—they even refused to refer to themselves as being from the right. We reject, we have a total disgust for such people who are nothing but opportunists and demagogues—opportunists just fashioning a political career. Our ideas were just not being represented.

The consequences of the crisis were viewed as threatening the traditional French way of life. The cataclysmic events of 1968 clearly called into question the relative stability of French society. French students and workers voiced their discontent with the Gaullist government and helped to precipitate the general's retirement. De Gaulle was still perceived as a traitor by the true believers on the extreme right of the political spectrum, and there was no mourning when he retreated into retirement for the second time. The center right, as represented by de Gaulle and his successors, was viewed as ineffectual and unable to control civil unrest. The eventual outcome of the crisis seemed to legitimize the Socialist-Communist alliance that developed in 1972. This frontiste argues that the left had already become dominant in many facets of French life:

> And after 1968, the right in power made many concessions to the left that was taking over just about everywhere. . . . The ideology

of the extreme left, called the leftist ideology in France, was omni-present . . . in the education system, in the culture, in the media. And I think that the creation of the National Front was a reaction to all of this. It was a reaction to the left's victory in the intellectual life, the media, and the culture of France.

A number of important factors converged to facilitate the creation of the Front: a renewed interest in pursuing electoral politics, the dominance of the left in the student sector, and the availability of Jean-Marie Le Pen. This member of the Front's Bureau Politique describes in detail how the Front filled an important political vacuum on the far right:

> In France, for over 30 years everything that touches the mind— that's to say the university, school, journalism school, the media, the press, the church, the unions, the associations—all of that, all the sectors that have something to do with people's minds, all of that was given up to the left. And that is in large part the responsibility of the mainstream right that governed the country for many years.
>
> Let's say that at that time already, Jean-Marie Le Pen understood the necessity, he was conscious already that the political majority of the period, the mainstream right, wasn't doing what was needed in light of the continual progress in all sectors of the left. It was after 1968, after the revolt of 1968, we already had had the capitulation of the mainstream right in all domains, and it is for that reason that the National Front was created at that time—in order to stand up also to the alliance between the Communist Party and the Socialist Party. At the time, there was the common program. For a very long time, the French Communist and Socialist Parties had remained divided, they were divided, they each followed their own path, and then one fine day in 1972, they created a common program in order to gain power. And it was in the face of this danger and the inability of the mainstream right to face these dangers, to contain these dangers, that the National Front was created.

Members of the far right felt the time had arrived for a new electoral initiative effort, but the resulting initiative came from a rather unexpected source. It was neither the experienced activists of the Poujadist campaign, nor the veterans of the OAS, nor the political operatives who managed the Tixier-Vignancour debacle, but rather the students of

Ordre Nouveau who initiated the resurrection of an electorally competitive far right. Ironically, the hardened political veterans briefly turned to youthful student activists for help in waging conventional political action.

The National Front and Ordre Nouveau

True to its original intentions to model itself after the MSI, Ordre Nouveau competed in its first electoral contest in 1970. This was clearly in reaction to the tentative electoral gains made by its Italian counterpart. Still dominated by students and youthful militants, Ordre Nouveau began to question its mission in French politics, and a serious debate ensued on whether the movement should start to engage in more conventional political activity. With some hesitation, as well as some internal dissension, Ordre Nouveau began to flex its electoral strength in 1970 by competing in a by-election in the twelfth arrondissement in Paris. Against a tough candidate who also appealed to the far right, Ordre Nouveau received 3.12 percent of the vote. Encouraged by this campaign, Ordre Nouveau began to concentrate its efforts on increasing its political influence throughout the country. At this time the group claimed over 3,000 members.

Once the decision was made, Ordre Nouveau and its ragtag crew of candidates competed in one election after another. Municipal elections were to be held in March 1971, and, in addition to a full slate of candidates in Paris, Ordre Nouveau contested a number of races throughout the country. In the capital, Ordre Nouveau received 19,529 votes representing 2.6 percent of the votes cast; in some other areas of the country its candidates reached double digits. The municipal list in Calais actually attracted 22 percent of the vote. Even though the extreme right was not actually winning elections, the youthful leadership was happy with these results. The movement was becoming firmly established in electoral politics.

This testing of the electoral waters continued for two years until the organization made a critical decision during the proceedings of its second convention in June 1972. The success of its Italian counterpart continued to fuel its electoral ambitions: "In the spring of 1972, the Italian neo-fascist movement realized its best score since its founding in 1946—8 percent of the national vote with a strong showing in Rome of

18 percent" (Milza 1987, 339). The group's leadership decided to try to replicate the Italian success, but the organization's militant image remained a significant obstacle. As the decision was made to participate even more aggressively in the 1973 legislative elections, Ordre Nouveau took a significant step to improve its public persona. The leaders, still hoping to replicate the moderate success of the MSI, urged the creation of a totally separate political party that would operate within the parliamentary system of the Fifth Republic as a legitimate electoral contender (Eatwell 1996).

Operating within the parameters of representative democracy was a radical departure for the extreme right. Previous extreme right movements such as the Action Française, the OAS, and Occident had never even considered working within the democratic limits imposed by the status quo. Thus, with the creation of the National Front, the French extreme right made an important strategic choice: it decided, for all practical purposes, to follow the rules of the game, to work within the legal parameters of the Fifth Republic (Chiroux 1974). In so doing, the extreme right, represented by the inchoate National Front, became the far right, a slight but nevertheless very important distinction that set the Front apart from its ideological ancestors. This development was indeed an admission by the far right that the Fifth Republic was here to stay; to further its own political agenda the far right would have to follow the rules originally crafted by and for de Gaulle, their most hated enemy. Dumont maintains that the decision to participate aggressively in the electoral arena initially created severe tensions within Ordre Nouveau: "For the most radical, the elections were nothing but a farce" (1983, 136). The leadership of the organization, on the other hand, felt it was a way to "extract itself from the political ghetto" (*Pour un Ordre nouveau* 1972, 11). Many of the movement's more strident activists expressed strong opposition to the electoral initiative; they argued that participating in a system they considered illegitimate would only weaken their resolve. Although the pro-electoral faction, most notably François Brigneau and François Duprat, ultimately prevailed, this disharmony was to reemerge quickly as control over the group became a contentious issue.

This desire to embark wholeheartedly on the electoral path eventually led to the creation of the National Front in October 1972. The synergy that existed between Ordre Nouveau and the newly created National Front is detailed by this member of the Front's Comité Central:

There was at the heart of the National Front an organization called Ordre Nouveau. Ordre Nouveau was a part of the National Front, but it maintained its autonomy. Ordre Nouveau was directed in particular by someone named Alain Robert. And in 1974, Alain Robert was the secretary-general of the National Front. He was at the same time the secretary-general of Ordre Nouveau.

A political party of this sort needs a leader. Ordre Nouveau, because of its extreme militant public image, was unable to offer a legitimate candidate for the presidency of this new organization from within its own ranks. The youthful leadership of the student movement lacked the political polish necessary for such a visible role. Furthermore, the leadership of Ordre Nouveau was tainted by its ties to the outlawed Occident as well as by its own questionable activities during the late 1960s and early 1970s. Therefore, it was forced to turn to the more main-stream elements of the far right for counsel. The elder statesmen of the far right advanced the candidacy of Jean-Marie Le Pen, who possessed an impressive political résumé that anchored him firmly on the French far right. As previously noted, he served as a Poujadist deputy and had managed Tixier-Vignancour's ill-fated presidential campaign; in addition, his close ties to the military as well as to the veterans of the Algerian conflict helped the sponsors of this new electoral initiative enlarge their circle of potential political supporters. Le Pen's extensive political experience made him uniquely qualified for the role of president of a newly created far right political party. Milza convincingly describes Le Pen as the best man for the job:

> He had participated in all the struggles of the extreme right since 1950, including the most violent ones. He was an ardent defender of a French Algeria after having been elected in 1956 under the Poujadist banner. But he isn't, strictly speaking, an ultra, and even less a fascist, while at the time the principal directors of *Ordre Nouveau* could not repudiate all ties with brownshirt totalitarianism" (1987, 341–42).

Milza goes on to argue that Le Pen's reputation as a "moderate (everything is relative)" made him the logical choice to lead a newly constituted far right party. Except for serious allegations about torturing Algerian prisoners during the height of that terrible conflict, Le Pen's adult political career up to this point was relatively free of violence. This was

especially true in comparison to the youthful activists in Ordre Nouveau and the hardline nationalist veterans of the OAS crisis. Moreover,
the fact that he emerged from the Algerian crisis essentially untarnished
but still possessing solid far right credentials made his nomination as
the National Front's first president a logical next step in a political career
that had officially begun when he was elected to the National Assembly
under the Poujadist banner in 1956.

Originally, Ordre Nouveau had hoped to keep tight reins on Le Pen.
He was viewed as a straw man by the student movement, a leader in
name only (Dumont 1983; Milza 1987). But Le Pen refused to serve in
this role; he decided early on that he was not going to be a puppet for
the militant roughnecks of Ordre Nouveau. Assuming as quickly as possible a dominant role, he led the new organization into the legislative
elections of March 1973. This first electoral initiative of the newly created National Front and its parent organization, Ordre Nouveau, ended
in failure. The campaign's rhetoric for this first political endeavor was
uninspired; it stressed far right themes that harkened back to the days
of Maurras and Action Française. The decline of France's *grandeur* and
the invasion by foreigners were political issues that failed to inspire the
electorate in 1973. This joint effort on the part of Le Pen and Ordre
Nouveau managed to field only 115 candidates, 285 short of its goal of
400. The actual election results were far from encouraging; the Ordre
Nouveau–National Front candidates received 108,661 votes, representing 1.3 percent. Le Pen, campaigning in the fifteenth arrondissement of
Paris, performed poorly; he received only 5.2 percent of the vote. Overall, this translated to an average of 2.3 percent in districts where the
Front had been able to muster candidates.

The radicals of the student organization reacted quickly, arguing that
the strategy had failed. They demanded that the organization abandon
its electoral initiatives and return to its militant roots. The complex mix
of youthful militants, student activists, former Poujadists, and hardliners from the OAS swiftly began to crumble. "Very quickly, the generational conflicts rendered this cohabitation difficult. The leaders of
Ordre Nouveau adapted poorly to their participation in a more moderate grouping; they preferred violent demonstrations" (Plenel 1984, 46).

The problematic alliance between old-style politicians and student
activists failed to last a year. Ordre Nouveau eventually suffered the same
fate as its immediate predecessor, Occident, when it was disbanded by
governmental decree in June 1973 because of its violent neomilitaristic

activities. Le Pen and the National Front were spared the government's wrath, and as the undisputed leader of the party, he proceeded to exercise complete authority over the organization. He was now free of interference from the students of Ordre Nouveau.

During the early years, many significant obstacles hampered the Front's development. The party's image as a far right conglomeration of political extremists isolated it from mainstream politics. This in turn contributed to the party's recruitment problems and precipitated internal disputes as well as personality conflicts. In addition, the Front was financially insolvent during the first ten years of its existence.

Being relegated to the far right fringes of French partisan politics made recruitment exceedingly difficult. The Front's inability to attract *notables* during the early stages of its development hindered its ability to nominate quality candidates at all levels of electoral competition. Indeed, in election after election throughout the 1970s, the Front was unable to field a complete list of candidates.

The developing National Front in the early 1970s was integrally connected to the maelstrom of the historical French extreme right from two distinct perspectives. This connection was evident in the Front's ideological foundations as well as in the early activists and leaders who were drawn to the party. Because of its direct links to preceding extreme right organizations, the Front's initial recruitment efforts were confined to the ranks of the defunct Poujadist movement, the remains of the banned OAS, malcontents from the Tixier-Vignancour campaigns, and the neomilitaristic Ordre Nouveau. The Front's political agenda appealed to the alienated and the disaffected, who were not viewed as part of the French political mainstream. Thus, the people who did join were viewed as political "marginals" by those outside the party and even by some within the organization itself. This former National Assembly deputy adeptly describes the type of people who were attracted to the Front during the party's early years:

> [A]ll the movements on the right were marginal and as always in fringe movements, or at least often, we find nothing but people on the edge. It's like a sociological law. I don't want to criticize those who were courageous, and it wasn't as if that's all there was in the Front, but in all the right-wing movements that I am familiar with and in those in which I have participated, one really had the feeling of being on the fringe.

Almost as quickly as it had supposedly unified the far right, the Front experienced dissension from within its own ranks. Dissatisfied with Le Pen's leadership, a small group of malcontents abandoned Le Pen and the National Front in 1974. Most notable among these dissidents were Alain Robert and François Brigneau, who founded an organization and publication called Faire Front before eventually creating the Parti des Forces Nouvelles (PFN), which competed directly with Le Pen's National Front during the greater part of the 1970s. This charter member, who deserted the Front in 1974 only to return to the party at the end of the decade, explains the situation:

> [A] short while afterwards, most of the people from Ordre Nouveau left to create a new organization which was the PFN, Parti des Forces Nouvelles. I followed my friend Brigneau to the PFN . . . We were in a war, a sort of permanent warfare between the National Front and the PFN which had at certain times very violent aspects to it. And which also preserved the division of the right.

Competition with the PFN, coupled with the Front's weak organizational base, precluded it from achieving success in its many electoral endeavors. As late as 1978, the two organizations were almost equal in membership. According to Husbands, "the Front claimed 7,000 members, the PFN about 5,000" (1981, 79). These *frères ennemis* (warring brothers) exacerbated the historically violent fractionalization that had always existed among the movements of the French far right. The constant competition for supporters and financing weakened both organizations and eventually led to the demise of the PFN in the early 1980s.[2] Le Pen's victory was costly; the division of the extreme right hindered the Front's ability to take advantage of the weakening position of the more mainstream right throughout the latter half of the 1970s. The gradual weakening of the center right paralleled an unprecedented rebuilding effort within Mitterrand's resurgent Socialist Party. Essentially, the fratricidal campaigns waged by the National Front and the PFN forestalled the political progress of Le Pen's movement for most of the decade of the seventies; moreover, it prevented the organization from exploiting the many dramatic changes occurring in the French party system.

The Front's early development was marked by political miscalculations, organizational weakness, and competition from the breakaway PFN, but there was one significant ray of sunshine for the Front and for Jean-Marie Le Pen personally. In 1976, Le Pen received a personal inheritance of 20 million francs as well as a palatial mansion, valued at 4 million, from Hubert Lambert, scion of a well-known industrial family. Questions immediately surrounded the curious circumstances of that inheritance and eventually prompted a court challenge from Lambert's cousin, Philippe Lambert. Hubert Lambert had joined the Front soon after its creation and was viewed as a rather eccentric figure in far right circles. He changed his will to favor Le Pen just nine months before his death. The circumstances surrounding his death continued to generate controversy when an old ally of Le Pen's, Jean Demarquet, publicly stated that Le Pen had in fact exerted undue influence over Lambert as he lay dying.[3] Although there is no way to know to what extent this infusion of cash into Le Pen's personal coffers benefited the Front directly, it clearly provided Le Pen the financial independence to devote himself to his political mission on a full-time basis.

The National Front on the Campaign Trail

The Front's forays into the electoral arena during the early years generated lackluster results. Although the outcome was basically a foregone conclusion each time a campaign began, the Front participated in all elections, at all possible levels. According to this membre fondateur and European Parliament deputy, "We were always running for something because Jean-Marie Le Pen wanted the people in the Front to stand for all of the elections." Le Pen refers to this period in the Front's history, from 1972 until 1983, as the "crossing of the desert." The party faced two major obstacles during the "crossing of the desert" in the 1970s: it found itself in a catch-22 situation because it lacked public recognition, and yet it did not have an organizational foundation capable of generating the much needed publicity. Jean-Pierre Stirbois, the now deceased secretary-general, who joined the party in 1977, stated, "I had imagined that the Front was a powerful organization, but quickly discovered that even if it had a leader, some ideas, as well as some quality volunteers, it lacked organization and an entrenched core of party militants" (1988, 27).

As previously noted, the first electoral initiative in 1973 ended in failure. The death in 1974 of President Georges Pompidou created the next significant electoral challenge for the National Front in the presidential election that followed. Furthermore, the candidacy of Jean-Marie Le Pen, as the representative of the National Front, was viewed as an important test of his individual popularity. There was a multiplicity of candi-

Table 2.1   The National Front's Share of the Vote in National
Elections, 1972–1981

Year	Election	Vote %
1973	Legislative	1.3
1974	Presidential	.8
1978	Legislative	.3
1981	Legislative	.4

dates claiming to represent the constituencies of the nationalist right: Le
Pen, representing the Front; Pierre Sidos from l'Oeuvre Française; Bertrand Renouvin, the candidate for the royalist group Nouvelle Action
Française; and Jean Royer, the deputy mayor of Tours. Le Pen received
only .8 percent of the votes and "passed the 1 percent barrier in only
8 of the 95 departments" (Perrineau 1989, 38). His second-place finish
among the many far right candidates was indicative of the Front's weak
electoral position in 1974 (see Table 2.1). Although Le Pen failed to have
a resounding impact on the presidential contest, "The televised campaign at least permitted him to get his name known, and according to
François Duprat the active members of the party doubled thanks to the
television appearances of Le Pen" (Dumont 1983, 153). This was Le Pen's
first direct contact with the national media during a televised campaign,
and if Duprat is to be believed, he performed admirably considering his
weak position among the candidates.

The fratricidal competition between the National Front and the PFN
dominated the 1978 legislative elections. The Front was dealt a cruel
blow by the government during this campaign: although the party ran
a slate of 137 candidates and met the minimum requirements for television and radio time, the government refused Le Pen and his party this
vital opportunity. The PFN did not suffer the same fate. Some would argue that the PFN's protected status was due to its support of the center
right during previous electoral campaigns.

Once again, the National Front performed poorly, receiving only .33
percent of the vote. In districts where it competed directly with the PFN,
the Front garnered .89 percent to the PFN's 1.6 percent. The constant
competition with the PFN had continued to weaken the Front's claim as
the legitimate and sole representative of the far right.

Yet Le Pen's organization suffered more than an electoral defeat during the 1978 legislative campaigns; tragedy visited the National Front between the first and second rounds of the election. François Duprat, an integral member of the Front's leadership and its master theoretician, was killed when his car exploded. Subsequent investigations revealed that he had been assassinated. To date, no one has been charged with the crime, but there remains a lingering doubt that his murder was in some way related to the vociferous conflict between the National Front and the PFN.

Surprisingly, the two competing organizations begrudgingly agreed to run a joint list for the 1979 European elections. The leaders of the two factious organizations, Jean-Marie Le Pen and Pascal Gauchon, originally entitled the joint list the Union pour l'Europe-droite des Patries, but the ceasefire proved to be short-lived; in fact, it did not survive the campaign. In a mere forty-eight hours, the PFN backed out of the agreement and eventually proposed its own slate of candidates for the elections. Le Pen, excluded from the elections, called for his supporters to abstain from voting.

In 1981, Le Pen's personal popularity suffered another serious setback. In France, a candidate's placement on the presidential ballot is predicated on the candidate's soliciting the support of 500 mayors, senators, National Assembly deputies, and so on. Le Pen and the National Front probably reached the nadir of their political life when he was unable to collect the necessary 500 sponsorship signatures. His inability to have his name placed on the presidential ballot was a foreboding of his poor political viability. The dearth of support from the mayors and political powerhouses precluded Le Pen from participating in the election that was to place François Mitterrand in power. Deprived of the chance to participate in the presidential contest, the Front was able to mount only a skeleton campaign for the legislative elections precipitated by Mitterrand's victory. The party ran a mere seventy-four candidates in the 1981 legislative contests.

The Front's inability to compete effectively in this series of elections —1979, European; 1981, presidential and legislative—highlighted the party's weak electoral position. The fact that the Front was squeezed out of the 1979 European elections by the Machiavellian maneuvers of the PFN, unable to secure the needed sponsorship signatures for the 1981 presidential contest, and powerless to conduct a credible legislative campaign in that same year, signified to many that the National Front was doomed to either perpetual insignificance or eventual extinction. Many political pundits, including Jean-Christian Petitfils, argued that

> The extreme right had disintegrated. It had ceased to play a role in the electoral arena. . . . Broken up into a myriad of minuscule islands, impotent *cénacles,* and phantomlike circles, it only exists as a historical vestige. More than ever its factionalists seemed like marginals, outcasts, and emigrants from the interior. (1983, 123)

These sentiments echoed the general consensus of observers of the French political scene. The poor performance of the extreme right during the late 1970s and early 1980s led Simone Veil, as noted in the introduction, to write a somewhat premature obituary for the French far right. Little did she know that soon after she had proclaimed the far right dead, the National Front would prove to be her primary competition during the 1984 European elections.

A Model of Party Development

The emergence of the French National Front provides an interesting example of change in a mature party system. Minor parties, such as the Front, that operate on the political margins offer interesting insights to the party system as a whole. In fact, Jaffré (1986) contends that the Front may be the only French political party currently addressing the fundamental social questions facing the country. In France, innovation and initiative seem to occur more often on the fringes of the party system, this is true of the Front on the far right as well as the various environmental groupings on the far left. How minor parties gain access to the mature party system is an interesting question for further inquiry.

According to Hauss and Rayside (1978) the development of new parties is inextricably linked to a set of political and institutional factors. Harmel and Robertson (1985) have also examined many of these factors of party development (see Figure 2.1). At the foundation of the model is the issue base, the decisive cleavage structure—the set of attitudes and beliefs—that provides the impetus for the new party (Lipset and Rokkan 1967). Hauss and Rayside agree with Lipset and Rokkan about the importance of social cleavages in the development of new parties, but assert that "their mere existence is not enough" (1978, 36). They argue that cleavages and/or strains "are necessary but not sufficient preconditions for the development of new parties" (39).

The cleavage structure that promoted the development of the National Front is inextricably linked to the historical legacy of the French far right. As previously discussed, the French radical right has been omnipresent in French politics; thus, in certain respects, the Front is but the contemporary manifestation of a much older political tradition. The anti-Semitism of Action Française and the leagues of the 1930s, the backlash politics of Vichy, the threatened shopkeeper class of the Poujadist era, and the fierce nationalism of the OAS melded to form the National Front. This inherent cleavage structure has been further radicalized by the Front's ability to manipulate public fears about immigration and *insécurité* (Lack of law and order). The political resonance of the Front's core issues coupled with the inherent radicalism of the French far right are important factors in the Front's political development. The addition of the posited institutional and political factors further enhanced the Front's political evolution. Institutional facilitators of new parties include the electoral system and the electoral focus of the system. Clearly, the electoral system has an impact on how the votes are counted and translated into seats. Proportional representation may encourage the electoral success of new parties, but it does not seem to have an impact on their creation (Harmel and Robertson 1985). Different variations on majority systems also play an important role in party development.

The French case is particularly interesting due to the variation in electoral frameworks. Under France's normal two-round electoral system, the National Front has performed poorly.[4] Its first major electoral breakthrough came in a proportional representation system, the 1984 European Parliament elections; the adoption of this system for the 1986 legislative elections further enhanced the Front's political future and facilitated the party's entry into the National Assembly. At different levels of the political ladder, other electoral frameworks are also employed. Regional elections follow a proportional representation format, whereas municipal elections have a dose of proportional representation in communes with more than 3,500 inhabitants.

Electoral focus pertains to the key electoral unit of party competition, whether a parliament seat or the presidency. Although the creation of political parties does not seem linked to the electoral focus (Hauss and Rayside 1978; Harmel and Robertson 1985), the French system may in fact be unique. The evolving nature of the Fifth Republic's hybrid presidential-parliamentary system (presidential politics arrived with the inauguration of the Fifth Republic) may have an impact on the development of new parties, for new as well as old parties need to be able to compete successfully in presidential elections (Lawson 1978; Bartolini 1984; Criddle 1987). For example, the precipitous decline of the French Communist Party over the past decade has been linked to its inability to compete in politics at the presidential level.

A second set of factors also has a direct impact on the development of political parties. Hauss and Rayside (1978) contend that these factors are more overtly political in nature, therefore having a greater influence on party development than the institutional factors. Four political facilitators are considered integral to the development of new parties: (1) the behavior of existing parties, (2) the level of mass commitment, (3) the leadership of new parties, and (4) the new party's organization.

The behavior of existing political parties is an important element in the creation of a new political party. Systems with responsive political parties do not foster the development of new parties. However, if the old parties lose touch with their electorates, the propensity for new political parties increases; in other words, the failures of the system's existent parties may promote the development of new parties. Moreover, the existing parties can legitimize or delegitimize new or excluded parties. Levite and Tarrow (1983) trace the progress of new and excluded parties in Italy and Israel by emphasizing the roles of the dominant parties in those systems. This process of legitimization is promoted or forestalled by the existing parties.

The relationship between the National Front and the existing parties is revealing here. For example, the decline of the French Communist Party roughly parallels the emergence of the National Front, as demonstrated in a detailed analysis of the Front's vote in Paris (Mayer 1987). The behavior of the existing parties has also served to legitimize the Front's presence (Schain 1987). The mainstream center right has, on two past occasions, entered into electoral alliances with the Front. This tactical maneuver on the part of the center right had two consequences, one intended and the other unintended. The choice to align itself with the Front helped the center right combat the left, but it also served to legitimize the Front in the eyes of the French electorate. More recently, the center right has taken a different approach, and since 1988 has refused all electoral alliances with the Front in the hope of completely marginalizing its influence and reducing it to pre-1984 support levels. In many respects, the mainstream right's behavior vis-à-vis the Front has lent credence to Le Pen's claims of martyrdom. At the same time, although the center right is unwilling to deal with the Front, this has not prevented it from attempting to usurp its political agenda; in fact, politicians on the left and the right have begun to expropriate the Front's political agenda. This heavy borrowing from the Front's political agenda has in turn enhanced its legitimacy.

A second potential political facilitator is the strength of the public's psychological ties to the party. If there is no commitment on the part of the electorate, the new political party will have a difficult time strengthening itself. If the electorate is engaged elsewhere, the new party will find little support.

Partisan attachment is an ambiguous concept in the French case. The seminal work of Converse and Dupeux (1962) uncovered a low level of party identification. Their study, conducted early in the history of the Fifth Republic, maintains that partisan politics in France operated somewhat differently than in other countries. Others argue that the French situation is atypical not because of low levels of partisan identification, but rather because of the discontinuities of partisan politics at the elite level (Lewis-Beck 1984). With respect to the National Front, there is a growing body of evidence to indicate that it is attracting an ever increasing number of disaffected voters from the opposite end of the political spectrum. Early analyses of the Le Pen vote indicated that the supporters of the Front are a diverse group. It is also important to note that although the Front has made some progress in increasing its mass-level support, a large percentage of French citizens still holds a decidedly negative view of Le Pen and his party; over 65 percent of the French polity believe that the Front represents a danger to democracy (Mayer and Perrineau 1993). This deep reservoir of anti-Front sentiment may portend a difficult future for the party.

A third key political facilitator is the efficacy of a new party's political leadership. Leadership is critical to the effective creation of any new organization. Elite perceptions of exploitable political cleavages may provoke them into action. Dalton underscores the importance of elite actions in "channeling the forces of social change" (1984, 399). Rose and Mackie also emphasize the significant role party elites play in party change: "The voluntary choices of party leaders affect the career of the party itself. They determine whether the party persists completely intact or with marginal modifications, undergoes structural change, or disappears" (1988, 557). Elite action or inaction is thus a critical component in the development of new political parties and in fact may be the

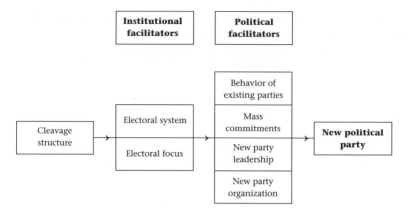

Figure 2.1   Creation of a New Political Party

ultimate determinant in system-level change. Whether the new group is a political party or a social movement, the role of its initial leadership is of primary importance. Resource mobilization theorists emphasize the role of the political entrepreneur at the early stages of a nascent movement's development (McCarthy and Zald 1977; Jenkins 1983). Political entrepreneurs such as the founding members of the Front play an important role in the party's development. In the case of the Front, the role of Jean-Marie Le Pen is most interesting. In many senses, especially during the early years, Le Pen *was* the National Front, and most previous studies on the Front have stressed his central role as the party's guiding force (Plenel 1984; Marcus 1995).

The final political facilitator is the party's organizational base. The Front's organizational base was essentially nonexistent at the party's creation, but as the party developed, its organizational needs became clearer. Although Hauss and Rayside (1978) argue that a new party does not need a strong organizational foundation to be created, it is clear that as a party matures, organizational strength may become more important.

As outlined in Figure 2.1, the institutional and political facilitators mediate between the cleavage structure and the creation of a new party. These facilitators help to transform the cleavage structure into a new political party. The importance of the political and structural facilitators in the creation of a party appears obvious, but change continues to occur once a party is created.

A life cycle approach to the development of parties may prove in-

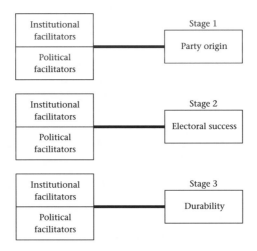

Figure 2.2   A Model for the Study of New Parties at Three Stages of Development

structive to the process of change in a mature party system. Such a development may be conceptualized as a three-stage process: (1) creation, (2) electoral success, and (3) durability (Pederson 1982; Janda and Gillies 1980; Harmel 1985). The impact of the different facilitators may change from one stage of the life cycle to the next (see Figure 2.2). Uncovering the variable influences of the facilitators at each level of the development process provides important information about political party development. The National Front is a compelling test case for this model of party development.

Elite Perspectives on Party Creation

Political party leaders serve as a repository of the party's oral history. As observers of the party's development, they possess unique knowledge that cannot be easily acquired through an analysis of mass-level survey research or electoral returns, and academic or popular media accounts are often based on secondhand sources that are unable to provide the rich details of political party development. The political elites who have participated in crafting the party's policy statements, managed and contested the campaigns, and served as the party's elected officials are uniquely aware of the party's evolution from creation to durability. It

Table 2.2 Facilitators of Party Creation

	Number of cases	Percentage citing as primary factor	Number of cases overall	Percentage overall
Leadership	13	48.1	23	85.2
Issues	11	40.7	21	77.8
Weak traditional parties	3	11.1	20	74.0
Presidential effect	—	—	4	14.8
Party organization	—	—	3	11.1
Media	—	—	2	7.4
Mass commitment	—	—	2	7.4
Other	—	—	3	11.1
Totals	27	99.9	78	288.8

Note: Overall percentage is over 100 because respondents were given the opportunity to name three factors.

is to these elites that we turn for their insights on the party's development.[5]

A number of interesting observations can be made from analyzing the responses of the Front elite. First, the uniformity of the responses is most significant. The consensus among the Front elite, at least with respect to the primary factors in the party's creation, is most revealing. Table 2.2 details these results. The respondents chose to name only three of the eight possible alternatives as the primary factor in promoting the Front's early development; the three most frequently cited factors are leadership, issues, and the weakness of the traditional parties. According to the party's primary decision makers, leadership and issues are of paramount importance in promoting the Front's creation. The combined influence of these two factors represents 88.8 percent of the first choice responses, and the behavior of the traditional parties accounts for the remaining first choice responses.

The overwhelming significance of political facilitators as opposed to institutional facilitators is readily apparent. The National Front elite regard two political facilitators, leadership and the weakness of the traditional parties, as crucial to the Front's creation. It is most interesting that no institutional factors are mentioned as first choice responses.

This agrees with the logic of Hauss and Rayside (1978), who argue that political factors play a more significant role in the creation of a political party than do institutional factors. A pattern similar to that of the first choice responses emerges when all possible responses are considered. The resulting distribution of the multiple responses reconfirms the importance of the three primary factors that comprise 82 percent of all possible responses.

Having discussed the import of the findings from a global perspective, it is important to consider the relative importance of the individual facilitators. At this stage of the party life cycle, a political facilitator, leadership, is mentioned more often than any other factor; 48.1 percent of the respondents contend that leadership is the most important factor in promoting the early development of the party, and 85.2 percent mention it overall. It is interesting to note that the respondents place leadership before issues in their discussions of the Front's early development. This analysis of the elite rankings in conjunction with the evidence garnered from the interview data lead to the conclusion that Jean-Marie Le Pen clearly played an instrumental role in promoting the early development of the National Front. For example, when asked to explain the creation of the party, this frontiste quickly answers, "First off, there was the personality of Jean-Marie Le Pen." This type of response is echoed by almost all respondents who mention the importance of leadership. This former National Assembly deputy deftly outlines the influence Le Pen exerts over the party:

> He is eminent . . . because of many factors. First, he has an understanding of things totally beyond the average person's. He knows how to put together a prospectus. Second, he is experienced politically. He has thirty years of political experience . . . things are automatic. Third, I believe that he has a real sense of friendship. He has exceptional charisma strengthened by the power of his convictions and his exceptional speech making abilities.

The importance of leadership in promoting the party's early development cannot be underestimated. Le Pen's role, or at least the party's perspective of Le Pen's role, is substantial.

Although the respondents rank leadership only slightly ahead of the issues that help to form the party's cleavage structure, the theoretical import of these findings is quite significant. Conventional wisdom maintains that a political party's creation is most contingent upon the existence of a defined cleavage structure. As Hauss and Rayside (1978) have argued, a cleavage is a necessary condition, but not a sufficient one. These data confirm this theory and elaborate upon it. They indicate quite clearly that the cleavage structure does play a dominant role, but it is the effective politicization of the cleavage structure by a skillful and forceful leadership that brings the creation of the party to fruition.

The issues of immigration and insécurité form the core of the complex cleavage structure upon which the Front is based. When asked to rank the factors that promoted the party's creation, the respondents cite issues as second in importance to leadership. Given the extremely volatile nature of the Front's primary issues, it is not surprising to observe that eleven of the twenty-seven respondents rate this facilitator as more important than leadership; approximately 41 percent of the respondents mention the Front's issues as the primary factor in promoting the party's early development, and close to 78 percent mention it overall.

A third possibility, the weakness of the traditional parties, receives the remainder of the first choice responses. The respondents uniformly criticize the poor performance of the majority party at the time of the Front's creation. This member fondateur is most critical of the mainstream right:

> In 1972, we believed that the time had arrived for the reestablishment of an authentic conservative movement. It was the initiative to reconstitute an authentic conservative party . . . a more dynamic and popular organization than the existent traditional parties such as the RPR, etcetera.

Although only 11 percent of the respondents cite this factor as the most important facilitator, 74 percent mention it overall as one of the factors that played a major role in the Front's creation. The leaders of the National Front are extremely critical of the other political parties in the system. They contend that before the creation of the National Front, France lacked a *droite de conviction* (truly committed right). The weakness of the traditional parties is viewed as an important contributor to the Front's success at this first level. Many of the respondents remark upon the faults of the traditional center right parties in France. This former member of the RPR maintains that the Front was created because there was a "lack of determination on the part of the other political parties."

Obstacles at the Creation Level

A comprehensive theory of new party development requires an under-standing not only of the factors that promote party development but also of those factors that may inhibit party development. Utilizing the identical set of factors, the respondents were asked to follow the same procedure and rank those factors they view as obstacles to the early development of the National Front. The results of this discussion are de-tailed in Table 2.3.

The Front's 1986 legislative campaign manifesto, *Pour la France: Programme du Front National,* begins with an attack on the media: "The National Front has fought for ten years in the media desert that protects the fortress of the Gang of Four" (1985, 7).[6] Completely in step with this party line, the Front's core elites are quick to name the media as the most important barrier to the Front's early development: a majority, ap-proximately 52 percent, name the media as the primary barrier to the party's creation, and close to 89 percent name them as an obstacle over-all. This indicates a striking consensus of opinion on the part of the Front's leadership. When discussing the Front's relationship with the media, the respondents contend that during the early years the party's activities were virtually ignored by the media and that, on those rare occasions when the Front did receive coverage, it was uniformly nega-tive. Some respondents maintain that negative coverage was better than no coverage at all.

The respondents do not differentiate between electronic and print media; instead, they seem to view the media as a monolith intent on destroying their fledgling party. This former National Assembly deputy, like many of his colleagues, reacts to the media assaults in an extremely personal and indignant manner:

> The dishonesty of the politicians and the journalists—the dishon-esty—there is no other term. I feel that it is dishonest to say of people who were never racists, nor xenophobes, nor fascists, nor Nazis, to insult them. . . . Me, I fought the Germans, and it really hurts me each time I hear that I am a Nazi, or a fascist . . . that really does something to me. I was in the French First Army.

Many of the respondents contend that the media play too active and too important a role in the political process. Some of the leaders articu-late this view by characterizing the media as a powerful lobbying force

Table 2.3   Obstacles to Party Creation

	Number of cases	Percentage citing as primary factor	Number of cases overall	Percentage overall
Media	14	51.9	24	88.9
Electoral system	8	29.6	21	77.8
Presidential effect	2	7.4	6	22.2
Party organization	2	7.4	6	22.2
Mass commitment	1	3.7	8	29.6
Weak traditional parties	—	—	2	7.4
Other	—	—	3	11.1
Totals	27	100.0	70	259.2

Note: Overall percentage is over 100 because respondents were given the opportunity to name three factors.

that carries out a nonstop direct assault on the Front, its leaders, and its ideas. A veteran of the party's parliamentary group is quick to view the Front's relationship with the media in warlike terms:

> We are directly under attack by the media. The media makes up a veritable fourth power in France: the crushing majority of the media, supported by an intellectual class that is oriented to the left and tied to the antinational lobbies. And we are accused—singularly the National Front and Jean-Marie Le Pen—are the continual object of a totally bewildering [process of] disinformation. For example, the qualitative of racism, although the Front is the only political party to have elected French Muslims. No other political party has French Muslims.

These sentiments are echoed by another frontiste who describes the conflictual relationship that exists between the Front and the media: "The media . . . is not only an intermediary, but an actor. The media is often an active player and also very often, it's necessary to say, an adversary."

The leaders of the National Front are justified in bemoaning their infrequent media appearances before 1984. The media, print or otherwise, were not interested in the Front's activities for one simple reason: they were not newsworthy. Unable to generate votes, weakened by political infighting, and pushed to the far right fringes of the political spectrum, the National Front was, during its early years, politically irrelevant. Simply put, the media was not interested in the Front because the Front was uninteresting.

In addition to the media, the leadership of the Front views the electoral system as a significant obstacle. This is the institutional factor most often mentioned by the respondents; nearly 30 percent contend that the two-round majority system was the Front's primary obstacle during the earliest stages of the party's development, and approximately 78 percent name it as an obstacle overall. The respondents claim that the two-round electoral system systematically favors the major parties in the system. One frontiste says simply that, "Among the obstacles, it's evident that the two-round majority system is a major obstacle."

As a new political party, the Front is severely disadvantaged by the two-round system. Because this system tends to foster the creation of electoral alliances between the first and second rounds, newer, smaller parties are placed in precarious political positions, for it is nearly impossible for them to enter successfully into advantageous alliances. Operating within an electoral system that was expressly designed to diminish the impact of smaller marginal political parties proved exceedingly difficult for the Front. This membre fondateur details the Front's tenuous electoral position during its early years:

> Yes, there were obstacles. The fact that we chose the democratic path, for a political party that means participating in elections. At the time, we had the two-round majority system. It's obvious that when you are starting a movement with very few financial resources. . . . [T]his type of electoral system is very unfavorable.

The leaders of the Front uniformly mention the combined negative impact of the media and the electoral system. According to the respondents, it was as if these two obstacles were working in tandem to create an incredibly hostile political environment for the nascent National Front in 1972. These two factors account for 64.3 percent of all responses offered by the leaders of the Front. Other factors mentioned include the level of mass commitment as well as the impact of the presidential effect and the party's weak organizational structure during its early years. But these three factors account for less than 30 percent of all the responses.

Overall, the respondents are more divided on the major obstacle than on the primary facilitator. This lack of consensus is evident by the fact that the leaders of the Front identify only three factors as the most dominant facilitator, but a total of five different factors are mentioned as the major obstacle. In addition, institutional factors are more likely to be viewed as obstacles than political facilitators; ten of the twenty-seven party leaders, accounting for 37 percent of the responses, contend that such institutional factors as the electoral system and the dominance of presidential politics inhibited the early development of the Front.

Conclusion

The history of the French far right clearly demonstrates the ideological legacy the Front inherited from its philosophical ancestors. French political culture clearly provides a hospitable environment for the development of far right political movements, and the ideological currents resurrected by the Front provided in essence a cradle in which to nourish the inchoate political party. In 1972, the preexisting cleavage structure combined with the contemporary social context in which the founders of the Front operated provided fertile ground for a new party. This context is a necessary condition, but alone it is unable to promote the development of a new political party. The stage was set, so to speak, but there were no players.

The preexisting cleavage structure and social context needed to be effectively politicized. The historical record in conjunction with the elite interviews trace the Front's early development to the student activists of Ordre Nouveau. Hampered by internal power struggles and conflicting political goals, they were able only to begin the process of creating a new political party; the leadership of Jean-Marie Le Pen was needed to bring the process to fruition. Le Pen is often incorrectly credited with creating the National Front, but as we have noted, the Front was actually created by François Brigneau, François Duprat, and Alain Robert, all leading activists in the now defunct Ordre Nouveau. Le Pen's contribution, and the Front's other leaders underscore this point, is that he more than any other contemporary far right figure was able to oversee the coalescence of the disparate elements that constitute the French far right (Charlot 1986). The multiplicity of groups, ideologies, personalities, and strategies that existed on the far right fringe of French politics made it difficult, if not nearly impossible, for this multiheaded Hydra to speak with one voice. Maurice Bardèche, Vichy apologist and postwar neofascist intellectual, resoundingly criticized the sorry state of the French far right just prior to the Front's creation: "The activists do not recognize their common ancestors. Some are fascists, others maurrassians, and certain others call themselves fundamentalists and each of these categories includes its own variants. They do not understand one another, nor do they understand the terms they employ: revolution, counter-revolution, nationalism, Europe. For each group they [the terms] have different meanings. How could they champion the same ideology?" (1970, 237). Le Pen's ability, especially during the party's early years, to ride roughshod over the many groups that make up the far right may well be his legacy to the movement that has occupied his entire adult life.

The elite rankings, the interview data, the historical record, and the survey data underscore the integral contributions of the preexisting cleavage structure and Le Pen's leadership in facilitating the party's early development, but the impact of these two factors was enhanced by a third factor: the behavior of the existing political parties. As Jacques Chirac transformed the Gaullist Party into a mass-based organization that would serve as the vessel of his own presidential aspirations, he increasingly neglected the overt nationalism and pretenses of *grandeur* that had been so tightly linked to the Gaullist legacy. This in turn created a void on the right that Le Pen and his political cohorts were only too happy to fill.

It was the conjunction of these three factors that promoted and sustained the development of the National Front during the party's formative years. This European Parliament deputy underscores the complex link between Le Pen's initiative and the behavior of the existing parties: "I believe that Jean-Marie Le Pen must have felt that the existing parties didn't measure up. . . . [T]hey did not correspond to what he wanted for France. He wanted to put a new movement in place."

The strength of these three factors enabled the struggling party to overcome the obstacles it faced during this difficult period in its development. As the data indicate, the media and the two-round majority electoral system served as significant obstacles to the Front's political viability. The determination of Le Pen and the ineptitude of the traditional parties helped the Front eventually reach electoral success. The factors that contributed to the Front's 1984 electoral breakthrough are the focus of the next chapter.

INITIAL SUCCESS: ELECTION

VICTORIES IN 1984 AND 1986

Le problème n'est pas la création, mais l'émergence.

—National Front regional councillor [1]

In the early 1980s, a resurrected and electorally competitive extreme right seemed to many to be a most unlikely possibility. No one could have predicted the sequence of events that was to lead to the resounding and unexpected results in the 1984 European elections. Only Jean-Marie Le Pen and his core group of supporters kept the faith as they crossed the electoral desert in the 1970s and early 1980s.

Many political parties are created, but few succeed in actually gaining electoral representation. Although legally chartered in 1972 as the nationalist and right-wing political alternative, the National Front failed to have any impact whatsoever in the French electoral arena until 1983. Le Pen and his political allies achieved their first significant electoral breakthrough in the 1984 European elections, but the path that led the party and its faithful supporters to that point was a carefully scripted effort that was drafted by the party's secretary-general, Jean-Pierre Stirbois. The political effort that led to the 1984 breakthrough consisted of the Front's participating in one election after another throughout the 1970s and early 1980s. The party had begun to outline its political identity, agenda, and goals, but until 1983 it remained unsuccessful in developing that identity, pursuing that agenda, and achieving those goals. After many years of disappointing campaigns and what appeared to be wasted efforts, the National Front finally gained national and international attention as well as a modicum of legitimacy in the 1984 European election. In this chapter, we examine the factors that contributed to this electoral breakthrough.

The success achieved in the European elections did not occur without intense political preparation. Before the 1984 election, the Front took a series of tentative steps in a sequence of municipal and legislative by-elections. "During 1983 the National Front succeeded in an electoral breakthrough in four stages: Paris, Dreux, Aulnay-sous-Bois, and Moribhan" (Plenel and Rollat 1984, 95). One regional councillor, discussing the emergence of the Front, contends that, "Initially, there was a precedent, which was the municipal [elections] of 1983." To better understand the sequence of events that led to the 1984 European electoral breakthrough, these tentative successes need to be examined in greater detail. The four elections that preceded the 1984 European contest are important because they set the stage for the Front's later successes; moreover, they underscore the importance local-level politics continues to play in France.

During the municipal elections of March 1983, the National Front competed in seven arrondissements in Paris. Le Pen stood for election in the twentieth arrondissement, a neighborhood that had had difficulty adjusting to the recent waves of immigrants. He received 11.26 percent of the vote, which propelled him to the municipal council of the arrondissement. Le Pen's decision to campaign in the twentieth arrondissement was an important strategic choice. The leading candidate of the left, Michel Charzat, contended that Le Pen "exploited an unhealthy climate which prevails in the popular neighborhoods where housing is decayed, the unemployment high, and the numerous foreigners poorly assimilated. . . . This xenophobic and poujadist vote is very disconcerting. There is a risk of radicalization" (in Plenel and Rollat 1984, 98). Charzat's astute commentary on Le Pen's campaign in the twentieth arrondissement foreshadowed quite elegantly the mainstream parties' relationships with Le Pen and his party for the next ten years.

The Front then achieved national prominence during the Dreux municipal elections of 1983. For years, Jean-Pierre Stirbois and his wife, Marie-France, had contested election after election in Dreux.[2] Their protracted labors on the campaign trail finally yielded dividends in 1983 (Perrineau 1993a). The Front's list, with the Stirbois duo at the helm, received 16.7 percent in the first round. The leaders of the center right in Dreux, who badly wanted to defeat the incumbent left, saw their opportunity, seized it, and merged with the Front in the second round. The mainstream right's decision to align itself with the Front conferred upon the insurgent Front forces a measure of legitimacy. Before the "Le Pen effect" of 1984, there was the Dreux effect (Rollat 1985). This local alliance highlighted a disturbing development: that to defeat the left, the center right was now willing, at least momentarily, to abandon its integrity as well as its political conscience and merge with the far right fringe elements found in the National Front.[3] At the national level, the leaders of the RPR and the UDF sharply criticized this alliance. The Front's success in the first round combined with the mainstream right's seal of approval made the Dreux municipal election a minor national sensation.

Another municipal by-election took place in Aulnay-sous-Bois in October 1983. At the time, the Front was riding a wave of success and profiting from the publicity generated by the election of Le Pen and Stirbois to the municipal councils in Paris and Dreux, respectively. To capitalize on their newfound legitimacy and notoriety, Stirbois and Le Pen made their way to Aulnay-sous-Bois to campaign personally for Guy Viarengo, the Front's candidate. Viarengo received only 9.3 percent of the vote, but this was enough to maintain the publicity boom this fortuitous series of minor successes was generating for the party. Although the results prevented Viarengo from competing in the second round of balloting, "[it was] nevertheless a confirmation of the rise of the Le Pen tide" (Milza 1987, 399).

The final, pivotal election for the Front in 1983 took place in December. Le Pen campaigned for election to the national legislature in a by-election in a district that comprises his hometown. His rising political profile and accomplished campaign skills helped him capture an impressive 12 percent of the vote. Furthermore, it is important to note that he performed this well without the direct appeal of his anti-immigration rhetoric. "Of all the regions in France, Brittany has the lowest level of foreigners—.09 percent" (Plenel and Rollat 1984, 96).

The 1984 European Election

Although this sequence of electoral surprises in 1983 created much-needed publicity, the Front's role as a political party of national importance was not established until the 1984 European parliamentary election, wherein the Front achieved its first national electoral success.

The political climate in 1984 differed markedly from that of 1972. Power, at both the executive and legislative levels, had shifted to the left for the first time in the history of the Fifth Republic. In raw political terms, this translated as Socialist control of the government for the first time since 1957. Jaffré contends that "The renaissance of an influential extreme right constitutes one of the most notable events of the left's period in power" (1986, 211). Ironically, the residual effects of the

Table 3.1   1984 European Parliament Election

List	Votes	Percentage	Seats	Percentage
RPR/UDF	8,470,687	42.75	41	50.63
Socialist Party	4,129,202	20.84	20	24.69
Communist Party	2,211,305	11.16	10	12.34
National Front	2,193,377	11.07	10	12.34

Note: Includes only those parties receiving seats.

left's first opportunity to govern the Fifth Republic turned out to be a renewed and electorally savvy far right.

Furthermore, political circumstances had continued to diminish the strength of the Gaullist legacy. The RPR, although the strongest political party on the mainstream conservative right, ran a unity list with the UDF in the European elections. Competing in the second European parliamentary elections under a system of proportional representation by national lists, the National Front campaigned with a list of eighty-one candidates. The Front's list attracted 11 percent of the total vote, which translated into ten European parliamentary deputies. The results of the 1984 European elections are outlined in Table 3.1.

Such a successful outcome was unprecedented for a far right party in the Fifth Republic; in fact, this was the far right's most impressive showing since the Poujadists were propelled to the center of the French political arena after the 1956 legislative election. After more than a decade of fruitless campaigns, Le Pen and his cohorts had finally made their mark in the legitimate arena of partisan politics. In reality, they were as surprised as anyone by the results. Stirbois, whose efforts in Dreux had laid the foundation for this breakthrough, was perhaps more surprised than anyone: "The day after, despite the interviews with journalists and FR3 [a French television network], I had a hard time believing it. Six months earlier, who could have ever predicted this political thunderbolt?" (1988, 87).

Although viewed as an election of marginal importance by many, the European contest did offer the Front its first taste of national success.[4] The unexpected outcome of the 1984 European elections revitalized the party's activists. After so many years of poor performances in the electoral arena, the Front finally was a legitimate participant in a bona fide legislature, albeit not in Paris but in Strasbourg. Not surprisingly, those in the National Front elite mark this election as an important milestone in their party's development. This frontiste echoes the sentiments of his compatriots:

> The election of 1984 was a sort of explosion. In particular, the French had had enough of listening to mealymouthed politicians. The 1984 election was a reaction against the existing political parties, decadence and decline, [wherein] the people displayed their confidence in Jean-Marie Le Pen.

As previously noted, the electoral system for the 1984 European parliamentary elections was one of proportional representation, with the parties running national lists. The Front took advantage of this different electoral system; Le Pen's name, the most recognized in the party, obviously headed its slate of candidates. Unlike proportional representation by districts and the traditional two-round system, the European parliamentary contest played to the Front's strength; the electoral system, the irrelevance of the *vote utile* phenomenon, and the low level of importance attached to the elections all worked to the Front's advantage.[5] The European elections were the first to highlight the Front's ability to mobilize its forces. Since then, the Front has been very successful in getting out the vote; whereas the supporters of the more mainstream political parties will often sit out the less important elections, the Front's loyalists go to the polls, thereby generating continued interest in this emerging political force.

One of the most striking developments of the 1984 European elections was that the Front entered the European Parliament on an equal footing with the French Communist Party. Georges Marchais's party posted its worst showing in the history of the Fifth Republic and began a decline that was to continue unabated throughout the decade and into the early 1990s. To the shock of the traditional parties and the media, over 2 million people voted for the Front d'Opposition Nationale pour l'Europe des Patries, the official designation of Le Pen's list of candidates. Seemingly overnight, after approximately eleven years in political purgatory, the National Front became a major player in French partisan politics. Immediately, the previously exiled political party began to attract unprecedented national and international media attention. The Front was now newsworthy.

The 1986 Legislative Election

With a tentative start during the European elections and continuing through the 1986 legislative campaign, Le Pen began an intense period of elite recruitment. He concentrated on enlisting the support and services of a new cadre of political elites; he not only wanted to promote their service to the organization by making them activists of the first order, he also wanted to convince these new elite recruits to become legislative candidates under the National Front's banner. His aggressive efforts began to pay substantial dividends during the early stages of the 1986 legislative campaign. The Front attracted such well-known politicians as Edouard Frédéric-Dupont, the doyen of French deputies, and such rising politicians as Yvon Briant and Bruno Mégret. Pascal Arrighi, François Bachelot, Charles de Chambrun, Michel de Rostolan, Pierre Descaves, Jean-Yves Le Gallou, Jean-Claude Martinez, François Porteu de la Morandière, and Jean Roussel were also recruited during this period. These individuals brought many important assets to the Front. They either possessed considerable political experience or they were well-known in their own professional circles; Arrighi and de Chambrun are good examples of the former, and Bachelot, Descaves, and Martinez represent the latter case. All of these individuals, except Le Gallou, were subsequently elected in the 1986 legislative contest. By joining the Front and having their names placed at the top of the departmental proportional lists, these newly recruited *notables* were essentially guaranteed a seat in the National Assembly, provided the Front held onto the 10 percent of the vote it had received in the most recent European elections.

The arrival of these *notables* infused the party with much-needed energy, resources, and expertise. Their abilities and high public profiles allowed them to move rapidly into the higher echelons of the party hierarchy, and the Front strategically maneuvered many of these individuals into high-profile positions within the party. This was a calculated move on the part of Le Pen and his inner circle to sanitize the movement's negative public image. This process of legitimization helped the Front appear more acceptable to the French professional political class. Rewarding these new arrivals with positions of importance not only helped ameliorate the Front's negative image but was also seen as a method to ensure the *notables'* loyalty. This *notable,* who joined the party during this period, recounts a typical route to membership in the Front:

Concerning my membership in the Front, I joined rather late in 1983 or 1984—beginning of 1984. I didn't have any faith in political activity. I was rather involved in rightist circles—I knew Le Pen, I especially knew Jean-Pierre Stirbois, and I knew and was a friend of Roger Holeindre. Because of these many connections they asked me to take on the responsibility of the movement in ———. It wasn't until after they asked that I joined. I joined and at the same time I had a position of importance.

Many of the *notables* who joined the Front during this period claimed to have always been sympathetic to Le Pen's political program but had hesitated to join because of the party's negative image. A common refrain among the new arrivals was "I always voted for Le Pen." Explaining his reasons for not joining the party sooner, this former National Assembly deputy says:

> I waited until 1984. . . . I was always a friend to Le Pen. In my capacity as mayor, I always gave my signature for the presidential elections, but I didn't become a member of the party until the European elections because I felt that I had to join in order for the Front to get the maximum number of European parliamentary deputies.

One respondent, a seasoned politician as well as a former Gaullist deputy, waited until late in 1985 before he accepted Le Pen's invitation to join the party. The Front's inability to attract votes had deterred him from placing his political future in the hands of a weak and fledgling party: "With no elected officials, no audience, it serves no purpose. I waited for a real party." Such sentiments illustrate succinctly the importance attached to a new political party's first national-level success. A new political party needs a national-level success to reach the second major threshold of the political party life cycle. The success the Front achieved in the 1984 European elections provided the party with elected officials, and these newly elected officials attracted an expanded audience of voters and new recruits. The former Gaullist deputy finally overcame his hesitation and answered Le Pen's call in 1985, once he was sure the party had elected officials and an audience. He was subsequently elected to the National Assembly in 1986 as a representative of this "real party." The Front's 1984 electoral breakthrough resulted in a plethora of political gains. It provided the Front with elected officials and incredible publicity, and it opened the doorway to a new and more respectable class of political operatives. The comments by the wary former Gaullist deputy underscore the complex relationship that exists between a party's initial electoral success and subsequent political advances.

Le Pen's role in this recruitment process was of paramount importance. The common refrain was "Le Pen and I have been friends for many years," or "Le Pen called me and asked if I'd help out." Obviously, Le Pen's personal invitation played an integral part in the recruitment process. No one else in the party had his stature or influence. The leadership displayed by Le Pen in attracting quality, name candidates cannot be underestimated. Another of the newly recruited *notables* emphasizes his personal relationship with Le Pen, but is also quick to mention the talents he himself brought to the party. He claims he entered "by the main door":

> I joined the Front because the president, Jean-Marie Le Pen, needed, in view of the legislative elections of March 1986, professionals—people having abilities of a sufficiently high caliber. And he did not want to have people in the assembly who weren't up to the task of dealing with the problems they would face at the National Assembly. In addition, he didn't want to have representatives who weren't able, at least, to discuss at an equal level with the other political parties. Since I have known him for thirty-four years, he asked me if I would accept or if I was interested.

The goal of this massive recruitment was to facilitate the Front's success in the 1986 National Assembly elections. High-profile candidates, the newly recruited *notables,* would head the departmental lists. Previous electoral results indicated that the Front would perform well in the 1986 legislative contest; under a national-level proportional representation system, as in the European election, the Front garnered 11 percent of the vote. Now, however, for the first time in the Fifth Republic, national elections were to be conducted under a district-level proportional system. This 1985 decision to change the electoral system fulfilled one of President Mitterrand's 1981 campaign promises, but his motives for the electoral modification were rooted in more purely political considerations. Approximately a year before the mandatory National Assembly elections, Mitterrand realized that the electoral system would need to be altered to cut the expected Socialist losses and possibly preserve his control over the legislature. In his attempts to safeguard the political fortunes of his own Socialist Party, Mitterrand facilitated the entry of the far right into the National Assembly for the first time in over thirty years.

If successful, the Front's influence, which at the time was isolated to a few areas, would be significantly extended. The change in electoral systems benefited political parties like the National Front, and that was why continued elite recruitment was essential; with one or two *notables* heading each of the district lists, the Front was well poised to enter the National Assembly. The optimal result would have been to have recruited at least one or two *notables* for each of the ninety-six constituencies in mainland France because, as this founding member of the Front says, "the first two or three on the list pull along the rest. . . . [Y]ou can put just about anybody in the tenth position and that has no importance."

The results of the election were more than encouraging (see Table 3.2). The Front performed admirably, capturing 9.7 percent of the vote and seating thirty-five deputies in the National Assembly. The ascendent National Front was now represented in the French legislature on a scale equivalent to that of the declining Communist Party. The massive recruitment had helped to sanitize the movement's poor image, at least for the time being. One of these *notables* immodestly attributes the Front's newfound success to the arrival of the new recruits:

> I believe that the quality of the candidates also played a role. We witnessed the appearance of some people, certain *responsables* who were willing to take risks by being candidates. A Martinez, a Mégret, or a Bachelot, they created problems of conscience for a lot of people who knew them because they were politically active: Mégret in the RPR, Martinez at the Faculté, and Bachelot in politics. Some people who knew them followed them. They also had an impact on the rank and file of the party. They [the rank and file] were able to say, "We have intellectuals in the party and not just skinheads." That was psychologically important for the rank and file. That was the strategy.

The presence of the new arrivals was strongly felt among the thirty-five-member parliamentary body. Sixteen of the Front's newly elected deputies had joined the party between 1984 and 1986; a few of these new recruits joined the Political Bureau or took on other important tasks in the party. In anticipation of the 1988 presidential elections, the Front continued its effort to appear as politically mainstream as possible.

Table 3.2 1986 Legislative Elections

List	Percentage	Seats in National Assembly
Communists	9.7	35
Socialists	31.6	208
Left Radicals	.3	2
UDF/RPR	42.0	129/145
National Front	9.7	35

The 1988 Presidential Campaign

Historically, the French far right has not performed well in presidential contests since the establishment of a directly elected executive. The debacle of the 1965 Tixier-Vignancour presidential campaign and Le Pen's 1981 humiliation at not obtaining the sponsorship signatures necessary to have his name placed on the ballot are the most glaring examples of the far right's weakness at the presidential level. As preparations for the presidential campaign began, Le Pen was determined to improve upon his previous presidential attempts. The presidential election of 1988 was not to be a repeat of those earlier disasters.

The National Front's presidential campaign started early. Returning to Brittany and his home town of La Trinité-sur-Mer, Le Pen announced his candidacy on April 26, 1987, a full year in advance of the elections. The National Front's leader, surrounded by his entourage, traversed the country for the entire period. The presidential initiative, with Bruno Mégret serving as campaign director, modeled itself after an American-style campaign. Mégret, one of the recently arrived *notables,* had an impressive political résumé. He was a founding member of the Comités d'Action Républicaines, a conservative think tank, as well as a recent political refugee from the RPR. Le Pen's decision to entrust the direction of his presidential campaign to a "new" frontiste signaled an important shift in the party's political orientation. This was clearly another step in the party's strategy to sanitize its ancien combattant image and extend its influence beyond the political ghetto of the French far right.

An indefatigable orator, Le Pen spread the gospel according to the National Front, seizing every opportunity to appear on television and radio. Many of the *notables* recruited during the 1986 legislative elec-

Table 3.3   1988 Presidential Election

Candidate	Votes	Percentage
Lajoinie (Communist Party)	2,055,995	6.8
Mitterrand (Socialist Party)	10,367,220	34.1
Barre (UDF)	5,031,849	16.5
Chirac (RPR)	6,063,514	19.9
Le Pen (National Front)	4,375,894	14.4

Source: *Les élections législatives. Supplement aux dossiers et documents du Monde 1988.*
Note: Includes only those candidates from the major political groups.

tions took on high-profile positions in the campaign, often serving as surrogates for Le Pen at the many campaign events Mégret organized throughout the country. The efficient nature of the campaign, its early start, and Le Pen's considerable campaign skills generated much interest in the Le Pen–Mégret political caravan. On the far right fringe of the political spectrum, history was indeed repeating itself. Mégret and Le Pen were now playing the roles that Le Pen and Tixier-Vignancour had played in the 1965 presidential contest; this time, though, Le Pen was the candidate and Mégret the master campaign strategist. Some would say that Mégret was a better strategist than Le Pen, but in all fairness, Le Pen proved to be a better candidate than Tixier-Vignancour.

Once again, the results surpassed the predictions of the preelection polls. Throughout the course of its early political ascent, the Front's actual vote totals have been consistently underestimated by approximately 3 to 5 percent in preelection studies conducted by the major French polling organizations. In the mid-1980s, French survey firms were repeatedly unable to ascertain the strength of the Front's mass-level support. Especially during the early years, survey respondents were unwilling to self-identify as Front supporters. Preelection polls for the 1988 presidential contest had forecast that Le Pen would be lucky to receive 10 percent; he actually received 14.4 percent of the vote, ranking fourth among nine candidates, with over 4 million casting their ballots for the leader of the far right (see Table 3.3). This represents a dramatic increase in the votes the Front amassed during its first national-level success in the 1984 European elections. The 1988 presidential elections also highlight the fidelity of Le Pen's supporters; exit polls indicate that

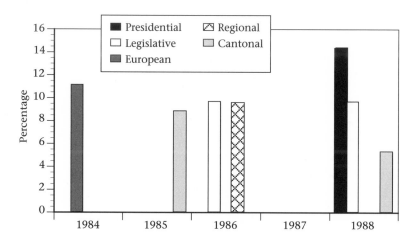

Figure 3.1   National Front Vote, 1984–1988

90 percent of those who voted for the Front in 1986 turned out for Le Pen in the first round of the presidential contest. This level of party loyalty from one election to the next surpasses that achieved by any of the other major candidates; moreover, it is an important indication of the growing levels of mass commitment generated by the Front in the mid-1980s. Figure 3.1 presents the results from each of the Front's electoral campaigns from 1984 to 1988.

Again, Le Pen's success contrasts sharply with the performance of the Communist Party's candidate; he outpolled the leading Communist candidate, André Lajoinie, by 2,319,899 votes. More importantly, Le Pen matched Lajoinie's score among the working class. In addition, there was solid confirmation that his rhetoric about immigration and unemployment was effective. In this election, the unemployed favored Le Pen over Lajoinie 2 to 1. The French political establishment was stunned. Perhaps most surprising was the narrow margin of 655,955 votes separating Le Pen and Raymond Barre, the former prime minister. These results represent an amazing achievement for a candidate who in 1981 had been unable to gather the 500 sponsorship signatures to have his name placed on the presidential ballot. Moreover, Le Pen's 4,375,894 vote total doubled the amount the Front received in the 1984 European elections, representing an unprecedented political progression in just four years.

The far right's presidential campaign of 1988 differed markedly from its previous electoral initiatives. In all respects, this was a professional political campaign almost American in its many staged events; in fact, Mégret had actually studied in the United States. His political experience and campaign savvy helped "Le Pen establish the historical record for the electoral implantation of the extreme right in France" (Perrineau 1989, 49).

Elite Perspectives on the Front's 1984 Electoral Breakthrough

When the Front's leaders were asked to rank those factors that they believed contributed to the party's 1984 electoral breakthrough, they mentioned only five of the eight possible factors as first choice responses: (1) the electoral system, (2) leadership, (3) the issues, (4) mass commitment, and (5) weak traditional parties. This is interesting in light of the fact that at the creation level, the party's leaders offer a more narrow range of only three first choice responses. This greater variability in the range of responses at the second stage of the party's development than at the first perhaps indicates the political complexities inherent in attaining the first major electoral breakthrough. Whereas the creation of a political party is a difficult endeavor, it is primarily dependent on two factors: effective political entrepreneurship and a mobilized cleavage structure. This contrasts sharply with a party's electoral breakthrough, which is dependent on a greater number of political and institutional factors.

The party elites mention the electoral system most often as the primary facilitator of the party's electoral breakthrough, with 35.7 percent rating it as the most important facilitator and 82.1 percent mentioning it overall (see Table 3.4). The primary significance of the electoral system's impact on the development of the Front cannot be underestimated. This former National Assembly deputy emphatically believes that, "Obviously, the system of proportional representation enabled us to survive."

The system of proportional representation utilized in the European elections mitigated the pernicious effects the vote utile has over the newer and smaller parties. Although Kitschelt argues that "it is unclear whether the proportional format of the European election in fact helped or hurt the National Front," the evidence clearly indicates that the Front has prospered in proportional representation frameworks and suffered in the two-round majority system (1997, 101).[6] The two-round electoral system focuses attention on the first-round vote choice; in the first round of voting for the National Assembly, a candidate must receive at

Table 3.4   Facilitators of Electoral Breakthrough

	Number of cases	Percentage citing as primary factor	Number of cases overall	Percentage overall
Electoral system	10	35.7	23	82.1
Leadership	9	32.1	21	75.0
Issues	6	21.4	17	60.7
Mass commitment	2	7.1	5	17.9
Weak traditional parties	1	3.6	14	50.0
Media	—	—	2	7.1
Party organization	—	—	1	3.6
Totals	28	99.9	83	296.4

Note: Overall percentage is over 100 because respondents were given the opportunity to name three factors.

least 12.5 percent of the *registered* vote to compete in the second round. Voters are consequently reluctant to cast their ballot for a party that only has a narrow chance of continuing on into the second round; thus, they feel compelled to cast their ballot for the major political parties, ensuring that their vote will play a role in the electoral contest. This vote utile phenomenon deters the voters from expressing their support for the minor parties in the system. This membre fondateur contends that the 1984 European contest was the first real opportunity for the voters to voice their support for the Front without feeling they had wasted their ballot:

> [It was the] first election where for us the vote utile played no role, because the European Parliament elections were proportional. Contrary to what is currently taking place, the people who voted for us don't feel like they were wasting their vote.

Although the electoral system is of primary importance in facilitating the Front's early political successes, it does not act alone. In addition to the electoral system, 32.1 percent of the respondents mention the party's leadership as the most important facilitator, and 75 percent name it as a general facilitator. The interrelationship between the electoral system and the leadership is particularly significant as a party develops beyond the creation stage and strives for its first electoral breakthrough. Combined, these two facilitators account for 67.8 percent of the first choice responses and 53 percent of the responses overall. Discussing an explanation for the 1984 election success, this frontiste points directly to the combined importance of the electoral system and the party's leadership: "Obviously, proportional representation. [And] the leadership, always . . . one of our strengths is that we have an excellent leader."

Two other responses, issues and the flaws of the mainstream parties, account for a significant number of the total responses; approximately 61 percent of the respondents mention the issues, and 50 percent mention the behavior of the traditional parties. As one would expect, the Front's leaders are especially critical of the behavior of the traditional parties; over 50 percent mention this political facilitator as a significant determinant in promoting the Front's 1984 electoral success. In his attempt to explain the party's 1984 electoral breakthrough, this former National Assembly deputy points directly at the mainstream political parties: "The incompetence of the other political parties. The rising rejection of the political class. That's to say their lack of conviction and their refusal to consider the real problems like immigration." The Front's criticism of the other parties is universal; it knows no ideological boundaries. The RPR, the UDF, the Socialist Party, and the Communist Party are each viewed as ineffectual by the elite of the French National Front.

To understand the foundation of this criticism, it needs to be placed in the appropriate context. At the time of the 1984 European parliamentary elections, the Socialist leadership was being resoundingly attacked for its inability to deal with France's economic woes. President Mitterrand was under siege because of a number of unpopular decisions and programs; the early 1980s was a period of high unemployment and failed Socialist initiatives in the industrial sector. In addition, Mitterrand also lost support in the early 1980s because of his stand on the omnipresent public-private school debate; the former situation led to the downfall of Pierre Mauroy, the first Socialist prime minister of the Fifth Republic, and the latter led to the largest public demonstrations since the 1960s. This perspective is effectively communicated by this Front leader:

> In the European election of 1984, I believe that the first factor was that the French population was fed up with the left which was in power. All the mistakes that were made, the extremism of the left which committed all the errors, the errors committed in 1981,

1982, 1983—that's what explains it. And the weak reaction of the traditional right parties.

The Socialist and Communist Parties were not the only mainstream parties to come under attack; the parties on the right were also being criticized. This respondent is resolute in her conviction that the behavior of the traditional rightist parties was a major contributor to the Front's victory in the European elections: "The dissatisfaction of the people with respect to the existing parties on the right." The parties on the center right are criticized for their inability to counter the left as well as for the unity list they constructed for the 1984 European parliamentary election. The joint list constructed by the RPR and the UDF provided the Front with a great opportunity. The Front elite believe the unified slate of candidates was vulnerable because of the political figure the mainstream right had chosen to head the ballot. Discussing the reasons for the Front's success in 1984, this former National Assembly deputy offers "for the European elections, the choice of a centrist personality— Simone Veil—as the head of the list. A controversial personality already at that time." The anti-Veil sentiment is echoed by another of his colleagues, who says, "a good part of the Catholic electorate was hostile because of her role in the legalization of abortion."

Clearly, the Front's 1984 electoral success depended on a complex mix of factors. At this second stage of the party's development, the Front elite point to both institutional and political factors as central to the party's success.

Obstacles to Electoral Success

Many factors influence the success or failure of a new political party's electoral endeavors. Having already noted those facilitators that promoted the party's electoral breakthrough, we now turn our attention to those factors that inhibited the Front's development at this second stage of the party's life cycle.

To determine the barriers to the party's continued progress, the respondents were asked to rank those factors that may have inhibited the party's electoral breakthrough. In the previous chapter, the adversarial relationship that exists between the National Front elite and the media was highlighted; according to the Front's leadership, this pattern of conflict with the media continued throughout the second stage

Table 3.5   Obstacles to Electoral Breakthrough

	Number of cases	Percentage citing as primary factor	Number of cases overall	Percentage overall
Media	22	81.5	24	88.9
Party organization	3	11.1	7	25.9
Mass commitment	1	3.7	12	44.4
Other	1	3.7	3	11.1
Weak traditional parties	—	—	3	11.1
Presidential effect	—	—	1	3.7
Totals	27	100.0	50	185.1

Note: Overall percentage is over 100 because respondents were given the opportunity to name three factors.

of the party's development. The vast majority of the respondents, 81.5 percent, contend that the media were the Front's primary obstacle to success at this stage of the party's development (see Table 3.5). There is almost total consensus on this point, with 88.9 percent mentioning the media as a general inhibitor. In fact, the Front's leaders exhibit signs of paranoia when they begin talking about the relationship that exists between the party and the media. This former National Assembly deputy's comments illustrate the animosity inherent in this volatile relationship:

> There were the same obstacles, we always know it's the obstacles of the media. They don't speak about us at all, it's like the iron curtain. It's very difficult for us, our rallies, our conventions, our meetings, we'll draw 15,000 people and there will not be a line in the newspapers. It's terrible, you can try to do everything, have a huge crowd and they don't speak about it. They say you do not exist.

Another frontiste asserts that the party's relationship with the media is more ambiguous. He contends that the media are both an obstacle to and a factor in the party's success and that it is better to have the media saying something about the party rather than ignoring them completely:

> It's the major obstacle . . . the image that they make of us. It's not at all contradictory. It helped us because they spoke of us. It's ex-

tremely important that they speak about you. We are in a media society: without television, without the radio you are nothing.

Although the negative view of the media dominates the discussion of obstacles, two of the elite respondents mention the media as a contributing factor in the party's 1984 electoral success. An important element of this perspective on the Front's relationship with the media is directly related to an appearance by Le Pen on a very popular political talk show, *L'Heure de Verité* (The hour of truth) during the campaign. This frontiste believes that Le Pen's appearance on the show had a great impact on the Front's progress in the 1984 election:

> It was the crystallization of the French who had common sense and were on the right around Jean-Marie Le Pen. The appearance on *L'Heure de Verité* . . . an important moment. It was an hour and a half where for once Jean-Marie Le Pen directly . . . someone didn't say what he thought, he said himself what he thought. It was a completely new phenomenon.

This "completely new phenomenon" was instrumental in the Front's 1984 electoral breakthrough. The antagonistic relationship that exists between the Front and the media is an important source of anxiety for the party's leadership, but Le Pen's appearance on *L'Heure de Verité* presented an incredible opportunity. Le Pen himself contends, somewhat immodestly, that this was a turning point in his and the party's history:

> Just like that, I must have changed. Just like that, I became an acceptable politician. Just like that, I must have changed my "look," just as they are saying today. And yet, I had changed neither my look, nor my message, nor my language, nor my behavior. What had changed, was that a television network, Antenna 2, granted me an "Hour of Truth." Sixty minutes, after a battle that has been going on for 28 years. An hour is nothing, but it was enough for me to get rid of the monstrous and carnival-like mask that all my opponents have so generously applied to me. (1984, 15)

Public opinion polls taken after Le Pen's appearance on the program highlighted the impact such national media exposure could have. The Front's support in the polls rose by 3.5 percentage points, from 3.5 to 7 percent (Ignazi 1989).

According to the leaders of the National Front, other obstacles besides the media that hindered the party's electoral progress are the party's organization and the level of mass commitment to the party. The condition of the Front's organization is mentioned by 11.1 percent of respondents as the primary obstacle and by 14 percent as a general inhibitor to electoral success. Jean-Pierre Stirbois, who had taken on the massive responsibility of modernizing the Front's organization, explicitly mentions the party's poorly anchored structure as he waxes nostalgic for the exciting days of the 1984 campaign in his book *Tonnerre de Dreux:* "We departed for a great and wonderful journey. The crossing of the desert is over. Our organization is still quite fragile, our resources are paltry, but our faith is great" (1988, 84). Surprisingly, only one respondent mentions the level of mass commitment to the party as a primary obstacle, but 24 percent cite this factor as a general obstacle. But it is the Front's complex relationship with the media that precipitates the sharpest and most pointed reactions from the Front leadership as they discuss their first electoral breakthrough.

Conclusion

A number of important points emerge from this discussion of the Front's political development during the first half of the 1980s. Perhaps most compelling is the party's uncanny ability to endure despite endless electoral failures, constant internecine competition, and media and public indifference. Despite these obstacles, the Front somehow managed to survive the innumerable campaign failures of the 1970s and emerge electorally victorious in 1983. By 1984, the National Front had emerged from the obscure shadows of the far right to become a nationally recognized political player of the first order. The election of thirty-five parliamentary representatives to the National Assembly and Le Pen's impressive showing in the 1988 presidential elections further solidified the Front's place in the French electoral system.

This is an amazing feat in and of itself, because far right movements are historically characterized by their transient and almost ephemeral nature. Such organizations were either outlawed by the government, as in the case of the OAS, Occident, and Ordre Nouveau, or they disappeared from the political scene because of a lack of interest or political resolve on the part of the leaders. The Poujadist movement and the Comité Tixier are prime examples of the latter.

A second important point emphasizes the central role of the electoral system in promoting the 1984 electoral breakthrough. The primary difference for the Front in 1984 as compared to 1972 was the fact that it was competing in an electoral system that did not automatically penalize newer, smaller parties. Essentially, the rules of the game had changed, and in 1984 those rules favored smaller political parties like the National Front. The Front was able to exploit its success in the 1984 elections and build upon it in the 1986 legislative contest that was conducted under a proportional representation framework. At the party's creation, the two-round majority system was considered an almost insurmountable barrier, with 78 percent of the respondents mentioning it as an obstacle, whereas in 1984, the proportional representation system of the European election was considered to be the primary facilitator of the Front's success, with 82 percent of the respondents contending that it was an important factor in that electoral breakthrough.

The shift in the National Front's electoral fortunes parallels the shifting electoral systems utilized in France. The French political elite have a perplexing proclivity to alter the rules of the electoral game as political fortunes wax and wane. The addition of the regional councils operating under a proportional representation system has also contributed to the Front's political development. The Front's political capital rose throughout the 1980s only to suffer a dramatic reversal as the electoral system was modified twice in the span of two years.

LEGISLATIVE LOSSES AND BEYOND

Le Front National doit s'en raciner dans la vie politique locale.

—Former National Assembly deputy [1]

For a new political party to elect its candidates on a consistent basis, have an impact at the policy level, and eventually participate in the governance of its country, that party must be able to endure. In the context of competitive democracies, this implies the successful completion of a sequence of milestones: party formation, electoral success, and durability. They encompass the political party life cycle developed in this study. In this chapter, we ask whether the Front has succeeded in becoming a prominent as well as permanent fixture of the French political landscape. If the answer to this question is yes, the Front has achieved the third stage of the political party life cycle: durability. Success at this stage implies that the party has been able to elect its candidates, participate in governance, and advance its agenda. The ability of the French National Front to meet these criteria is an important element of its continued political survival. Although the Front has continuously exerted its electoral strength in the European Parliament elections, success in National Assembly elections remains elusive. The party's influence in the regional and municipal elections has produced representative gains, but its ability to gain access to the National Assembly appears stalled. Durability, as defined in this context, implies electoral success not only at the European level but also in the more competitive and meaningful national-level political setting.

After its initial victory in the European elections, the Front was somewhat able to ameliorate its predominantly negative image. It was no longer the perpetual loser of French partisan politics; the party had sampled success, and it was determined to capitalize on its newfound accomplishments, no matter how modest they might be. To quell its critics and detractors, the Front badly needed to be tested in elections of real political importance, what Reif (1985) calls a first-order national election. Modestly successful in a few minor local-level contests as well as in the 1984 European elections, the Front felt compelled to replicate these results on a grander scale; thus, after the European victory, Le Pen and his party sought legitimacy on the national level. The election of thirty-five deputies to the National Assembly in 1986 conferred upon the fledgling party an enhanced sense of political legitimacy. Le Pen's personal success in the 1988 presidential election also marked an important point in the party's political development. With his 14.4 percent of the vote in the presidential race, Le Pen and his party were clearly a rising force in the French electoral arena. It was against this backdrop of escalating success that the Front mobilized its forces for its next political challenge.

The 1988 Legislative Elections

In some ways, the 1988 legislative contest was similar to the 1986 election; it followed Le Pen's unexpectedly strong showing in the first round of the presidential race, just as the 1986 contest had followed the Front's electoral breakthrough in the European elections. Although the time lag was greater in 1986, the impact was the same: the Front was viewed as a rising political force. But the situation facing the Front was more complex in 1988 than in 1986. A number of serious obstacles were to prevent a simple repeat of the 1986 victory: the reintroduction of the two-round electoral system, the hasty call for new elections with such a limited campaign period, the combined list of UDF and RPR candidates, and the loss of a number of prominent *notables.*

The election in 1986 of a Conservative majority in the National Assembly led to the rapid reintroduction of the two-round electoral system. Soon after assuming power, the RPR-UDF alliance pushed another modification of the electoral system through the National Assembly. Le Pen's fierce reaction was rather misguided, given all the work that had been invested in improving the party's image: "In depriving my 2,700,000 voters representation in the National Assembly, Mr. Pasqua [a high-ranking cabinet member of the center-right ruling coalition] clears the way for my constituents to be tempted to turn to violence. When legal means are not possible, the extremist approach is legitimated" (in Ysmal 1989a, 128). Cohabitation, the tenuous alliance between a Socialist president and a Conservative prime minister, was not expected to last. With this in mind, the Conservative majority hoped to further weaken the Socialists and also mitigate the influence of the surprisingly energetic National Front by resurrecting the two-round system.

Obviously, the return of the single-member constituency system served the interests of the Conservative-controlled cabinet, just as the switch to district-level proportional representation had served the interests of Mitterrand and the Socialist Party (Cole and Campbell 1989). In addition, it placed the National Front and the other smaller parties, such as the Communists and the factious French Greens, in a precarious position. This return to the old electoral system served to diminish the strength of the minor parties and in turn improved the chances for a government to acquire a solid majority, thereby exacerbating the centripetal nature of the system.

Mitterrand's precipitous call for legislative elections caught the Front unprepared. In the aftermath of the presidential election, the Socialists' aborted opening to the center had proved unworkable. The president was confident he could repeat the success he had enjoyed in 1981 by dissolving the legislature in the wake of his recent presidential victory. The unexpected decision to hold new elections placed the Front at a serious strategic disadvantage: it was completely unprepared for the dissolution. In her informative memoir, the late Yann Piat argues, "The news not only surprised Le Pen and his staff, it also panicked them" (1991, 192). As previously noted, the Front's prior political successes were the result of intense and well-planned campaigns. Le Pen's 1988 presidential bid illustrates the Front's ability to wage a campaign of national proportions. He had campaigned hard, gathering support for the mammoth undertaking of his presidential campaign, with Mégret directing and supported by a complex campaign machinery. Le Pen may have been the star and the main attraction, but he was ably supported by a traveling band of national speech makers who represented him across France. Mitterrand's quick election call provided neither the necessary amount of time nor the resources to wage a similar campaign.

In addition, the quick construction of joint lists by the RPR and the UDF also complicated the Front's position. The alliance, called l'Union du Rassemblement et du Centre (URC), covered the entire country and had as its goal to squeeze the National Front out of the legislative elections. As was his custom, Le Pen reacted quickly, vehemently criticizing the alliance: "The single candidacy seems to me to be a violation of the spirit of the two-round electoral system . . . Wherever the UDF and the RPR campaign with single candidates, they run the great risk of seeing the Front's candidate continuing into the second round" (in *Le Monde*, May 19, 1988). The URC could not take this threat lightly in view of Le

Pen's strong performance in the presidential race. His 14.4 percent was the strongest showing ever for a candidate of the extreme right; if Le Pen's success carried over into the legislative elections, two rightist candidates would split the vote and lead to a swift Socialist majority.

The brief campaign period also made it difficult for the Front to solidify its candidate base. A number of *notables* had either defected or been banished from the party in the interim; most prominent among this group were Yvon Briant, Bruno Chauvierre, Guy Le Jaouen, Olivier d'Ormesson, and Edouard Frédéric-Dupont. The defection of even a few *notables* proved exceptionally burdensome to a fledgling party like the National Front and served to highlight the weaknesses inherent in the Front's candidate pool.

Although there were certain minor similarities between the 1986 and 1988 legislative elections, the 1988 contest presented the Front with a host of obstacles. Unlike the 1986 National Assembly election, the 1988 election required strong candidates in all 570 electoral constituencies. The 1986 election was contested through party lists organized at the level of the ninety-six departments; no longer could one or two *notables* pull the other candidates on their district-level list to victory. The reversion to the traditional two-round system served to mitigate the impact of Le Pen's strong performance in the presidential contest. Furthermore, the two-round system necessitated that each candidate run his or her campaign as a solo political entrepreneur. Although the Front fielded candidates in all districts, the experience and quality of these individuals varied significantly from one constituency to the next. The return to the two-round system only highlighted the fact that the Front lacked experienced candidates; moreover, it did not have a ready stable of elected officials at the regional and municipal levels from which to draw its legislative candidates. This former National Assembly deputy maintains that the quality of the Front's candidates is a serious concern: "The primary problem is the training of its cadres—recruitment and training. The National Front suffers greatly because of the lack of training of its cadres and because of the lack of quality of these people."

In 1986, proportional representation by districts had worked to the Front's advantage; the far right had returned to the National Assembly in force with a parliamentary group of thirty-five deputies. The results of the first round in 1988 were far worse than expected: the Front received only 9.7 percent of the vote, and not a single Front candidate received a

Table 4.1   1988 Legislative Elections

List	Percentage	Seats in National Assembly
Communists	11.3	27
Socialists	34.8	274
Left Radicals	1.1	2
UDF	18.5	130
Gaullists	19.2	128
National Front	9.7	1

Source: *Les élections législatives. Supplément aux dossiers et documents du Monde 1988.*
Note: Unaffiliated deputies and splinter groups are not included.

majority of the first-round vote; therefore, no frontiste was elected out-right in the initial round of voting.

On the national level, Le Pen's success in the first round of the presidential elections was not replicated by the Front's candidates in the legislative elections (see Table 4.1). The Front's 9.7 percent of the vote represented a net loss of slightly more than 2 million votes between the presidential election and the legislative contest. In a mere two months, the Front's vote had declined precipitously. The party and its candidates proved unable to capitalize on Le Pen's strong showing in the presidential race: "The vote of the Front's candidates was below Le Pen's vote in 115 electoral districts by a margin [of] 4 to 14%" (Mazzella 1989, 20). In a matter of just a few weeks, the Front's political stock had significantly decreased in value. Some of the Front's leadership directly attributed this massive loss of votes to the party's inability to field a national slate of experienced and quality candidates.

From the Front's perspective, the presidential results did not create the same momentum for the legislative campaign as the 1984 European elections had done for the 1986 National Assembly elections. The Front's primary achievement in the first round was its success in maintaining its 1986 share of the vote under a discriminatory electoral system designed to eliminate minor parties. It became necessary to do damage control because of the dramatic shift in the Front's political fortunes between the presidential and legislative contests. One member of the Front's

Political Bureau insists that one should not compare Le Pen's 1988 presidential results to the 1988 legislative outcome:

> We cannot consider that the shift from 15 to 10 percent between the presidential and legislative elections corresponds to a step backwards. We need to compare what is comparable; therefore, compare the 1988 legislative election with the 1986 legislative election. From this point of view we can see that the score is the same. This election was much more difficult because the system was a majority one. URC ran combined candidate lists in order to block our progress.

The reversion to the two round system had forced a shift in strategies; rather than waging a true national campaign, the Front felt compelled to concentrate its energies in the regions where it had the most strength. The Bouches-du-Rhône region, in the south, was a Front stronghold; Le Pen had received 26.4 percent of the presidential vote in the region. Very early in the short campaign, it had been decided that the party's leaders—Le Pen, Bruno Mégret, and Jean-Pierre Stirbois—would "parachute" into this region to contest legislative seats. Parachuting candidates into new districts is a common practice in France, where residency requirements are much less stringent than in the United States, for instance. This risky strategy provoked dissension within the party ranks. Some argued that losses by the party's most public spokesmen in what were areas of great geographic strength would magnify the party's frailties. The decision to parachute Le Pen, Mégret, and Stirbois also alienated many of the local militants. Yann Piat, the Front's only incumbent female deputy, argued against this strategy:

> The militants did not at all appreciate this opportunism that did not conform with the image of a political leader: a Breton in Marseilles. The local party leaders felt abused, tricked by the Parisian predators who were acting just like the predators from all the other political parties. Because I understood the southerners . . . I tried to explain to him [Le Pen] that he had not made a judicious choice. I told him what no one else had the courage to: that his choice had offended the local militants. (1991, 193)

On a national level, although the Front essentially repeated its 1986 performance of 9.7 percent, the number of candidates able to contest the second round was small; only thirty of the Front's candidates succeeded in capturing the requisite 12.5 percent of the registered vote needed to continue into the second round, and over a third of these candidates were concentrated in the south of France. If the Front's surviving candidates decided to stay in the race and contest the second round, the right would surely lose; neither the Front nor the combined URC lists would survive triangular (three-candidate) races in the region. Such triangular races would find two rightist candidates facing a single leftist candidate, ultimately leading to the defeat of the right. Some mainstream conservative leaders quietly considered negotiations with the Front; they understood that the resurrected two-round system necessitated compromise among the various political factions on the right side of the political spectrum.

The URC and the Front were forced into negotiations to prevent Socialist hegemony in the Bouches-du-Rhône region. The mainstream center right claimed eight of the Bouches-du-Rhône constituencies by virtue of the fact that their candidates achieved the highest vote totals of all the right-leaning candidates in each of those districts. Jean-Claude Gaudin, the departmental secretary for the UDF, quickly negotiated a deal with the National Front to protect his candidates.

Politicians of the left and the moderate right fiercely criticized this "pact with the devil." Michel Rocard, Mitterrand's new Socialist prime minister, vehemently attacked the URC coalition for its electoral accords: "Do you really imagine, for an instant, that the agreement is limited to Marseille, as if gangrene were but a localized infection? And how can you accept that in Republican France racism, rejection of foreigners, and xenophobia could be so completely trivialized?" (in *Le Monde,* June 9, 1988). His words were echoed by Simone Veil and other centrists. On the other hand, some politicians attempted to place the blame on the Socialists and Mitterrand's abrupt decision to dissolve the National Assembly. Former president Valéry Giscard d'Estaing argued that "The local party officials make decisions imposed upon them by the current electoral system and not because of any personal choices. We are undergoing the disastrous consequences of the dissolution" (in *Le Monde,* June 9, 1988).

The arrangement called for the Front to withdraw its candidates in eight of the districts in the Bouches-du-Rhône region. Surprisingly, in a unique show of unity, the Front also agreed to withdraw a number of incumbent candidates in other regions of the country. This agreement included such incumbent deputies as Jacques Peyrat and Albert Peyron from the Alpes-Maritimes region; Charles de Chambrun (Gard) and

Table 4.2   Percentage of Votes for National Front Presidential and Legislative Candidates, 1988

District	Presidential vote (Le Pen)	Round one legislative candidate	Percentage difference
3 Marseille	29.86	29.37	-.49
4 Marseille	29.76	27.93	-1.83
5 Marseille	27.25	27.02	-.23
7 Marseille	32.58	34.41	+1.83
8 Marseille	29.18	32.83	+3.65
9 Aubagne	26.37	25.77	-.6
10 Gardanne	26.12	26.01	-.11
11 Marignane	28.74	25.82	-2.92
3 Hyeres	25.62	26.26	-2.36
Averages	28.39	28.05	-.34

Source: *Les élections législatives. Supplément aux dossiers et documents du Monde: 1988.*

Pierre Ceyrac (Nord) were also electoral victims of the Marseille agreement. The decision to suspend the candidacies of those frontistes from outside the Bouches-du-Rhône region carried with it important political overtones; the Front was clearly making a statement to the mainstream right that it could be counted on in the future to make deals that would block the path of the Socialists and Communists. In addition, the withdrawal of its candidates implied that the Front had become more than a fringe party: it was now a serious player in the political arena, able to wheel and deal with its ideological confrères on the right of the political spectrum. The 1988 legislative contest marks an important step in the Front's electoral progress; it represents the only legislative election in which the center right entered into an alliance with the National Front.

The relationship between Le Pen's score in the first round of the presidential election and the scores of the nine remaining Front candidates is described in Table 4.2. Le Pen's supremacy as the party's top vote-getting attraction is evident in that in only two of the nine races did the score in the legislative elections surpass Le Pen's share of the vote in the presidential elections. Pascal Arrighi, a local figure of some renown, added two percentage points to the Front's presidential score in the seventh Marseille, and Le Pen's personal presence in the eighth Marseille dis-

Table 4.3 First-Round Total Right Compared with Second-Round Front Performance, 1988

District	Total right, round one	Front candidate, round two	Percentage difference
3 Marseille	58.21	49.57	−8.64
4 Marseille	40.34	36.46	−3.88
5 Marseille	56.85	48.61	−8.24
7 Marseille	47.30	42.55	−4.75
8 Marseille	48.22	43.57	−4.65
9 Aubagne	51.50	47.96	−3.54
10 Gardanne	50.39	43.96	−6.48
11 Marignane	51.91	44.13	−7.78
3 Hyeres	61.70	53.72	−7.98
Averages	51.82	45.61	−6.21

Source: *Les élections législatives. Supplément aux dossiers et documents du Monde: 1988.*

trict improved upon his score by 3.65 percent. Although the candidates in these elections were unable to build upon the presidential vote, they did quite well when the Front's entire national slate is taken into consideration. These candidates had outpolled the URC candidates and as a result of the alliance were well placed for the second round. The Front's strong showing in the region was due to the presence of eight incumbent deputies as well as the political hold it was beginning to develop on the region's electorate. In the districts where the Front candidates contested the second round, the combined vote for the rightist candidates in the first round ranged from 40.34 percent in the fourth Marseille district to 61.7 percent in the third Hyeres district (see Table 4.3).

A number of the Front's candidates had been well placed for the second round; six of the nine candidates went into the second round with a combined right vote of 50 percent or more. Yann Piat, in the third Hyeres, had the greatest margin, with a combined right vote of 61.7 percent; Jean Roussel, in the third Marseille, also had a good chance of winning reelection, with a right total of 58.21 percent. The prospects were darker for Le Pen, whose combined right total was only 48.22 percent. For Le Pen to retain his National Assembly seat, he needed to improve upon the right's first-round score by 2 percent, and he had to hope that

Mitterrand would be unable to mobilize those Socialist voters who had abstained in the first round. The other parachuted candidates, Mégret and Stirbois, were somewhat better placed than Le Pen; the total right vote for Mégret in the tenth Gardanne was 50.39 percent, and Stirbois entered the second round with 51.91 percent in the eleventh Marignane.

The deal between Gaudin and Le Pen did not produce the desired results for the Front's candidates (see Table 4.3). To the contrary, the results of the second round were without a doubt disastrous: the Front's candidates were unable to preserve the winning margins from the first round; to a candidate, the second-round scores were uniformly less than the right total for the first round; and every Front candidate lost ground between the first and second rounds. In the first round, the average total right vote for the nine races covered by the agreement was 51.82 percent; in the second round, this figure dropped to 45.61 percent. Ronald Perdomo, in the ninth Aubagne, lost only 3.54 percent of the vote, whereas Roussel, in the third Marseille, lost 8.64 and ultimately lost the election by only a few hundred votes. Essentially, the Front derived no benefits from the electoral alliance with the conservative majority. In the end, only one incumbent Front deputy, Yann Piat, was elected to the National Assembly.

In addition to losing its parliamentary representation, the Front lost the myriad resources that come with such a delegation. The end of its role as a parliamentary party translated into a financial disaster for the party. Traditionally, the Front required its parliamentary deputies to tithe a portion of their earnings back to the party; with no deputies, the only tithing would now come from its other elected representatives in the European Parliament and the regional councils. In addition, as a parliamentary group, the Front had been able to offer some of its activists positions as legislative assistants; this ended when all but one of the party's sitting deputies was defeated. Another consequence of losing its legislative presence was a concomitant decline in the party's ability to generate media interest in its policy agenda.

The results of the second round underscored the Front's electoral vulnerability under the two-round majority system, as it was unable to hold on to the URC voters in the second round. Although the traditional right coalition consented to the Front agreement, it failed to actively support it during the campaign. The leadership, as described by this member of the Political Bureau, felt betrayed by the URC coalition:

We were penalized by the poor transfer of votes from URC. We mobilized 75 percent of URC's voters. That's a loss of 25 percent, which
is not bad because . . . Everybody was saying, "It's scandalous, this
agreement, it's shameful, it's dishonorable, it's unacceptable. . . .
I prefer to vote Socialist rather than for the National Front," said
Mme Veil and others. When the voters listen to that all day on the
television and the radio, it's quite good that only 25 percent refused to vote for us.

The electoral agreement was much more favorable to the URC candidates. Nationwide, approximately 86 percent of the Front's voters supported the URC candidates in the second round; the Front, on the other
hand, received only about 66 percent of the URC vote in the second
round (Cole and Campbell 1989). The 20 percent positive shift in the
direction of the URC coalition helped the UDF-RPR coalition elect six
deputies in the Bouches-du-Rhône region, but the largest party in the
region—the party with the biggest mass-level following—the National
Front, was completely shut out of the National Assembly. The Front's
only successful candidate, Yann Piat, was actually from the Var region.

The debacle of the 1988 legislative elections forced the Front into a
period of reflection and internal political tumult. The hardliners in the
party felt vindicated; they argued that it was impossible to work with
the center right, citing the poor transfer of votes from the mainstream
right's electorate. Considering the enormity of the electoral defeat, one
would have thought the Front had reached its lowest point, but the
worst was yet to come. Le Pen's inability to control his vicious rhetoric
was the first step in a new downward spiral. If the electoral defeat was a
setback, the months that followed found the National Front in a political hell of its own making.

Close to the anniversary of his infamous "detail" remark, Le Pen again
provoked national outrage by his anti-Semitic excesses. In a television
interview in 1987, Le Pen had cavalierly dismissed the Nazi gas cham-
bers as a "detail of history." After making the remark, Le Pen continued
his conversational self-implosion by introducing the specter of the historical revisionists who deny the Holocaust. One would have thought
that Le Pen had learned from that 1987 gaffe and would henceforth try
to steer clear of such anti-Semitic rhetoric. But, close on the heels of the
1988 legislative loss he made a terribly offensive pun; he attacked Michel

Durafour, a Jewish minister in the Socialist government, by linking his name to the word *crématoire*. Once again, Le Pen's rhetorical excesses prompted national outrage, but Le Pen responded quite differently after this second distasteful episode. Although he had made what constituted an apology after the detail remark, he remained on the offensive after the "Monsieur Durafour-crématoire" comment.[3] Within days, this second public display of Le Pen's anti-Semitism prompted the resignation from the party of two important political allies, Pascal Arrighi and François Bachelot. Bachelot was most public about his split from the party and immediately told a group of journalists, "I am ashamed of having collaborated with this movement" (in Piat 1991, 206). It is most interesting that he used the verb "collaborate" to explain his tenure in the party; given the explosive nature of the word in contemporary France, one wonders if it was intended or not.

The Front's troubles would not end with this episode. Yann Piat, much to Le Pen's chagrin, began to exert her political independence. She balked at the party's insistence that she continue to tithe a portion of her deputy's salary; she also refused to vote as instructed by the party's Political Bureau. In a most surprising move, the Front's leaders chose to exile her from their political family. Given that she was the party's only representative in the National Assembly, one would have thought that the Front would have tried to be more solicitous. Also, for a party that desperately needs to improve its support among women, it was political suicide to have the all-male Political Bureau publicly sanction its only nationally elected figure.

The last and perhaps most significant event in this downward spiral was the death of the party's secretary-general, Jean-Pierre Stirbois. As noted, Stirbois and his wife, Marie-France, were instrumental in the Front's first early political successes; he had worked tirelessly to help improve the Front's organization and his death created an important void in the party's cadre of political leaders. But although Stirbois's death was dutifully mourned by the party faithful, it was also viewed as an opportunity by some of the party's more forward-looking leaders.

The 1989 European Parliament Elections

As previously noted, the National Front was severely penalized by the return of the two-round electoral system. Unable, because of institutional barriers, to translate 10 percent of the votes into a 10 percent share of the

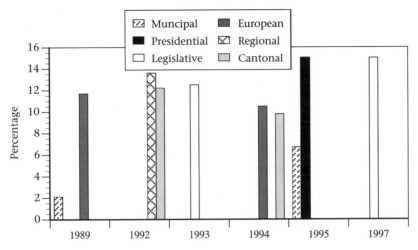

Figure 4.1   National Front Vote, 1989–1997

deputies in the National Assembly, the Front was forced to view the outcome of the 1989 European elections as a do-or-die proposition. Because of the party's weak showing in the summer of 1988, the importance of the European contest increased exponentially.

The French voting public had grown weary of political campaigns and elections because of the unusually charged electoral cycle. The previous year had included five separate elections, and the constant campaigning during this time period served to diminish further the relevance of the European contest for the average French citizen. As the campaign approached, the voting public was faced with a plethora of choices. In France, the campaign for the European elections was rendered even more complex with the appearance of fifteen separate lists competing for seats in the European Parliament. The supporters of the governing Socialists and the combined UDF-RPR list stayed away from the polls in massive numbers. Campaign fatigue and a general lack of interest in the elections contributed to the 51.27 percent abstention rate. In their defense, French citizens were understandably fed up with elections and campaigns; in a matter of six short years, they had been called to the polls ten times (Marcus 1995). The results of all the elections from 1989 to 1997 are presented in Figure 4.1.

The National Front succeeded in retaining the support of approximately 11 percent of the French public and cemented its presence in the European Parliament with its second party group of ten deputies.

The Front's presence in the European Parliament was thus assured for the next five years. Although the Front performed well, the media spotlighted the Greens' list, spearheaded by Antoine Waechter. The French Greens made a dramatic showing in the European contest by improving on the 3.7 percent Waechter received in the 1988 presidential race by more than 6 percent. The 1989 European elections, at least in France, provided a showcase for the minor parties.

The 1993 Legislative Elections

Preelection prognostication had been highlighting a Socialist debacle since Michel Rocard had been forced to form a minority government in the aftermath of the 1988 elections. The regional and cantonal elections of the previous year presaged the Socialists' poor performance in the contest for the National Assembly. Even before the election, voices on the right called for Mitterrand's resignation because the right did not have the stomach for a second round of cohabitation. Mitterrand had become a severe liability to the Socialist Party's candidates; he was now more unpopular than at any other point in his twelve years in office. Musical chairs in the prime minister's position further reduced the public's confidence in the governing Socialists; Rocard, Edith Cresson, and Pierre Bérégovoy were all rotated through the prime minister's office in a span of two years. The Socialists' inability to manage the country's blood supply, the poor performance of Edith Cresson as France's first woman prime minister, and the public's impatience with Mitterrand's ineffectual leadership portended a difficult if not disastrous election for the Socialists.

It was against this backdrop of an imminent Socialist collapse that the Front began its 1993 legislative effort. With only one incumbent deputy in the National Assembly, the Front started the campaign season with a serious handicap.[4] Unlike the 1988 legislative contest, the Front did not have a core group of incumbent National Assembly deputies who could generate popular and media interest along the campaign trail, although the absence of a cadre of incumbent deputies was somewhat mitigated by the inroads the party had made at the local level. In the 1992 regional elections, the Front received 13.9 percent of the vote, a 4.2 percent improvement over its score in the first regional elections held in 1986, when it had elected 137 regional councillors. The Front's investments at the local level paid excellent dividends in the most recent regional elections, where its success at the ballot box enabled it to seat 239 regional councillors, a 74 percent improvement in the Front's regional council representation.

Public opinion polls also demonstrated the vitality of the Front's political progress. A poll taken in October 1991 found that 32 percent of French citizens agreed with the ideas defended by Jean-Marie Le Pen (Mayer and Perrineau 1993). Pollsters had been regularly asking such questions since the Front first appeared on the national political landscape in the aftermath of the 1984 European elections. The score achieved in October 1991 represented a record high for the Front; fully one-third of the French citizenry now believed that the policies advocated by the Front held merit.

Although Le Pen and his core group of advisors had long labored to improve the Front's standing, the party had not singlehandedly transformed public opinion. In fact, other political leaders helped to make the Front's ideas more palatable to the French polity. Mainstream politicians on the left and the right were now publicly agreeing with the Front on its core issues of immigration and security; the Front's concerns about immigration in particular were now seemingly appropriate conversation topics in polite political circles. Former president Giscard d'Estaing wrote an extensive article for *Figaro Magazine* lamenting the "immigrant invasion." Former prime minister Chirac openly discussed the "noises and odors" of immigrant neighborhoods. Former RPR interior minister Charles Pasqua's harsh rhetoric had long courted the anti-immigrant vote; his extremist sympathies were mentioned by this membre fondateur of the Front, when she matter-of-factly stated, "Pasqua shares many of our values."

The shift in rhetoric was not confined to politicians on the right. Prominent Socialist figures also began echoing the Front's concerns. While in office, Prime Minister Edith Cresson advanced the idea of government charters to return illegal immigrants to their home countries. But Cresson did not stop there; she added fuel to the fire by making xenophobic comments about the Japanese and the British. Even Michel Rocard, in milder terms, had stated that France could no longer receive the world's poor, and it was during the Rocard premiership that work permits were canceled for those with refugee status. The once vilified rhetoric of the Front had become decidedly mainstream. It would be naïve to assume that these comments were rhetorical slips by the system's mainstream politicians; clearly, these were well-calculated comments made to usurp the Front's core constituency. The Front's excellent showing in the regional elections combined with the favorable shift in public opinion forced the mainstream parties to take the far right's challenge more seriously than ever before.

After the election, the Union pour la France (UPF), a center right alliance of the UDF and the RPR, emerged victorious, capturing 449 of the 577 seats in the National Assembly, the greatest margin of victory for the conservatives since 1815. The Socialist losses were worse than anyone had expected; they received less than 20 percent of the vote, their poorest electoral performance since 1968. The number of Socialist and allied deputies plummeted from 282 to 67. With all the election returns counted, the Socialists represented hardly even a credible opposition. The humiliating losses of the governing party were further compounded by the fact that many prominent Socialists lost their seats in the National Assembly, among them Michel Rocard, Lionel Jospin, and Roland Dumas. Although the story that emerged from the election focused on the crushing defeat of the governing Socialists, the National Front's performance in the elections also provoked commentary.

The Front's 12.7 percent of the first-round ballot represented more than 3 million votes, the Front's best showing ever in National Assembly elections. In fact, the Front added 700,000 votes to its 1988 legislative elections total. Its score in this election reflects a slight decrease in support when compared to its 1992 regional council vote, but because the two electoral systems are so different, this decline is essentially insignificant. Overall, given the low-key nature of the party's campaign, there was much to celebrate in the party's performance. The Front's unexpected electoral progress in these elections prompted Prime Minister Raymond Barre to say "I didn't think such scores were possible for the National Front's candidates" (in *Le Monde* March 23, 1993).

The Front's increased visibility at the local level through its work at the regional, cantonal, and municipal levels translated into a solid performance in the 1993 legislative elections. Although the discriminatory nature of the electoral system still served to handicap the Front, approximately 100 of the party's candidates had passed the 12.5 percent threshold in the first round; in the prior legislative elections only 30 candidates had been eligible for the second round of balloting. On the evening of the vote, Le Pen appealed directly to those who had supported the Front's candidates during the first round: "The success of the right being guaranteed, the voters can in the second round correct the scandalous results that give, for example, twenty-five seats to the Communists who only received 8 or 9 percent of the vote, and between zero and two seats to the National Front which had 13 to 14 percent. This must be done in order to insure a pluralist Assembly where the voices of the nationalist voters can make themselves heard" (in *Le Monde* March 23, 1993). The Front's efforts at the local level clearly paid off handsomely in the 1993 legislative contest. The large number of frontistes who were eligible for the second round buoyed the Front's hopes for a renewed presence in the National Assembly. Nevertheless, the postelection optimism would not last long. Of the many Front candidates who were well placed for the second round, only a very few could reasonably expect to be elected, and then only if they received unqualified support from the mainstream right's first-round voters. This did not occur. The party was once again shut out of the National Assembly. Marie-France Stirbois, the party's only incumbent deputy, narrowly missed reelection by 105 votes.

The 1994 European Parliament Elections

The political circumstances of the 1994 European Parliament elections differed markedly from those of the 1989 electoral contest. During the five-year interval, all countries registered a decline in support for European Union (EU) policies (Grunberg 1995). The greatest decline in pro-EU sentiment was evident in Belgium, where public support for the EU declined by nineteen points from November 1990 to May 1994; France, with a documented decline in support of eighteen points, was tied for a close second with reunited Germany. Public perception of the benefits derived from EU-level policymaking had shifted sharply. Unlike the cautiously optimistic economic scenarios that greeted the 1989 European elections, the 1994 contest occurred as many of the countries in the Union were facing heightened economic concerns. Chief among these was the stagnant level of job creation and the still high level of unemployment; in addition, the rising costs of "cradle to grave" welfare policies were coming under increased scrutiny. All of these problems increasingly were topics of concern in the French domestic political arena. France especially was unable to create new jobs to combat its decade-long experience with double-digit unemployment. Economic fears coupled with deep seated questions about impending monetary union focused increased attention on the 1994 European elections.

The closely fought battle over ratification of the Maastricht treaty clearly underscored the discontent French citizens felt about granting additional powers to the European bureaucrats based in Brussels. In addition, the referendum vote cut across the dominant cleavage structures of French politics (Buffotot 1993). Opposition to the treaty emerged from all points on the political spectrum, and an odd alliance of politicians from all ideological persuasions vocally opposed the treaty. Given that the principal leaders of the country's two largest political parties, the RPR and the Socialists, agreed on the need to ratify Maastricht, its narrow margin of victory was more than just a repudiation of Mitterrand, it was also an important indication of the citizens' discomfort with the increased integrative efforts inherent in the Maastricht initiative. Clearly, the French populace would no longer follow the dictates of their leaders when EU policymaking was at issue. The salience of European issues had increased, as evidenced by the preelection polls, the heated debate over the Maastricht treaty issue, and the cliffhanger of the final vote (Subileau 1996).

In France, this shift in attitudes sharply altered the political context in which the European elections were conducted. The Front, which had always been guarded about France's role in the EU, had become over the ensuing five years increasingly negative in its policy pronouncements vis-à-vis increased integrative efforts. In fact, Jean-Marie Le Pen, in another example of his astute political sensibilities, seized the initiative and became a leading voice against the ratification of Maastricht; moreover, he campaigned aggressively against Mitterrand's Maastricht referendum. The Front's detached and rather guarded approach to EU-level initiatives had become openly hostile by the 1992 vote on the referendum.

Prior to the Maastricht referendum, the majority of anti-EU voters were monopolized by the Front and the Communist Party. With the arrival of former UDF rising star Philippe de Villiers on the political scene during the Maastricht debate, the anti-EU vote had more options. De Villiers's slate, Majorité pour l'Autre Europe, and Jean-Pierre Chevènement's list, l'Autre Politique, were joined by the Chasse-Pêche slate of candidates.[5] Like de Villiers, Chevènement was a dissident, having created his own list to protest the pro-European policies of his former colleagues in the Socialist Party. Politics, at least in the European context, had changed, as the Front faced competition from a number of anti-EU and anti-Maastricht forces.

With the increased competition for the anti-EU vote, the Front needed to maintain its share of the vote at least at the level of the last European contest, and it hoped to replicate its score in the 1993 legislative election. As the Front entered the European campaign, the stakes were high and the competition for anti-EU voters was uncharacteristically keen. In the end, the results were neither disastrous nor cause for celebration; they were merely acceptable: 10.5 percent of the total vote. This was, in reality, a decline of three percentage points from its 1993 legislative score, but given the fact that the anti-EU vote was courted by more political groupings than ever before, the Front was happy and modest about its electoral stability in this election. The Front's 10.5 percent enabled it to seat eleven deputies in the European Parliament.

1995 Presidential Elections

The first of an eventual nine candidates, Jean-Marie Le Pen announced on September 18, 1994, yet another attempt to secure the French presidency for himself and his loyal followers in the National Front. The official beginning of his presidential campaign coincided with the Front's annual Fête des Bleu-Blanc-Rouge celebration. Le Pen's third attempt at gaining France's highest political office began with characteristic vigor as he claimed he would put an end to the many corruption scandals that had plagued the ruling elites of both parties in the Fifth Republic. His attacks on the scandal-plagued political class and his vehement denunciations of increased European integration served him well during the campaign. These issues were prominent in the public consciousness during the campaign season, and his successful exploitation of them helped to further legitimize his presidential campaign. Immigration coupled with the related issue of insécurité still constituted the core of his political agenda, but these other issues further enhanced his credibility as a presidential candidate. The fact that the Maastricht debate had split the center right and that fissures had also developed within the Socialist camp over the same issue lent an air of legitimacy to Le Pen's harangues about increased integrative efforts. Such seemingly mainstream politicians as Jean-Pierre Chevènement, Philippe de Villiers, and Charles Pasqua began to parrot Le Pen's rhetoric when they attacked the Maastricht referendum.

Up to this point, the party had clearly accepted the legitimacy of the Fifth Republic's institutions, but Le Pen added a new element to his campaign proposals during this election. His promise to create a new Sixth

Republic once he was elected president propelled the Front's rhetoric to a new level. The creation of a new Republic was presented in calculated terms: Le Pen argued that a new Republic was needed to replace the scandal-plagued institutions of the current Republic. This marked an important development in the party's political program in an otherwise rather unremarkable campaign.

Chirac's campaign, without mentioning the Front or Le Pen, was clearly influenced by the hot-button issues that the Front had introduced to the political debate. He emphasized the pressing social issues — the social fracture — currently facing France. He promised specifically to solve the difficult unemployment problem, while also discussing the crises facing those living in the more urban centers of the country. His emphasis on these issues was in essence a blatant attempt to poach from the National Front's political agenda. But Chirac was not the only candidate to borrow from the Front's political lexicon. The candidacy of de Villiers was predicated on only two issues: a repudiation of the Maastricht treaty and an attack on the corrosive corruption plaguing the French political class. De Villiers, a political refugee from the UDF, had broken with his center right compatriots and used this theme to enter the European Parliament in 1994. In each successive election since the Front's electoral breakthrough, more of the Front's themes were being usurped by more of the political mainstream.

No one seriously thought Le Pen had even the remotest chance of being elected president, but the election was nevertheless of great symbolic importance to the National Front and its many millions of supporters. The party had achieved some important electoral victories prior to the presidential contest, but each subsequent election leading up to the 1995 contest marked a decline in the Front's vote totals. The Front amassed 13.6 percent of the vote in the 1992 regional elections, which declined to 12.7 percent in the 1993 legislative elections and then to 10.5 percent in the 1994 contest for the European Parliament. Although the party continued to play an important part in the electoral process, it did not benefit from a rising electoral tide as it began this next campaign (Shields 1995).

Jean-Marie Le Pen occupies a unique role in contemporary French partisan politics. Omnipresent since the 1950s, he has succeeded in carving for himself and his party an important place in the electoral arena. Le Pen's third presidential campaign proved once again to be a high-energy affair. He traversed the country speaking to the party faithful — all the while collecting the 30 francs a person that is charged for admission to a National Front "event."

Since the beginning of the Fifth Republic, French presidential politics has become increasingly linked to a strong and structured political party apparatus. Candidates require the support of a well-organized and disciplined political machine to survive the rigors of a presidential campaign. Over the previous ten years, Le Pen, with the help of Carl Lang and Bruno Mégret, had built such an apparatus. His party had become a well-established national force capable of competing in all elections at all levels. Candidate training workshops, campaign manuals, and an authoritarian intraparty discipline had created a formidable political machine. In the years since the first European Parliament election success, the Front had transformed itself from a marginal *groupuscule* on the far right fringe into a well-organized, deeply entrenched political machine.

Election results indicated quite clearly that candidates with firmly structured party support were the most successful in the first round (Szarka 1996). After the results of the first round were counted, Le Pen had improved upon his 1988 record-setting score. He captured 15 percent of the vote, nearly 200,000 more than he had collected in the previous presidential race and the highest total ever for a candidate of the far right. Le Pen was immediately thrust into the spotlight with his 4,570,000 voters. His share of the first-round vote would weigh heavily on the candidacies of the two remaining competitors, presidential perennial Jacques Chirac and a surprisingly vigorous Lionel Jospin (see Table 4.4).

Through his surrogates, Chirac openly courted the Le Pen voters. Alain Juppé, president of the RPR and future prime minister, maintained that "those who had voted for Le Pen had 'legitimate concerns that should be taken into consideration' notably 'those that deal with security in our cities and suburbs as well as the preservation of a certain form of national identity'" (in Shields 1995, 36). Others discussed the possibility of reinstituting proportional representation for National Assembly elections, an important element of the Front's political program. Once again, Le Pen's legitimacy was further enhanced by the mainstream parties; at each step of the Front's development, the mainstream politicians increasingly pandered to the Front's voters by liberally borrowing from Le Pen's rhetorical arsenal. Before the second round, in an attempt to remain in the media spotlight, Le Pen tried to generate suspense regarding how he would instruct his 4,570,000 supporters to

Table 4.4   1995 Presidential Election, First-Round Results

Candidate	Vote total	Percentage
A. Laguiller	1,615,653	5.30
R. Hue	2,632,936	8.64
L. Jospin	7,098,191	23.30
D. Voynet	1,010,738	3.32
E. Balladur	5,658,996	18.58
J. Chirac	6,348,969	20.84
P. de Villiers	1,443,235	4.74
J.-M. Le Pen	4,571,138	15.00
J. Cheminade	84,969	.28

Source: Perrineau and Ysmal 1995.

vote. He eventually announced that he planned to cast a blank ballot. Once the second round ended, postelection surveys showed that 21 percent of his supporters followed his lead and cast either blank ballots or abstained completely; 51 percent voted for Chirac and 28 percent of the far right's candidates chose the Socialist candidate, Lionel Jospin. The second-round choices of Le Pen's 1995 electorate differed markedly from the second-round choices of his 1988 electorate. In 1988, 65 percent of Le Pen's first-round supporters had voted for Chirac, and only 19 percent chose Mitterrand—another clear indication of the Front's increasingly popular electorate (Jaffré 1995).

Early Elections: The 1997 Legislative Campaign

After the hectic pace of the electoral calendar of the early 1990s, the Front and the nation were ready for a respite from campaigning. Legislative elections were scheduled for the spring of 1998, and the Front's successes in the regional and municipal elections in the early part of the decade would provide the party with its strongest and most experienced candidate pool ever. With its 1995 mayoral victories in Marignane, Toulon, and Orange, the Front settled into its new role as a party of government, albeit on the small but important stage of local politics. With its own cadre of *notables,* the National Front was no longer on the outside looking in.

Not known as a political risk taker, President Jacques Chirac nevertheless surprised the French political class and called for legislative elections eleven months ahead of schedule. His decision to dissolve the National Assembly is unprecedented in the history of the Fifth Republic. In the past, presidents have dissolved the legislature to generate an electoral majority or in response to a national crisis. Chirac did not face either of these circumstances; he had an overwhelming majority in the National Assembly, and the country, although restless because of continued unemployment, was far from the brink of a crisis.

During the months prior to Chirac's announcement, the National Front experienced incredible media scrutiny. It was either directly or indirectly the focus of much of the nation's news reporting for the five months prior to the elections. It would not be an exaggeration to say that from February to June 1997, the national media were uniformly fixated on the ever expanding role the Front was now playing in contemporary French life.

Because of campaign irregularities, the 1995 municipal election results in Vitrolles had been annulled. Vitrolles, a dreary suburb on the outskirts of Marseilles, suffers from 19 percent unemployment (well above the 12.8 percent national average). With its large immigrant population and depressed social and economic situation, Vitrolles would be an important test of the Front's new electoral strategy. Having duly noted its exceptional strength among the working classes in the 1995 presidential elections, the Front had begun to take extraordinary measures to seduce this sector of the electorate. Over the previous few years, Bruno Mégret had made Vitrolles the center of his personal political empire, but he was prevented from contesting the election because of financial misdeeds during the previous contest. He was barred from running in the municipal election, but he handpicked his surrogate. Catherine Mégret, the granddaughter of Russian Jewish immigrants and Bruno Mégret's wife, served as her husband's anointed replacement. In a runoff election with the tarnished Socialist incumbent mayor, Mme Mégret became the Front's fourth mayor in a medium-size city. This runoff election demonstrated, once again, that the Front could indeed prevail in a face-off with its leftist opponents.

Less than two weeks after the Front's Vitrolles victory, opponents of the mainstream right's immigration reform proposals engineered a series of demonstrations in the streets of Paris. Thousands of cultural leaders had already signed a petition that expressed their opposition to the law's most vilified proposal; in an eerie echo of the Vichy era, the mainstream right proposed to require French citizens to inform the local authorities of the comings and goings of their foreign guests. For the cultural intelligentsia this rather minor component of a much larger piece of legislation was viewed as a step back to the time when the French were required to turn over their Jewish neighbors to German authorities. Although the protests were organized ostensibly to protest the Debré immigration reforms, they were also viewed as an opportunity to rebuke the National Front for its victory in Vitrolles. Not since the 1990 desecration of the Jewish cemetery in Carpentras had anti-Semitism, racism, and xenophobia been so central to the political debate. Some sources estimated that 100,000 citizens participated in the series of Parisian protests.

The National Front maintained its grasp on media attention when it held its party convention in Strasbourg over the Easter holidays. Between 2,000 and 3,000 frontistes converged on the city to celebrate their Vitrolles victory and plan their agenda for the upcoming legislative and regional elections in 1998. The French conventioneers were joined by other far rightists representing movements and political parties from the Netherlands to Croatia and from Finland to Greece. The presence of so many avowed far rightists, of both the French and imported variety, prompted a massive counterdemonstration. Estimates of the number of counterdemonstrators ranged from 30,000 to 50,000 people; they journeyed from all over France, many arriving en masse in what were named "freedom trains," to participate in the anti-Front festivities.

This series of events, which began with the Vitrolles victory and ended with the anti-Front rally in Strasbourg, placed the Front on the defensive as it prepared for the hastily called National Assembly elections. The 1997 legislative campaign was a decidedly low-key affair for the National Front. One of the most noticeable differences between this campaign and previous Front efforts was that large-scale rallies and massive demonstrations, which had become so integral to the Front's electoral strategy, were largely absent from this effort. The party leaders decided early in the short campaign that it was better to run a more discrete campaign because of the number and sheer intensity of the many anti-Front rallies during the previous months. Le Pen's decision to sit out the campaign also offers a partial explanation for this new strategy; he thrived in the country's big meeting halls and was always a major attraction for the party faithful, but his absence from the campaign as a candidate necessitated a shift in strategies. Most of the party's previous electoral successes were long-drawn-out affairs that had required intense planning and detailed organization; the short campaign period, just over a month, gave the party only enough time to get its candidates in place and develop an agenda.

Although the Front seemed caught off-guard by Chirac's decision, the results of the first round were cause for celebration. The Front's strong showing in the first round of balloting clearly illustrated the success the party has had in building a truly national organization. The fact that it waged a credible campaign in such a short time, and without Le Pen on the ballot, underscores the progress the party had made in the past ten years. In addition, the party's ability to improve on its 1993 legislative score and match Le Pen's 1995 presidential score clearly highlights the fact that the party had become more than just a one-man movement. In the past, it had always been easy to dismiss whatever progress the party made in nonpresidential races because its results were always inferior to those of Le Pen's. The 1997 election clearly marked a turning point in the Front's political development. Jean-François Jalkh, the party's national secretary for elections, commented on the day of the first round, "It shows that the party is firmly anchored, that now it can exist without Le Pen" (in *Le Monde,* May 27, 1997). Such comments by a party leader would have been viewed previously as heresy, but this election presented the party with a new and original set of opportunities. The party was finally beginning to emerge from Jean-Marie's shadow.

Le Pen's decision not to participate in the legislative elections came as a surprise to most political observers. With political campaign experience that dated back to the Poujadist era, Le Pen had dutifully carried the banner of the far right for decades. Although he maintained that he wanted to be free to challenge Chirac in the 2002 presidential contest, most political observers concluded that Le Pen decided to sit out the race to avoid another embarrassing loss. His absence from the actual electoral contest presented the party's candidates with an important test.

Although Le Pen may not have been a candidate in these elections, his presence nevertheless was apparent throughout the campaign. In a stroke of public relations genius, Le Pen convinced the media to turn their spotlight on him and the Front prior to the first round of balloting. In this blatant effort to seize control of the headlines, Le Pen said that he "preferred an Assembly of the left, rather than an Assembly of the right" and argued that such an outcome "would paralyze Jacques Chirac's plan to dissolve France into the Europe of Maastricht" (in *Le Monde* May 21,

1997). The fallout from his outburst was instantaneous: immediately, Le Pen's two main lieutenants, Bruno Gollnisch and Bruno Mégret, *les deux Bruno,* took to the airwaves to curtail the uncertainty that their leader's comments had engendered. Without overtly contradicting him, *les deux Bruno* argued that Le Pen's comments had been misinterpreted and that he had never actually called for his supporters to oust the governing center right in favor of the left.

With 15.24 percent of the total vote, the Front emerged from the first round of balloting with a new title; it was now without question the third most important political force in the country. Again the party found itself at the center of the political debate. One hundred thirty-two of its candidates surpassed the 12.5 percent threshold of registered voters, and thus qualified for the second round. Never before in the history of the Fifth Republic had this many far right candidates advanced to the second round of balloting. The mainstream right, although heavily wounded by the results of the first round, refused to consider any electoral deals with the celebrating frontistes. Although it controlled 15 percent of the electorate, without the benefit of reciprocal candidate withdrawals the Front found itself again pushed to the margins of the political contest; without electoral allies, the Front could not expect to become a significant presence in the National Assembly. But even though it again found itself on the margins, the Front weighed heavily on the electoral future of the center right, this time by the sheer volume of its support. Ironically, because of the center right's unwillingness to deal with the far right, Le Pen's party became the arbiter of the elections.

Between the two rounds of voting, Le Pen demonstrated his uncanny ability to remain central to the debate without actually being a candidate. On May 30, Le Pen campaigned with his daughter, Marie-Caroline, who had emerged as the top vote recipient in her constituency in Mantes-la-Jolie. In a highly publicized episode, Le Pen entered into a shouting and shoving match with Socialist candidate Annette Peulvast-Bergeal and some of her supporters. The pictures that emerged from this episode show an enraged Le Pen clearly shouting at Peulvast-Bergeal, whom he has pinned up against a wall. The headline on the Front page of *Le Monde* the next day read "Jean-Marie Le Pen rediscovers the habits of his youth in Mantes-la-Jolie."[6]

The second episode, rather than involving an allegedly criminal act, was only an exercise in supremely poor taste. At a massive rally at the

Paris Palais des Sports, Le Pen jubilantly performed for the party faithful, symbolically offering the head of one of his greatest critics, Catherine Trautmann, the mayor of Strasbourg, to Marie-France Stirbois. This public display of sophomoric bad taste could not have come at a worse point in the party's development. The beheading of Trautmann and the attack on Peulvast-Bergeal provided little incentive for those center right voters who remained undecided about their second-round choices to cast their ballots in favor of the remaining Front candidates. The image the Front needed to entice the bourgeois voters of the RPR and the UDF was one of stability; it needed to project the image of a party capable of governing. These episodes did little but reenforce the traditional stereotype of the French far right as street thugs undeserving of the mainstream public's political support.

In the second round of the elections, the Front's decision to contest all but one of its 131 eligible races provoked a crisis within the center right. Charles Pasqua, former interior minister, courted the Front's supporters by appealing directly to their concerns about immigration:

> [T]o vote for the Socialists, is to vote for the abrogation of the immigration laws . . . [we need] to do even more, implement quotas, accept only those people with limited work contracts, and if we need to, we should suspend family reunification. (in *Le Monde* May 30, 1997)

One could argue, as did center right leader Jean-Claude Gaudin, that the Front essentially handed the election to the Socialists by maintaining its candidates wherever possible. Seventy-six of the Front's second-ballot contests were three-person races, where a frontiste faced a candidate from the center right as well as one from the left. The center right lost forty-seven of those three-person races, well above the margin it needed to hold onto the majority of the National Assembly. It is impossible to say with certainty that the outgoing majority would have held onto all of those seats, but the Front's power also extended beyond those three-way races. Even in those races where the Front did not have a second-round candidate, it played an essential role in defeating the center right. In such contests, over 50 percent of the Front's first-round voters cast their ballots for the center right, but 25 percent abstained in the second round and almost 20 percent voted for the leftist candidate. The Front's presence as well as its absence played an essential role in these elections. Although only one frontiste, Toulon mayor Jean-Marie Le Chevallier, won election to the National Assembly, the party's power to influence the election was instrumental in the center right's defeat.[7]

Elite Perspectives of Party Durability

The party's core leadership was asked to rank those facilitators that they believed would be most crucial to the party's continued development; their responses included five factors. The range in responses at this third level of party development is strikingly similar to what appeared at the second stage of the party life cycle. In fact, of the five responses offered, four were also mentioned in relation to the party's electoral success. The most notable difference at this level is the omission of the electoral system as a factor. The habit of the French political elite to modify the rules of the electoral game explains this change. The electoral system, having reverted back to the two-round majority system after the 1986 legislative election, is no longer viewed as a facilitator of success, but rather as an obstacle. In Table 4.5, the electoral system is replaced by a new facilitator—the party's organization.

Contrary to previous assumptions, the level of mass commitment appears to play only a minor role at this stage of the party's development. When asked to choose the most important facilitator for this third level of the political party life cycle, only two respondents named mass commitment; it ranked last out of the five factors mentioned as the primary facilitator. The impact of the presidential effect, an institutional factor, is not even measurable from these data. Not one respondent mentioned it as vital to the continued development of the party at this level.

Five individual factors were mentioned as first-choice responses; in order of importance, these factors are (1) leadership, (2) party organization, (3) weak traditional parties, (4) issues, and (5) the level of mass commitment. At this stage, leadership continues to play a dominant role; moreover, throughout this study, the data underscore the primacy of the party's leadership as the party's political elite discuss the Front's development during the earlier stages of the life cycle model. This political factor is consistently viewed as the first or second most important facilitator at every stage of the political party life cycle. More specifically, at this stage of the life cycle model, ten party leaders, 38.5 percent, regard the party's leadership as the principal facilitator for the Front's future progress, and 65.4 percent mention it as a general facilitator.

Table 4.5   Facilitators of Party Durability

	Number of cases	Percentage citing as primary factor	Number of cases overall	Percentage overall
Leadership	10	38.5	17	65.4
Party organization	7	26.9	14	53.8
Weak traditional parties	4	15.4	8	30.8
Issues	3	11.5	15	57.7
Mass commitment	2	7.7	12	46.2
Media	—	—	5	19.2
Other	—	—	3	11.5
Totals	26	100.0	74	284.6

Note: Overall percentage is over 100 percent because respondents were given the opportunity to name three factors.

The historical record and the comments of the Front's elite clearly illustrate the extent to which the party has relied on the prodigious leadership skills of Jean-Marie Le Pen. In 1988, the party elite stressed that Le Pen's leadership was essential to its continued growth; his central role in the party and the elections that it has contested since the date of the interviews confirms their interpretation of the party's evolution. Le Pen was central to each electoral advance; obviously, this is doubly true in the party's presidential campaigns. No other frontiste was capable of generating the enthusiasm and the votes that Le Pen did in the 1995 presidential election. From 1988 until 1997, Le Pen remained the party's most important asset, and the elite respondents clearly understood his importance to their growing political movement. The party's performance in and Le Pen's absence from the most recent legislative contest demonstrate that the Front is finally beginning to emerge from Le Pen's shadow and become more than a one-man movement.

During earlier discussions of the party's creation and initial electoral breakthrough, the relative unimportance of the party's organization compared to such factors as leadership, issues, and the electoral system was noted; in its early development, improving the party's organizational base was less important than promoting Le Pen and sounding the alarm about the immigrant problem. In fact, only four respondents mentioned the party's organization as an important factor in its development during the first and second stages of the party's life cycle. The Front tended to rely almost exclusively on its leadership and the appeal of its political message while it capitalized on the vagaries of the French electoral system. This perspective changed radically when the Front's leaders were asked to discuss which factors would promote the party's development beyond its initial electoral successes. The respondents argued that the party's organization would become an important and politically strategic factor in the party's future political maturation. When asked to evaluate the party's chances of becoming a permanent fixture in French politics, seven respondents contended that the party's organizational structure would play the most important role in the Front's reaching such a goal. When all first-choice responses are considered, organization is surpassed only by leadership; when all possible responses are examined, 53.8 percent of the respondents mention the paramount importance of the party's organization. This places it third in total responses after issues and leadership, an important consideration as we ponder the Front's future role in French politics.

The data indicate that the leaders of the National Front clearly recognized the necessity of improving the party's skeletal organization. They advocated a variety of approaches to improving the party's organizational base. This emphasis on organization is apparent at three levels. First, the respondents stressed the need to upgrade the party's local-level organization. Second, a number of respondents emphasized the importance of improving the quality of the party's activists and candidates. Finally, some respondents perceived a need for an organizational makeover; they believed that in the future the party will need to downplay its negative image and begin to collaborate more extensively with other political parties and politicians. Many individuals within the Front elite agreed with this frontiste, arguing that the Front "needs to build itself up at the local level." The party's leaders feel that it is imperative for the party to concentrate on contesting all elections through a well-structured local-level network of National Front federations. This membre fondateur contends that the Front's rapid progress during the 1980s can actually be viewed as an impediment to continued success. His contention is based on the fact that the party's organization was insufficiently developed to deal with the early successes:

We must participate in all the elections, especially the local, municipal, and canton elections. . . . I think that we have to establish ourselves this way. One could say that we started at the top. One could say that we started at the wrong end. In politics, it's normal for a movement to begin with the local elections, and then the legislature, and the senate. It's just the way things worked out that we emerged in the European elections. . . . We are beginning to experience the consequences of not having respected the rules of construction. It's like with a house, you never start with the roof. If we had been better established locally in the municipalities, the regional councils, we would have had without a doubt more success.

Furthermore, this same frontiste links the party's organization to its leadership when he says "Me, I'd put in first place the organization of the party. Organization is extremely important. We need a group of leaders." The reference to a "group of leaders" implies that he understands that the party needs to continue recruiting people who are capable of serving in leadership capacities within the party's hierarchy. It also implies that the party needs to develop its own leadership cadre system.

To compete in the electoral arena, a new political party needs not only voters, but also candidates. Previous chapters have highlighted the Front's difficulty in attracting candidates. Its poor showing in the 1988 legislative election emphasized the problems the Front has had recruiting quality candidates. The progress made in the 1993 contest was in part due to the party's success in the 1992 regional council elections, but although the party improved on its 1988 score, it was still denied representation in the National Assembly. This charter member argues that the Front has often been beset with "mediocre" candidates:

We have often had candidates, who even if they live in the neighborhood, were unknown politically as well as socially. . . . It's not easy to find candidates. And sadly, I have to say that we have often had mediocre candidates and that also has an impact on the results. Obviously, with a proportional system, the first two or three on the list pull along the rest. . . . [Y]ou can put just about anybody in the tenth position and that has no importance. But with an [electoral] system by districts, each candidate is as important as the next. Certainly this election proves that in an extraordinary manner. For both the Socialists and URC, it's the people who have been established in a district for a long time who got the best results.

Another perspective on the candidate problem is offered by this former National Assembly deputy, who feels that "The problem is with the training and the quality of the candidates." The poor quality of candidates will not be solved by recruiting from within the ranks of the party, according to this respondent: "We must reenforce our party with activists. To enrich our party with activists, we have to go and find them outside our membership ranks."

As the National Front leaders pondered their party's future development in 1988, they clearly understood the need for an increased organizational presence. The death of Jean-Pierre Stirbois in 1988 provided an opportunity for an infusion of new ideas and new practices. Bruno Mégret and Carl Lang, respectively the national delegate and the secretary-general, filled the void created by Stirbois's death and began an organizational overhaul of the party apparatus. The elites interviewed for this study played a role in developing the party's new, more structured organization framework; their responses clearly underscore the fact that they were acutely aware of the party's needs in this area.

The party's organization was recast over the past ten years. Militant and candidate training became a priority as the party established workshops throughout the country to brief its activists on everything from where to post a flyer to how to respond to specific questions from potential voters and the media. Special summer sessions were held annually to indoctrinate the candidate hopefuls in the Front's preferred campaign strategies. The party also published a manual, entitled *Militer au Front,* that serves as an activist cookbook. In the aftermath of the 1988 legislative elections, the elite respondents had determined that the party's organization was central to its future growth; in hindsight, we can see that the improvements they made in the party's organization led to its becoming a permanent fixture in the French political horizon.

In addition, the Front's image problem was an important consideration for a number of the party's leaders. As noted in previous chapters, whether justified or not, the legacy of the extreme right continues to haunt the National Front and isolates the movement from the mainstream of French politics. This charter member contends that the Front needs to make a real effort to change how it markets itself: "We should not change our ideas, but perhaps we need to make the message more polite. When I say make it more polite, I mean more tactful, but also clearer and more presentable." Another of his colleagues takes this argument one step further and believes that the Front needs to become less "marginal." He argues that the party can do this by making overtures to the center right:

> The Front needs to become less marginal, that's to say it needs to offer its hand to deputies whose beliefs coincide with its own, and it should help in breaking up this false parliamentary right comprised of the RPR and the UDF. It needs to stop going its own way. . . . [T]he technocrats of the traditional right need to return to the spineless center . . . and we will become a federation of organizations on the right by agreeing to collaborate with the best of them.

Others believe just the opposite: that the Front suffered because of its alliance with the URC coalition during the 1988 legislative elections. They believe that the Front was betrayed by the traditional parties and caution their colleagues against entering into future alliances with the other political parties on the right. This is a debate that remains unresolved today. In some ways, the center right has made the Front's decision for them, because since 1988 it has refused to enter into an electoral agreement with the Front. In 1993, the mainstream right clearly did not need the Front's votes, but in 1997 the tables had turned; the mainstream right's decision to isolate the Front's 131 second-round candidates clearly contributed to its downfall.

According to the party's leaders, the behavior of the system's dominant parties is the third most important factor in promoting the Front's future development. Four respondents, 15.4 percent, mention this factor; this figure doubles to 30.8 percent when all responses are considered.

Other factors also continue to play a role at this level of the party life cycle. Although only 11.5 percent of the respondents mention the Front's core set of issues as the most important factor in the party's future development, 57 percent mention it when all responses are considered. This actually makes issues the second most important facilitator overall after leadership.

Obstacles to Continued Development

The respondents' perception of the Front's future was also affected by factors they believed would inhibit the party's further development (see

Table 4.6   Obstacles to Party Durability

	Number of cases	Percentage citing as primary factor	Number of cases overall	Percentage overall
Electoral system	12	46.2	18	69.2
Media	9	34.6	22	84.6
Party organization	2	7.7	6	23.1
Other	2	7.7	2	7.7
Mass commitment	1	3.8	4	15.4
Presidential effect	—	—	1	3.8
Weak traditional parties	—	—	1	3.8
Totals	26	100.0	54	207.6

Note: Overall percentage is over 100 percent because respondents were given the opportunity to name three factors.

Table 4.6). The Front presents a unified vision when discussing these factors: two obstacles, the electoral system and the media, account for 80.8 percent of the first-choice responses. This seems to underscore the findings of the previous chapters. In contrast to the discussion about the Front's electoral breakthrough, the electoral system is now viewed as a serious impediment to the party's continued development. The pernicious impact on small parties of the two-round single-district majority system is obvious from the results posted by the Front in all the legislative contests since 1986. Although the Front maintained its share of the vote between the 1986 and 1988 legislative elections, it received only one seat in the National Assembly. In 1986, 10 percent of the vote translated to thirty-five deputies, whereas in 1988 the same vote share equaled only one deputy. In 1993, when the Front recorded its best score in legislative elections up to that point, it was rewarded with no representation in the National Assembly. The discriminatory nature of the two-round system is illustrated by a study done by *Le Monde* after the 1993 legislative elections. According to the study, if the elections had been held under a proportional representation system similar to the one that had been utilized in 1986, the Front would have seated sixty-four deputies in the National Assembly. This score would have represented an increase of twenty-nine deputies over the Front's 1986 parliamentary group (*Le*

Monde March 3, 1993). The 1997 elections presented the Front with its best legislative score ever, but it was again denied meaningful representation. The electoral system continues to be a significant obstacle to the system's smaller parties. Close to a majority of the respondents, 46.2 percent, mention the electoral system as the most important factor inhibiting the Front's continued development; 69.2 percent cite it as an obstacle overall.

The irritation the Front elite manifests toward the media diminishes somewhat at this third stage of the political party life cycle. At the first two stages, the data highlighted the strong negative reactions registered by the respondents when discussing the media, with 88.9 percent naming them an obstacle to success. At this third level, the media rank second to the electoral system, with 34.6 percent of the respondents naming them as the primary obstacle to the party's continued growth; when all responses are taken into account, the media surpass the electoral system, with 84.6 percent of the respondents mentioning them.

When discussing the media, this respondent echoes the sentiments of many of his colleagues: "We have a veritable conspiracy facing us." Some of the respondents take partial responsibility for the treatment they receive in the media; another frontiste voices this perspective when he says, "It is clear that we don't know how to communicate. We must stop worrying people with our tone and our style." The manner in which the media depict the Front and its members is of great concern to the respondents. They recognize the problem, but many are at a loss as to how to solve it. This former National Assembly deputy seems almost resigned to the situation:

> We have an image problem, a problem with the media. It's a huge problem. No one really believes that we are really Nazis, fascists. . . . An American journalist came to see me during the campaign in Nîmes and he said, "You don't seem like someone from the National Front." They have made us out to be diabolic.

The respondents mention two other factors as obstacles. Interestingly enough, 23.1 percent of the respondents feel that the party's organization is a significant obstacle to the Front's future development; previously, many of the respondents believed that improving the party's organization was the most important task in assuring the Front's future development. In addition, 15.4 percent overall cite the party's low level of mass support as a major obstacle; many of the respondents believe that the Front's poor image in the media is linked to its difficulty in generating greater mass-level support.

In the aftermath of the 1997 legislative elections, the National Front's future seems assured because the party's organizational improvements are beginning to pay significant benefits. The elite respondents interviewed for this study are politically astute; they understood the party's weaknesses and its faults, and have doggedly improved the party's organization over the past decade while continuing to benefit from Le Pen's charismatic leadership. Some would argue that Le Pen has used the Front to promote his egomaniacal desire to remain in the political limelight, but in reality the relationship has clearly been reciprocal. Le Pen has remained in the forefront while the party's *fonctionnaires* labored in the shadows, creating an impressive political machine that will remain standing once Le Pen leaves the political stage.

THE POLITICAL AGENDA

OF THE NATIONAL FRONT

Pendant des siècles, la France, l'Europe et le christianisme ont

lutté contre l'envasion des musulmans.

—Former National Assembly deputy [1]

The French National Front is the most visible and vocal far right political party in Europe today. Because of its unprecedented durability and political success, the Front has become a decidedly potent force in contemporary French partisan politics. As noted in previous chapters, this is a relatively recent phenomenon given that the party was created in 1972. As the party's electoral presence increased, its ability to influence the political debate has also expanded. Since its electoral breakthrough in 1984, the Front has increasingly had an impact on the more mainstream political parties. In addition, the Front has proven quite capable of adapting its political agenda to the changing political climate. In this chapter, we examine the changing nature of the Front's political agenda. The elite interview data provide an important base from which to study the Front's political appeal. The Front's policy statements and campaign manifestos demonstrate how the party has modified its political message to profit from a growing sense of French anxiousness about the country's political and economic future.

In the popular and even the academic presses, the political agenda of the National Front is often reduced to one issue: immigration (Mitra 1988). That restrictive reading of the Front's political agenda is called into question in this chapter; detailed, face-to-face interviews with the core leadership of the Front reveal a wide range of issue concerns, but a comparison of these results to findings from public opinion studies reveals congruence on but a limited range of issues. Dissonance on other issues may help to explain the Front's electoral glass ceiling.

Issues and Representation

In representative democracies, political parties provide an important mechanism that links the governing elites to the masses; linkage mechanisms of one sort or another are a necessary and fundamental aspect of democracy in increasingly complex societies. Theoretically, if not always in reality, political party leaders are presumed to represent their constituents.

Representation can be operationalized in various ways. Party leaders may share many of the same socioeconomic characteristics of their constituents, indicating that the leaders have backgrounds similar to those they represent and thus have undergone many of the same socialization processes. This is perhaps representation in its purest form: individuals of the same socioeconomic class representing the concerns of their peers in the society's legislative arenas. On the other hand, representation may take a decidedly different form: leaders may hold political views that correspond to those of their supporters, or the political leaders may represent their supporters in both ways, sharing similar socioeconomic backgrounds as well as corresponding views on the important political issues of the day. These two forms of representation have been studied extensively.

Representation can be examined by analyzing the political issues that are of primary importance to the Front elite and comparing these with the issues identified as most important by the French public. In this chapter, we first consider the extent to which the National Front is speaking for all French citizens. This is done by asking National Front elites questions originally conceived for the Euro-Barometer surveys of the French public. The purpose is to ascertain to what extent the Front's leaders espouse the issue concerns of all French citizens, not just their partisan supporters.

Next, we undertake a more thorough consideration of the Front's primary political concerns. The Front's leaders were asked to name the three most important political problems facing France; an attempt is then made to ascertain to what extent the party leaders' priorities mirror those of their partisan supporters in particular, and those of the French population in general. This is accomplished by making direct comparisons between the leaders' priorities and those of the party's supporters and of the French population. The party's long-term political viability is inextricably linked to its ability to anchor itself within the broadest political context possible. If the National Front is unable to expand its issue base, it will undoubtedly fail to increase its core constituency and may eventually suffer the same fate as the Poujadist movement of the 1950s.

Thus, the purpose of this chapter is to compare the political views of the Front elite to those of the French public. In simple terms: Does the Front, as it so often claims, really say what all French men and women are actually thinking?

The Front attempts to emphasize its ties to the French public by claiming to be the true representative of the nationalist popular right. A common saying among Front loyalists is "Le Pen says out loud what everyone is thinking." The Front's campaign literature routinely stresses the party's ideological solidarity with the French public by such slogans as "Two Frenchmen out of three agree with us about reducing the number of immigrants." This clearly is an exaggeration, but French public opinion surveys do show that the Front's policy agenda is indeed attractive to a significant percentage of the French public. Fully one-third of the public agrees with the ideas promoted by *lepénisme* (Mayer and Perrineau 1993). More recent public opinion surveys indicate that a majority, albeit only 51 percent, express support for *some* of the Front's agenda (*New York Times,* November 10, 1996). The influence of Le Pen's ideas clearly extends beyond those who are willing to cast their ballot for him or his party's candidates.

Comparing the attitudes of the National Front elite to those held by the general French population is a form of collective correspondence (Weissberg 1978). This approach to the issue of representation draws links between elite attitudes and those of the general population by examining the ideological and political differences and similarities that exist between these two groups. As Dalton argues, "When the distribution of public preferences is matched by the distribution of elite views, the citizenry as a collective is well represented by the elites as a collective" (1988, 206). If the National Front is as extremist and iconoclastic as some would argue, one would expect to find little correspondence between the specific issue concerns of the Front elite and the general French public. But if there is extensive issue convergence between the Front's leaders and French citizens, the extremist label pinned to the Front may be somewhat unwarranted.

Finally, it is imperative to note that, in the case of the National Front, the analysis of issue correspondence not only indicates whether the party is representing the French public and its constituents; it also has important ramifications for the party's future political viability. Essentially, it can be argued that as the ability of the National Front elite to represent the views of all French citizens is documented, important information about the party's political future is uncovered.

Issue Concerns of the French National Front

To determine which issues play a major role in the Front's political platform, general patterns of correspondence between the Front's views and those of the French public are examined. Again, the purpose is to ascertain whether the Front is completely out of touch with the political sentiments of the French population, as is routinely portrayed in the media.

By replicating an issues battery from the twice-yearly Euro-Barometer, the attitudes of the Front's leadership are directly compared to those of the French public on a number of important political issues (see Table 5.1). For the purpose of discussion, these issues are divided into three categories: (1) economic issues, (2) moral issues, and (3) societal issues. The data reveal whether and to what extent the respondents at the elite and mass levels agree with the statements listed in the table. A very high score or a very low score indicates agreement within the samples considered, whereas the closer a score is to 50 percent, the less consensus there is within the two samples.

Findings reveal that the Front is most attuned to the concerns of the general French public with respect to societal questions. In this category are such divisive political issues as immigration, security and violence, and racism, issues that have in fact served as the Front's philosophical and political core. Findings for the four questions in this subset of issue concerns show that the average difference between the Front's position and the position of the French public is 14.3 percent. Given the high negative ratings that the party and its leader routinely receive, this is an important finding.

As one would expect, given its campaign rhetoric, the party's leadership presents a unified stance on the immigration issue. An overwhelming 95 percent of the Front's leaders agree with the statement that there are too many immigrant workers in France, and 76 percent of the French population concur. Immigration is an issue that has played an essential role in the Front's political appeal, and from these data it appears

Table 5.1   Issue Correspondence between National Front Elite and French Public

	Front elite	French public
Economic issues		
Too many unemployed don't want to work	88	88
Unemployment is often very distressing	100	97
Trade unions are absolutely necessary	67	75
The government should intervene less in the economy	95	57
Employees deserve to have more rights in their company	40	85
Differences in incomes must be reduced as far as possible	15	78
Moral issues		
The family should remain the basic unit of society	88	90
There are some books that should be censored	52	47
Homosexuals are people just like others	24	54
One should be ready to sacrifice oneself for one's country	100	46
Liberalization of abortion is a good thing	0	66
Societal issues		
Violence is continuously on the increase	88	90
The courts of law can be trusted	43	54
We have too many foreign workers	95	76
There is too much talk of racism	100	75

Source: Euro-Barometer, 21 April 1984, and author's interviews with the leaders of the National Front.
Note: Tables entries are the percentage agreeing with each statement.

that a significant segment of the French population holds views similar to those of the Front elite. Such a high degree of agreement on the immigration question indicates that a vast reservoir of popular support may exist for the National Front, at least with respect to this one issue. The question of whether there is too much talk of racism is closely related to the issue of immigration; furthermore, the results for these two questions are nearly identical. All of the elite respondents agree with the statement that there is too much talk of racism, and 75 percent of the French public express the same sentiment.

Another important issue for the Front revolves around the notion of insécurité. Although not a perfect indicator of this concept, the violence question taps into the anxiety people feel for their personal safety and the security of their possessions. This political message has played exceedingly well to urban populations, who feel threatened by the combination of high crime rates and large influxes of immigrants. With 90 percent of the French public and 88 percent of the Front's leadership agreeing with the statement that violence is continuously on the increase, an important correspondence between the Front and the French public exists on this issue.

The National Front is most out of touch with the total French electorate when it comes to issues dealing with moral concerns. In this subset of issue concerns are questions dealing with abortion, patriotism, homosexuality, censorship of books, and family values. Overall, on the five questions dealing with morality issues, the average difference between the Front's leaders and the general population is 31.4 percent, a significantly higher difference than observed with the societal questions.

This divergence is most obvious with the abortion issue. Although 66 percent of the French public maintain that the liberalization of abortion is a good thing, none of the Front leaders agree with this statement. Certain frontistes, such as Vice President Martine Lehideux and Political Bureau member Michel de Rostolan, are leaders in the French anti-abortion movement, and anti-abortion policies are central to the Front's political agenda. The party's antiabortion stance is actually related to two other issues: a strong moral opposition to abortion, and their belief that French citizens are engaged in demographic warfare with non-French immigrants who have higher fertility rates than French citizens. De Rostolan dramatically equates the issue of abortion to France's lost generation of World War I in his book *Lettre ouverte à mon peuple qui meurt* (An open letter to my people who are dying): "One hundred sixty thousand abortions in 1985—and I am only counting the official statistics—that equals, in nine years, one and a half million children who were never born, who were destroyed even though they were already conceived. To say it another way, abortion costs our country the equivalent, each year, of about one half of the yearly dead in as bloody a conflict as the Great War" (1987, 68). The Front is vehemently antiabortion and has supported legislation to create a maternal salary "for those women who will provisionally give up their professional lives in order to raise their children" (*Passeport pour la Victoire* 1988, 101), contending that such a policy will help to decrease the number of abortions. In addition, the Front argues for such "pro-family" legislation because it believes that such proposals will help increase the historically moribund French birthrate.

The Front appears more patriotic than the French populace; 100 percent of the Front's leaders feel it may be necessary to sacrifice oneself for one's country, compared to only 46 percent of the populace. Obviously, nationalism serves as an important cornerstone of the Front's philosophical foundation. The mainstream right, in the post–de Gaulle era, has increasingly refrained from blatant appeals to French nationalism. The National Front, on the other hand, observed this void in the nation's political discourse and promptly filled it with a rhetoric reminiscent of de Gaulle's most strident appeals to nationalism. The Front's ability to exploit the nationalism issue has paralleled a decline in the Gaullist Party's populist appeal. Although Le Pen is known for his nationalistic fervor, Mégret is also a master at framing the Front's rhetoric on this issue: "Because France is an ancient nation and she is accustomed to a leading role, she is unable to survive without greatness . . . During every era, she has found herself at the center of the great events that have fashioned Europe and the world, sometimes in a dominant position, and other times in a defensive position, but always as a privileged actor on the world stage. Today, in order to remain loyal to herself, she must once again claim her place among the great nations: For her greatness is an essential element of her existence" (1997, n.p.).

Another indicator of the respondents' traditional perspective on moral issues is the question dealing with homosexuality. The Front exhibits greater homophobic tendencies than the French population, with only 24 percent of the Front elite agreeing that homosexuals are "like other people," compared to 54 percent of the French population.

Two issues in this category present a different picture. Both the Front elite and the French public agree with the central role of the family in French society. And, surprisingly, a similar picture emerges on the issue of censoring books; both respondent groups share a mixed opinion on this issue. Recent events in the towns of Marignane and Orange, cities captured by the Front in the 1995 municipal elections, underscore the Front's willingness to censor books, magazines, and newspapers it finds objectionable. In September 1996, Marignane's municipal library ended its subscription to *Libération,* a left-leaning daily newspaper that is widely popular in France. Two other popular leftist publications have also been removed from the library's stacks, whereas a number of far right publications have been added. In Orange, the Front passed many of the same edicts prompting the resignations of the library's four professional librarians. Jacques Bompard's administration in Orange has also placed a moratorium on buying books about North Africa. Other episodes dealing with the Front's control of funds for cultural festivals and the designation of cultural awards have followed the same pattern: Promote the nationalists at the expense of their leftist opponents. The four cities where the Front now controls city hall clearly demonstrate that the party is not only waging a political war, but that when given the chance to lead it will engage in a cultural war as well.

Economic issues constitute another important part of the Front's political agenda. The degree of issue correspondence on these economic concerns varies greatly according to the specific question; the data reveal a 29.4 percent average difference overall between the two respondent groups. On some issues, such as unemployment and the role of trade unions, the elite respondents' concerns mirror those of the French public, whereas with respect to employee rights and reducing income differentials, the data present a marked lack of issue correspondence. Overall, the elite respondents represent a united front when it comes to advocating free market initiatives. They also claim to encourage private initiative and want the government to make greater progress with privatizing industry. In three other areas, the French public does not share the Front's economic views. Income inequality is an important issue, with 78 percent of the French advocating measures to redress the problem of income inequality, whereas only 15 percent of the Front's leaders feel the same. Although 95 percent of the Front's leaders think the government should intervene less in the economy, only 57 percent of the French population agree with the Front on this issue. The contrast between the Front's economic views and those of the French public is most noticeable when the indicators address issues relating to the government's proper role in managing the country's economic future. The French public express greater confidence in the government's ability to effectively manage the economy, and the Front elites argue for less governmental interference in economic affairs. This split between the party's leaders and its mass-level supporters was reconfirmed in a 1990 study of the Front's convention delegates (Ysmal 1991).

Issue Priorities of the French National Front

Another method of examining issue correspondence is by comparing the issue priorities of the party elite to those of its supporters and to those of the total French polity. The issue priorities of the respondents were determined by asking them to rank what they believe to be the

Table 5.2   Issues Priorities of National Front Elite

	Number of cases	Percentage citing as primary problem	Number of cases overall	Percentage overall
Social Problems				
Immigration	12	42.8	20	71.4
Declining birthrate	7	25.0	14	50.0
Education	1	3.6	2	7.1
Security/Violence	—	—	4	14.3
Generational problems	—	—	1	3.6
AIDS	—	—	1	3.6
Economic Problems				
Government control	3	10.7	8	28.6
Unemployment	1	3.6	3	10.7
General economic	1	3.6	2	7.1
Cultural Problems				
Moral crisis	1	3.6	5	17.9
Loss of national identity	1	3.6	3	10.7
Cultural decline	—	—	1	3.6
Political Problems				
Right's future	1	3.6	1	3.6
Unified Europe	—	—	1	3.6
National preference	—	—	1	3.6
Totals	28	100.1	67	239.4

Note: Overall percentage totals more than 100 because respondents were encouraged to give more than one response.

three most important political problems facing France. This exercise provides a second opportunity to examine to what extent the National Front is attuned to the issue concerns of the French public in general and its own partisan supporters in particular. Table 5.2 details the issue priorities of the National Front elites by listing those problems they mentioned as most important and then summarizing all their issue concerns. In this analysis, the problems that concern the Front are divided into four categories: social, economic, cultural, and political. Again the data reveal that the Front is most preoccupied with social issues. A Front leader, elected to the European Parliament, insists that it is "especially the societal problems, more so than the political problems," that are of primary importance. These include immigration, the declining *French* birthrate, and crime.

The National Front has been accused of being a one-issue political party because of its close identification with the immigration question. This interpretation is too simple in the extreme. Immigration plays an essential role in the Front's political rhetoric, but it is far from the only issue. Underestimating the Front's appeal has been a way for French academics and political pundits to diminish its impact and dismiss the party as a mere aberration. The party's skillful manipulation of the immigration issue has generated a great deal of visibility vis-à-vis the electorate. Le Pen's provocative statement, "Three million unemployed is three million immigrants too many," is an economic fallacy, but a politically powerful sound bite.[2] And not surprisingly, the most significant political problem facing France, according to the leadership of the National Front, is immigration. Although the leaders of the Front are concerned with a number of crucial issues, immigration is most frequently cited as the number 1 problem. Interestingly, given the image of the Front as a one-issue party, immigration is not mentioned by a majority of the leaders as the country's primary problem: approximately 43 percent of the Front elites point to immigration as the number 1 problem facing France; 71 percent of the respondents include this issue in their list of three.

Many French citizens feel threatened by the Islamic immigration from North Africa, and the Front has expertly manipulated their misgivings to its political advantage. As the Front approached its twenty-fifth anniversary, immigration remained an explosive issue in contemporary French politics. The recent controversy in the winter of 1997 over the Debré immigration reforms well illustrates this point; in another attempt to usurp the Front's political strength on the issue, the conservative administration of Alain Juppé advanced a series of strict immigration reforms. As opposition mounted to the most controversial measure, a requirement that French citizens inform local authorities of the comings and goings of their foreign guests, the government removed it from the legislation, despite the fact that more than 70 percent of the population supported the reforms.

The drama inherent in the country's inability to address the immigration issue has pushed the Front's rhetoric to hyperbolic levels. Latent racism becomes overt as this former National Assembly deputy explains his animosity to North African immigrants:

> [F]or centuries France and Europe have fought back the invasion. France, Europe, and Christianity fought back the Muslim invasion. We were successful for a thousand years, more than a thousand years, for fifteen hundred years in pushing them back, and now in fifty years Europe will be conquered by Muslims.

This message plays exceedingly well in cities with large immigrant populations, such as Marseilles. In fact, the National Front has become the top vote getter in the Bouches-du-Rhône region where Marseilles is located. However, not all of the leadership is as sensational in its approach to the Islamic immigration. Although still stressing his concern about the problem, this charter member compares the current immigration to previous influxes of immigrants and concludes that the import of the present immigration is much more ominous:

> I believe that there is a major problem in France today and that is the immigration problem. Understanding it from abroad is hard. France has a social welfare system that is very attractive as well as a language that is equally attractive for the countries of the Maghrib and black Africa because they know how to speak French and therefore they have a tendency to come here quite easily. Previously, France was able to absorb, historically, immigrants coming from Poland, from Italy, and from quite a few other countries. [This previous immigration] was accomplished without problems, in small doses, because those people had the same culture as our own. The Maghrib problem is very different. This Islamic problem is quite different, because Islam mixes together religion and politics.

This same individual, in a classic case of blaming the victim, contends that not only is it impossible to integrate the Muslim immigrants into French society, it is the immigrants themselves who are responsible for whatever racism exists:

> Law is a product of religion in Islam. They don't know how to adapt to the laws of French society. They are unable to be integrated. Previous immigrations were accomplished in a more normal manner in small doses and these people were very quickly integrated into

the country. We have a flood of Islamic immigrants that it's just impossible to absorb. They create ghettos, and in my opinion they create the racial phenomenon. I fear that in Marseilles there will be an explosion. You must understand that people are witnessing their surroundings fall into disrepair, they no longer can find their heritage, and in certain neighborhoods of their city they are just no longer allowed in.

The Front's leaders are adamantly opposed to the continued importation of Islam from North Africa. The emergence of Islam as the second most practiced religion in France creates a palpable anxiety on the part of many French citizens (Wieviorka 1993). Over 65 percent of the French believe that there are too many Arabs living in France, 61 percent say there are too many Muslims, and 57 percent no longer feel comfortable in their own surroundings. The Front has expertly manipulated these fears to enhance its political standing. This member of the Political Bureau believes that "People experience a sort of inverse colonization that manifests itself when a mosque is built near their homes." Others point to the fact that the increased presence of North African Muslims is an affront to French identity. A former National Assembly deputy argues that immigration is linked to a loss of national identity:

> If I were to elaborate on the loss of identity, it's the primary problem, it's the immigration problem which isn't at all like the immigration before or after the Second World War. That was an immigration of people who came to France, generally from other European countries, thus possessing the same civilization with the desire to become French citizens. And now it's an immigration from the third world, thus coming from different civilizations to settle in France but living with their own culture and their own customs, thereby creating communities which are antagonistic to the French community and thus destroying our national identity and placing the future of our country at risk.

Immigration, according to the Front's leadership, is linked to a variety of problems, the increase of insécurité being one of the primary offshoots.[3] Only 17 percent of those interviewed in a 1993 survey linked increasing crime to the "large number of foreign workers," but 54 percent expressed being seriously worried about their personal safety (Le Gall 1994). This provides an important reservoir of untapped support for the National Front. In a masterpiece of manipulation, this Central Committee member links immigration to a host of social ills:

> Certainly, the most important problem has to be the issue of immigration because around this revolves all the other problems. Immigration is a problem with our national identity. France is swamped by immigrants and it risks losing its soul, its culture, its heritage— simply put, its identity. It's also a problem of security. Domestic security, because the people who come from these other countries, often African countries, come generally to find here what they can't find at home: much more favorable working conditions, salaries which are evidently a lot higher, and the whole social welfare system.

His diatribe against immigration continues as he links it to the unemployment issue:

> Apart from the legal immigration, there is the clandestine immigration, the unauthorized immigration that creates an enormous domestic security problem when you have people coming into the country without papers, without work contracts.

The discussion of immigration ends as he insists that the immigrants are responsible for the drug problem: "We can see it with the drug problem since 70 to 75 percent, maybe even more now, of the drug traffickers come from African countries."

Immigration is not the only social problem that disturbs the far right. This frontiste claims that France's low fertility rate is inextricably linked to immigration: "I think that at the top of the list is the low fertility rate, with its corollary, the immigration from the third world. Both are intimately tied together. You could say these are the two most important." When asked to explain why a low fertility rate is cause for concern, he responds:

> I think that is quite clear—France, like most of the countries of Western Europe and Eastern Europe for that matter, is a country which is liable to blow up demographically. The French population is in a vertiginous drop and that has consequences for everyday life.

As previously noted, this issue prompted its 1986–88 legislative contingent to advocate maternal salaries and strict controls on abortion.

Although distinct from the immigration problem, many of the Front's leaders think that the high levels of immigration serve to exacerbate the situation caused by the decline in the French birthrate; 25 percent of the respondents point to the decline in French fertility as the primary problem in France, and 50 percent name it as a problem overall. The low French fertility rate is clearly an important preoccupation of the Front. This frontiste, who abandoned the RPR to join the Front, maintains that "France is no longer having babies. In Paris, one baby out of three is born to a foreign mother. If we continue down this path, in a few years France will no longer be France." Many of those in the Front leadership, such as this Political Bureau member, view this issue with as much concern as they do the immigration question:

> First, the decline in birthrates . . . it's a problem which no one is addressing, but it threatens the very survival of French society as well as other Western societies such as Germany and Italy. It is certain that if in two generations, which is nothing in the long view of history, the situation is not reversed very rapidly, France will be, in two generations, a nation of 35 million with half its people being over fifty years old.

The urgency with which the respondents view the declining birthrate question is obvious; they contend that it is the second most important problem in France. The Front's perspective on the severity of the situation is evident by the comments of this Front leader, who represents the party in the European Parliament:

> If there are no more young people, I believe that we will witness the death knell of Europe, perhaps the end of a civilization. We have fertility rates in the European countries of 1.2 . . . the only country replacing its generations is Ireland . . . such problems are even more serious when one considers the vigorous fertility rates in the African, Asian, and North African countries—the entire third world.

These data reveal that the Front's leaders are also preoccupied with a second set of political problems, essentially economic in nature. Economic concerns have been central to the Front's political platform since the party's creation. Its initial emphasis on free market economics tended to differentiate it in an important way from the mainstream right, which had historically endorsed a strong state presence in the country's economic life. Although this aspect of the Front's agenda has been overlooked by many, it has, in actuality, been an important element in the Front's efforts to attract new members from beyond the political ghetto of the nationalist right. François Bachelot, Pierre Descaves, Jean-Yves Le Gallou, and Bruno Mégret are representative of frontistes who were primarily motivated by the Front's economic agenda. The impassioned rhetoric that accompanies the immigration debate tended to overshadow the Front's neoliberal economic program. Long before the Front became widely known for its vehement opposition to immigrants and immigration, it had published in 1978 a short work entitled *Droite et démocratie économique* (The Right and Democratic Economics). The Front's free market proposals are best explained by Le Pen himself, as he discusses the central themes of this publication:

> [It] constitutes a preface to all the current developments in liberal economics. Another way to say it is, that we were "Reaganites" before everybody else, even before President Reagan himself, who wasn't elected until 1980! Thus, since 1978, the National Front has analyzed the crisis, the reasons for France's economic decline. And, since that time, we have advocated the reinstitution of liberal economics—competition, the end of exchange controls, reduction in public spending and the number of public sector employees, and the intervention of the State in economic matters. Simply put, we were on the cutting edge seven years in advance, which is rare for political parties. . . . Today, Chirac wants to appear modern and is imitating us. Reducing taxes, privatizing industry, getting the state out of banking, all of that, we were speaking of it seven years before him. For us it's not a last minute election trick. (In Bachelot 1986, 73)

Economic issues account for approximately 18 percent of the first mentions and nearly 50 percent of all the responses. This former National Assembly deputy insists that the state has overextended itself:

> We must reduce the state to its essential functions, that is to say, defense, diplomacy, and justice, and completely remove it from all the other tasks. It [the state] has no business in the economy, in energy or transportation or the services—we must free the state.

The Front is primarily concerned with the excessive control that they think the government exerts over the French economy. This issue is mentioned by 10.7 percent of the respondents as France's most important problem, and approximately 29 percent include it in their list of three. The party's campaign literature underscores the Front's desire to purge the French economy of its Socialist taint: "In order to get rid of socialism, we must make the public sector private." Another member of the Political Bureau contends, "we have a directed, Socialist economy, with the state playing a large part in everything."

Concern about unemployment, although mentioned by only four of the frontistes, has served as an important part of the Front's overall economic program. In 1988, the Front published a manifesto, *Pour une vraie économie libérale* (For a true liberal economy), in which it extolled the virtues of the free market. In this publication, the Front argued that the answers to France's economic ills were to be found in the models applied by Margaret Thatcher in Great Britain and Ronald Reagan in the United States: "Unemployment is not our fate. The dynamic economies of the free world have proved this once they satisfied one condition, namely, break with socialism and the planned economy of the technocracy. In Great Britain, Mrs. Thatcher's policies, over the last three years, have permitted the creation of more than a million jobs. In the United States from 1981 to 1987, eight million jobs have been created in seven years, permitting the country to have the most favorable unemployment rate in fifteen years" (16). This economic agenda was also tied to France's role in the emerging European Union. In recent years, the Front has become vehemently opposed to any increased integrative efforts, but throughout the 1980s, the party extolled the virtues of the European Community. In fact, the Front advocated quick progress to total monetary union: "And to all this we must add the necessity of rapidly creating a circulating European currency that will be the motor for the construction of an efficacious Europe, and the realization of the biggest market in the world. And if we are able to liberate our own business enterprises they will be the beneficiaries" (47).

The Front's most prominent leaders were also singing the praises of the European Union in the 1980s. In 1986 before the National Assembly, Bruno Mégret, who has since become the party's primary strategist, argued eloquently for the creation of a European patriotism that would extend beyond individualized nationalistic concerns: "Europe is a community of myths, of norms, of values, of history, of religions, of ethnicities, in brief a community of culture and civilization. And if the construction of Europe must be accomplished, it should first be done by being conscious of this, by the exaltation of a European sentiment, by the birth—above and beyond national patriotism—of a prideful Europe" (*Passeport pour la victoire* 1988, 59). Jean-Pierre Stirbois also discussed the need for France to remain at the heart of the European Union. In his book *Tonnerre de Dreux,* Stirbois unequivocally endorses the European integrative enterprise: "Imagining France with a solitary future is impossible. To avoid dependence and survive, to find again the common values that have made the civilization and the power of our continent, we cannot shirk the pressing need of the time: to link our future to that of Europe's and be the motor of her future. How can we not see that the future of Europe's peoples lies in their union so that we can face together the problems of the modern world" (1988, 156).[4]

The dawn of the new decade heralded the beginning of the Front's anti-Europe rhetoric and its retreat from its purely pro-market agenda. Mégret was one of the first to sound the alarm: "The Europe of Brussels [is] the Trojan horse of 'worldly' propositions" (1990, 161). Once again sensing possible political opportunities, the National Front has become progressively protectionist and continually more hostile to the free market policies advocated by the European Union. Kitschelt (1997) endorses Safran's (1993) contention that the Front remains wedded to neoliberal economic policies, but a close examination of the Front's economic agenda in the 1990s reveals a decided shift away from this perspective (Marcus 1995). Originally critical of the many strikes that paralyzed the country in 1995, the Front has zealously embraced the country's working classes in an effort to enlarge its support among this group. As it has increasingly embraced the problems of the working class, it has begun to mute its decidedly pro-market policies.

Its rhetoric against the European Union in general and the Maastricht treaty in particular has become increasingly aggressive. Here it works both sides of the coin: it manipulates workers' fears about the changing global economy and at the same time waves the flag of nationalism by arguing that any increased integration will further weaken France and deprive it of its sovereign rights as a great nation:

> Today, France's identity is threatened by the global vision of the political establishment. Faced with the cosmopolitan projects that mix together people and cultures, the National Front wants to be the rampart of our national identity. Far from being racist or xenophobic, Jean-Marie Le Pen is fighting to defend the French so that

they are given priority before foreigners and so that their fundamental rights will be respected. The Europe that is being built in
Brussels, with the complicity of the French political class is the
first step toward this globalization. For the National Front, Europe
is not just a large marketplace, she is before everything else a
community of civilization. The Europe that is being fashioned in
Brussels, according to the utopian schemes of the Eurocrats who
are dreaming of a super-European state involved in everything, is
destroying the nations and opening Europe to the immigrants of
the Third World as well as to American and Japanese products.
(National Front's home page on World Wide Web 1997)

The retrenchment from its previously closely held liberal economic policies combined with its more heated attacks on the European Union
underscore the Front's ability to anticipate the changing political winds.

Cultural concerns make up the third category of political problems
mentioned by the respondents; in particular, 18 percent believe France
is confronting a serious moral crisis, the fourth most mentioned problem overall after immigration, declining birthrates, and too much government control of the economy. Those respondents who cite France's
moral crisis tend to agree with the sentiments of this former National
Assembly deputy:

France is a country which has profoundly turned away from Christianity. There is no moral point of reference, it's a country where
people speak rarely of God. From my perspective it is the fundamental problem in France today."

In addition to the perceived moral crisis, the Front leadership believes
that the core of French society is being threatened. They refer to the loss
of their national identity as an extremely critical cultural problem. The
discussion of these sentiments tends to take on a xenophobic dimension, as in the comments by this member of the party's Political Bureau:

We are going to have a profound transformation of our national
identity. You see it every day. I can tell you that in the district
where I have campaigned . . . certain parts of the city are populated by no one but foreigners. When I say a foreign city, I mean a
city where you see Islamic butcher shops, where you see mosques,
or where you see people dressed as they would be in the Maghrib,
etcetera.

One of his colleagues, a founding member of the Front, discusses her visit to an immigrant neighborhood in Paris: "There wasn't a single white person. There were hundreds of people in the area, and there wasn't one white person." As she realizes the import of her comments, she stops and says, "I'm not talking about the color of one's skin, I'm talking about their nationality." This high-ranking frontiste echoes the comments of his colleagues as he decries the loss of French culture and the eventual possibility of a multicultural France:

> I would say that the primary problem is a cultural problem, and that French culture and the French nation are threatened. I'm a strong supporter of the defense of French culture. I also support the National Front's positions on immigration, the nationality code, and national identity because these are essentially questions of culture rather than legal or political issues. I'm not one of those who is going to accept a multiracial or a multicultural France.

Another former National Assembly deputy contends that the danger in France's losing its national identity lies in the difficulty the country will have participating as an equal in the European Union:

> My third biggest fear is that we are losing our cultural identity for a sort of cultural melting pot which has no foundation. . . . We are unable to be a strong component of the European federation, the great common market.

Problems of a more purely political nature are mentioned by only three respondents. One argues that the demise of the right is France's primary political concern, and two others contend that European unification and the issue of national preference in employment and social security problems are important concerns.

What is perhaps most interesting with respect to the Front's perspective on the country's most important political problems is that more than half of the respondents did not place immigration at the top of their list. Immigration is a serious problem, according to the Front's leadership, but it is definitely not the only problem; surprisingly, 57 percent of the respondents name issues other than immigration as the most important problem facing France. These data call into question popular media's depiction of the Front as a one-man, one-issue movement.

In addition to immigration, eight other problems are mentioned by the respondents as being the nation's most important. Only two other problems received more than one mention apiece; these are the decline in the birthrate and government control of the economy. Problems mentioned only once are education, unemployment, general economic concerns, the moral crisis, the loss of national identity, and the weakness of the traditional right.

A Comparison of Issue Priorities

The discussion of the Front's issue priorities, although extremely valuable in providing information about the closely held political beliefs of the respondents, only allows this information to be viewed in a vacuum, somewhat isolated from the concerns of the Front's partisan supporters and the general French population. By drawing direct comparisons between the issue priorities of the National Front and the masses one can more clearly see how concerned the general public is with the Front's political agenda.

   The first observation to be made when examining the public's concerns over a series of elections is that the National Front and its supporters are preoccupied with different political problems than are the general French public (see Table 5.3). According to the Front's leadership and its political supporters in 1988, immigration was the leading political problem facing France. An overwhelming 71 percent of the party's leaders mentioned the immigration issue when asked to name the major political problems facing France. Although this figure drops to 59 percent when we consider the issue priorities of National Front supporters, it remains the primary political problem for these individuals. Obviously, this issue has served to mobilize support for the National Front. Interestingly, the Front's supporters became more concerned with immigration issues during the 1993 election, but their preoccupation with this question leveled off again in the 1995 presidential contest.

   On the other hand, immigration is only the seventh most frequently mentioned political problem when the 1988 issue priorities of the entire French population are examined. In 1988, only 22 percent of the total population mentions immigration as a major concern. For the French public in general, we note the same pattern as with the Front's supporters: an increase in concern about immigration in 1993 with a retrenchment in 1995. Overall, French citizens in general are more preoccupied with the unemployment crisis, which they name the most important problem in all three years; it even supplants immigration as the most

Table 5.3   Issues Priorities of Front Elite Compared to Front Supporters and Total
French Population, 1988, 1993, and 1995

	1988			1993		1995	
Issue	Front leader-ship	Front sup-porters	Total French popu-lation	Front sup-porters	Total French popu-lation	Front sup-porters	Total French popu-lation
Immigration	71	59	22	72	31	65	25
Violence/Security	14	55	31	57	34	57	31
Unemployment	11	41	45	64	68	73	81
Taxes/Government control	29	24	20	—	—	—	—
Social Security	—	21	24	—	—	25	37
Competitiveness of the French economy	—	21	23	6	11	—	—
Education	7	20	29	23	42	—	—
Social inequalities	—	18	31	26	32	—	—

Sources: Perrineau 1989, 1993b, 1995; author's interviews with Front leadership.
Note: Respondents at the mass levels were provided a list of political issues; the Front leadership
was asked to name three important political problems facing France. Totals are more than 100
because respondents were asked to give more than one response.

important issue for the Front supporters in 1995. Only 11 percent of
the Front's political elite mention unemployment. For both mass-level
populations we see an important increase in the number of people who
express deep-seated concern about France's unending unemployment
crisis. As we will see in our discussion of the Front's organization in the
next chapter, the Front has become more sensitive to this issue and has
taken concrete measures to address it.

The Front's fixation with France's low fertility rate is not replicated
in either the sample of Front supporters or in the general population.
In fact, it is not even found among the top thirteen political problems
facing France for the two samples at the mass level. Another issue missing from the two mass-level samples is the Front's preoccupation with
moral decline.

For the Front supporters in 1988, immigration is followed by vio-
lence/crime in second place and by unemployment in third. By 1995,
Front supporters are actually more concerned with unemployment than
they are with immigration, even though immigration remains an im-

portant source of anxiety. For the French population as a whole, unemployment is the most important problem in all three years.

Simply put, the National Front's preoccupation with immigration and low fertility rates is not shared by the general French population, and, although Front supporters emulate the party leadership's concern about the immigration issue, the level of shared issue priorities diminishes rapidly after that point is considered.

Conclusion

Comparison of the Front's political agenda to the issue concerns of the general public reveals significant agreement on certain issues. This is especially true when political problems are viewed in isolation, without respondents making relative choices among a wide range of issues. The core leadership of the Front and the general public express surprisingly similar views with respect to such issues as immigration and crime; more than 75 percent of the French public think there are too many immigrant workers in France. Given that the Front's core constituency remains stalled at 15 percent, one could argue that this provides fertile recruiting ground. On the other hand, when the Front's political agenda turns to economic and moral concerns, the degree of issue convergence decreases. This is especially true with such issues as abortion and the reduction of income inequality; when these issues are examined, it becomes clear that the Front leaders' views are far removed from those of the average French citizen.

Although many French citizens express views that are similar to those of the National Front elite, striking differences emerge when the respondents are asked to rank their issue concerns. The Front's priority issues are not those of the French public. Moreover, except for the volatile issues of crime and immigration, the political problems that trouble the Front's leadership are not the same issues that concern the Front's own partisan supporters. French citizens are clearly not concerned with the multiplicity of morality questions that seem to dominate the political mindset of the Front's leaders; neither the Front's supporters nor the French public in general consider abortion and the country's perceived moral decline to be issues of great priority. On these issues, the Front is clearly out of touch with the French public. Moreover, the support that the Front received because of its stance on immigration and crime seems to be undercut by broad disagreement on economic and moral issues. Essentially, one could argue that the Front represents French citizens only up to a point, and that point revolves around the two linked issues of immigration and security. The National Front obviously faces the problem of broadening its political agenda as well as bringing it into greater harmony with French public opinion.

Fifteen years after the Front's electoral renaissance, immigration and insécurité remain important issues for the party's political elite. On the other hand, its decidedly pro-market neoliberal economic agenda has been replaced by an opportunistic protectionism that shamelessly courts votes in the country's working-class neighborhoods. This shift in its economic agenda may have prompted the defections of some of the party's more recently recruited elites, but it also allowed the Front to make serious inroads within the country's working classes.

The bête noire of immigration now shares center stage with the Eurocrats in Brussels and the imperialistic Americans. After a long period of pro-American sentiment that was related to a genuine appreciation for Ronald Reagan's strong anti-Communist rhetoric as well as his free market policies, the Front has clearly shifted toward an anti-American stance.[5] In the buildup to the Maastricht referendum, the Front's anti-EU rhetoric reached a feverish pitch. And, although the Front sang the praises of the market-driven U.S. economy in the 1980s, it now attacks those same policies with a vengeance. The Front's leaders have rediscovered the nationalistic rhetoric abandoned by the Gaullists and have moved it to the center of their own political agenda. During the height of the 1997 legislative campaign, Le Pen drove his anti-U.S. rhetoric to new levels when he said that France is "at war with the United States which wants to dominate the world" (in *Le Monde*, May 31, 1997). The savvy leaders of the National Front have refashioned their political appeal, and in so doing, they have not only secured their place in the political debate, they have slowly but surely deepened their political support.

THE LEADERSHIP AND

ORGANIZATION OF

THE NATIONAL FRONT

C'est vraiment très disparate, la droite révolutionnaire.

—National Front Political Bureau member[1]

Much has been written about the French National Front since it emerged from electoral obscurity in 1984. Schain (1987) effectively traces the Front's attempts to achieve political legitimacy during the 1980s. Other scholars have examined this far right political party by paying particular attention to the bases of its mass-level support (Jaffré 1985; Mitra 1988; Perrineau 1993b). But little attention has been paid to the elite composition and recruitment patterns of this important political actor (Ysmal 1989b). Birenbaum (1992b) and Ysmal (1991) do report on findings from a self-administered closed-ended survey conducted at the Front's 1990 convention held in Nice. Over 1,000 delegates were interviewed for that survey, but it provides little detailed information about the party's principal leaders. For example, 36 percent of those interviewed held no positions of importance within the party, and only 26 percent held elective office. Detailed information about the party's internal organization and the myriad related pseudo-political groupings has also been largely absent from the English-language literature.

This chapter fills the void that the Nice survey of the party's convention delegates could not. We begin with a discussion of the leading frontistes—the party's primary decision makers—who were interviewed for this study. The focus of attention then shifts to the social composition of this particular elite group. In addition, three different pathways to power within the hierarchy of this political party are identified and examined in detail. The chapter concludes with a discussion of the Front's internal organization, with special attention paid to the current membership of the party's Executive Bureau, its primary decision-making body. The vast network of ancillary organizations that has emerged around the Front are also presented.

The National Front Elite

Holding a leadership position in the National Front is a time-consuming endeavor. The elite respondents represented here were required, by virtue of their position in the party, to wear many hats simultaneously. For example, many of the respondents held positions within Le Pen's presidential campaign as well as within the party's organization. Although this overlap of members and positions helps to further strengthen the ties that exist between the party and its membership (Gaxie 1977), it was also symptomatic of the Front's organizational weaknesses in the late 1980s. By tightly integrating the members that it did have into the party's organization, the Front turned a weakness into an advantage. Because so many leading frontistes exercised so many different functions within the party, their desire to see the party succeed and endure was intensified. New parties that are struggling to maintain their position within an established party system are singularly dependent upon the political ambitions of their leadership; the following discussion of the positions held by the elite respondents illustrates the tenuous and extremely vital link that exists between the Front and its individual leaders. Elected officials as well as professional political party operatives were interviewed. Twenty respondents held elective office representing the Front in a variety of political forums. In a relatively short time, between the years 1984 and 1986, the Front had successfully competed in three separate electoral arenas: the European Parliament, the newly created regional councils, and the National Assembly. In addition, all respondents held leadership positions within the party. Appendix 1 outlines the elective offices and internal party positions that the elite respondents held at the time the interviews were conducted.

The Elected Officials

The Front first achieved national success in the 1984 European parliamentary elections. Ten of the Front's candidates were elected to the European Parliament, representing 11 percent of the total vote. Two of the Front's European Parliament deputies were interviewed for this study.

The Front had also achieved some success at the regional level. The increased importance of local government, with the Socialist initiative for decentralization, made election to the regional councils an attractive option for individual politicians and their respective parties. This was especially true for new political parties like the National Front, because the regional councils increased the number of available political positions. Moreover, the proportional representation system used for the regional elections increased the chances that minor parties would gain regional representation. The first regional council elections were held simultaneously with the 1986 legislative elections, and the Front achieved representation on twenty-one of the twenty-two inaugural regional councils. Seven regional councillors representing five different regions were interviewed for this study; three of the seven regional councillors served as presidents of the Front's regional groups. Another five respondents were either mayors or elected municipal council members at the time of the interview; the five people who held these positions had not been elected to their respective municipal-level positions under the banner of the National Front. They represent but a few of the many RPR and UDF party members who began migrating to the Front in the 1980s.

The party's initial electoral successes continued when, in 1986, it seated its first parliamentary group, consisting of thirty-five members, in the National Assembly. At the time the field work was conducted, the Front was a vocal and highly visible force in the national legislature (Birenbaum 1992a). The party was representing the agenda of the far right in the National Assembly for the first time since the 1950s, when the Poujadists burst onto the political scene. But electoral success was accompanied by intraparty conflict. Between 1986 and 1988, four deputies left the Front, ultimately decreasing the size of its legislative contingent to thirty-one members; this was only one member over the number necessary to sustain its parliamentary group. Fifteen of the Front's thirty-one member legislative group were interviewed for this study.

All the respondents are experienced political campaigners, having competed in electoral politics numerous times during their tenure in the Front. As one founding member said, "Le Pen wanted us to stand for all elections." At the time of the interviews, twenty-eight of the twenty-nine respondents were campaigning for the 1988 legislative elections.

Table 6.1 Composition of National Front Political Bureau, as of 1998

Bernard Antony[a]	*Jean-Marie Le Chevallier*
Christian Baeckeroot[b]	Jean-Yves Le Gallou
Jean-Claude Bardet	Martine Lehideux
Damine Bariller	**Jean-Marie Le Pen**
Michel Bayvet	Fernand Le Rachinel
Martial Bild	Samuel Maréchal
Yvan Blot	**Jean-Claude Martinez**
Jacques Bompard	Serge Martinez
Jean-Marc Brissaud	**Bruno Mégret**
Dominique Chaboche	Pierre Milloz
Michel Collinot	Philippe Olivier
Pierre Descaves	**Jean-Pierre Reveau**
Jean-Michel Dubois	**Michel De Rostolan**
Bruno Gollnisch	**Jean-Pierre Schenardi**
Roger Holeindre	**Pierre Sirgue**
Pierre Jaboulet-Vercherre	**Marie-France Stirbois**
Jean-François Jalkh	Franck Timmermans
Alain Jamet	Jean-Claude Varanne
Jacques Lafay	Pierre Vial
Carl Lang	**Georges-Paul Wagner**

[a] Names in italics indicate frontistes who were members of the 1988 Political Bureau; at that time, the Political Bureau included only twenty members.
[b] Names in boldface refer to those frontistes who have represented the Front in the National Assembly. All of the Front's National Assembly deputies served from 1986 to 1988 except for Marie-France Stirbois, who was elected in a by-election and served from 1989 to 1993.
Source: Interviews with the National Front leadership.

The Party Officials

The members of the National Front's Political Bureau were well represented in this study. At the time the interviews were conducted, the Political Bureau consisted of twenty members; eleven consented to interviews. At the initiative of Jean-Marie Le Pen, the Political Bureau was recently enlarged to forty members. Table 6.1 lists the current members of the party's Political Bureau.

The structure of the Executive Bureau, Le Pen's personal office, has also been further codified and enlarged within the past few years. Eight members now serve on the Executive Bureau, which functions as the true locus of power within the organization. Five of the eight current members of the Executive Bureau were interviewed for this study.

The leadership of the National Front often occupy more than one position of responsibility within the party's hierarchy, illustrating what Putnam calls "simultaneous overlap" (1976, 110); this was especially true when it was a relatively new and growing party. This overlap in positions of authority provided me with access to the Front's essential personnel.

The 1988 organizational chart of the National Front lists forty-three individual positions of importance. Many of these posts reflect a shadow cabinet in the style of an opposition party. The individuals interviewed occupied eighteen positions of importance, as detailed in the party's organizational chart. In addition to the positions listed in the Front's chart, there are seventeen auxiliary organizations directly aligned with the National Front; six leaders of these auxiliary groups as well as the individual responsible for their overall administration were interviewed for this study. The Front's Central Committee is also well represented in the sample; twenty of the respondents were members at the time of the interviews.

Thus, the respondents embody the leadership of the National Front. Not one of the twenty-nine respondents is merely a militant or activist. These people are either elected representatives or high-ranking party officials. Their knowledge of the Front is of an intimate nature.

Political Recruitment

The study of the National Front's recruitment processes is important for a number of reasons. First, it provides a greater understanding of the individuals within the party's leadership cadre. The picture we have of the National Front is most often the one provided by the popular media; this study offers a corrective to those popular journalistic accounts aimed more at sensationalism than objective study. Second, by providing an analysis of the different pathways to power within the party's organizational hierarchy, this study uncovers important information about the party's future electoral viability. Finally, this analysis underscores the primacy of Le Pen, in recruiting elites and acting as the gatekeeper to higher level party positions.

Political recruitment is not a haphazard process. Aspiring politicians do not suddenly appear at party headquarters and clamor for leadership positions within the party's hierarchy. They are recruited. The various pathways these individuals follow as they become politically engaged are important because they "encourage leaders to behave in certain ways and not in others" (Putnam 1976, 69).

How individuals gain access to elite status within a political organization is essential to a greater understanding of how that organization operates and how it represents itself to the wider political community. Moreover, the process of selection and recruitment of potential elites is crucial to a political party's continued existence because it determines who will hold the positions of power within the party's hierarchy. In addition, successful elite recruitment is essential to leadership succession, another important factor in determining the party's future political viability.

In their seminal study of politicians and bureaucrats, Aberbach, Putnam, and Rockman (1981) found that access to elite status within political parties was clearly biased in favor of university-educated, urban-reared males from politically active families. Such biased recruitment manifests itself at each stage of the three-part elite recruitment process identified by Seligman, King, and Kim (1974): certification, selection, and role assignment. But this bias is in fact twofold: not everyone is drawn to every organization, and not every organization is open to all recruits. In the case of the National Front, bias in recruitment does indeed occur at each stage of the process.

For the purpose of this discussion, political recruitment is defined as the exact point in the political process where the goals of the individual converge with those of the political organization. Seligman approaches political requirement in the same manner, arguing that "the relationship among candidates, sponsors, and selection is reciprocal" (1971, 4). The reciprocity inherent in the recruitment relationship is integral to the entire process. A discussion of recruitment from this perspective implies that the motives of the party as well as those of the aspiring politician must be given careful scrutiny. A party's motives may change with new developments in the political environment, and different individuals may have different motives for actively participating in the day-to-day operations of a political party.

Not all scholars of elite recruitment agree with this perspective. Marvick, for example, contends that "the self-activating effort of the person himself" is less important than organizational considerations (1976). Although this may be true for well-established political parties that have the luxury of slowly selecting and carefully grooming potential leaders, the situation is different for newly created or minor parties such as the French National Front. These parties, more often than not, find places for all new recruits who are "self-activating" into politics. Political recruitment within the Front involves a complex mix of correct timing, organizational requirements, and candidate motives.

Motivation is a key element in the recruitment paths followed by the respondents of this study. In fact, motivation coupled with timing and socioeconomic characteristics detail three separate paths to leadership in the Front. Furthermore, organizational imperatives are inextricably linked to the various recruitment paths. It is also important to note that organizational imperatives change as the party's political viability changes.

The Social Profile of the National Front Elite

Before turning to the analysis of the actual recruitment paths it is important to consider the composition of the entire leadership cadre, that is, its sociodemographic characteristics. The fundamental purpose in ascertaining the sociodemographic characteristics of the National Front elite is explanatory in nature: it will fill a void that exists in the literature on the National Front by systematically describing the leaders of this new, vital, and increasingly important political party. Much can be learned about the National Front by asking and answering such questions as Who are these people? Where do they come from? What attracted them to the National Front in the first place? A paucity of information exists about the National Front elite. The only other detailed study of the Front's leadership was originally conducted in 1978 as part of a larger project on middle-level party elites (Ysmal 1989b). Although this study is referred to for comparison purposes, it must be emphasized that the middle-level elites project studied individuals who were not the primary decision makers in the party. The interviews discussed here include the highest ranking officials of the French National Front. Due to the lack of systematic research on the leaders of the Front, describing the composition of this elite is an important research endeavor.

The National Front must bear some responsibility for the dearth of information that exists about its leadership. The leaders of the National Front typify what Wagstaffe and Moyser call a threatened elite (1987); the Front's primary decision makers feel especially victimized by the

French media, and because of this they have been reluctant to grant interviews.

Twenty-nine leaders of the French National Front, four women and twenty-five men, were interviewed for this study. Women are not well represented in the Front hierarchy; top-level party positions have not been made available to them. The Front had only one sitting female in the National Assembly, and only one of the Front's ten European Parliament deputies was a woman. In the summer of 1988, Yann Piat, the only female National Assembly deputy, was also the only woman on the twenty-member Political Bureau. Two of the four women interviewed were members of the party's Central Committee. Women have made few advances in the years since the elite interviews were conducted. Although the size of the Political Bureau has doubled in the intervening years, women's representation has remained constant; Martine Lehideux and Marie-France Stirbois are currently the only female members of the Political Bureau.

The absence of women in the highest positions of power within the party parallels the gender gap that exists in the Front's electorate: men are significantly more likely to cast a ballot in favor of the Front than women. This has been a recurrent problem, plaguing the Front since its creation. The party's image as a group of disgruntled veterans still opposing Algerian independence is not particularly appealing to French women.

Approximately 45 percent of the elite respondents are under 45. The average age of the respondents was 49 years old at the time of the interviews; the youngest respondent is 27 and the oldest 70. The Front is very hospitable to young political entrepreneurs. Young voters also find the Front's proto-nationalist, anti-immigrant message very inviting; in the 1993 legislative contest, the Front received the support of 15 percent of those between 25 and 34 years of age. At the elite and mass levels, the Front is a very young party. Furthermore, the party's share of the youth vote has increased since its first electoral success in the 1984 European elections. This may in part reflect the success of its youth organization, which claims over 15,000 members. The youthful character of the National Front was also replicated in its parliamentary group, where 41 percent of its deputies were under 45, as opposed to 30 and 32 percent for the UDF and RPR, respectively (Ysmal 1989b).

Conservative movements in France have historically been linked to the Catholic Church. Although the far right in general has followed this pattern since the early days of Action Française, the leadership of the National Front breaks from this tradition. A variety of religious beliefs are represented in the sample, including an agnostic, an atheist, a nonpracticing Muslim, and a member of the Unification Church. The great majority of the respondents, 86.2 percent, are Catholic, but only 27 percent profess to attend mass on a regular basis. Although nonattendance of mass is a typical French phenomenon, many of the respondents express sentiments similar to this one, who explains his nonpracticing Catholicism in this manner: "I disagree with the modern church which aggravates me." The "modern" church is too leftist for many of the respondents. A number of the Front's leaders express an affinity for the anti-Vatican II teachings of the deceased Archbishop Lebfevre. Eleven of the respondents, approximately 38 percent, state they never attend church. These findings coincide with those of Percheron (1987), who studied the regional councillors elected in 1986 and observed that the leaders of the Front are less likely to be influenced by the religious cleavage that has for so long been a part of the left-right division in France.

The elite of the National Front is well educated. Only three of the respondents had not passed the baccalaureate examination; two had attended the prestigious Ecole Normale d'Administration; and the vast majority, 75 percent, had continued their studies beyond the baccalaureate.

The social class of the Front elite, as determined by occupation, does not differ markedly from that of the other two conservative parties, but there is a difference in the class of origin among the three. Cayrol and Jaffré (1980) find that 51 and 46 percent of the middle-ranking elites in the UDF and RPR have their origins in the upper classes (liberal professions and *cadres supérieurs*), whereas only 38 of the Front's highest ranking officials have their origins in these same classes.

Like any other political movement, the National Front is not a homogeneous group of individuals. This heterogeneity is apparent in the twenty-nine leaders that were interviewed for this study, their previous political experiences, education, family background, and so on. For example, some members of the Front's leadership have been involved in extreme right movements since the days of Action Française, whereas others are participating in politics for the first time. Family background is another variable that demonstrates the differences in the respondents' political socialization; some respondents are from politically active families, and others claim to be from apolitical households.

According to some observers of the Front, the most obvious division in the National Front elite is between the hardliners and the moderates. One respondent, a former National Assembly deputy, describes the split in the following manner: "There are two different schools of thought, they are not really factions, just groups of individuals. There are the old-timers, the founders, the fathers of the church, and then there are those who joined later." This division seems apparent to the casual observer. The hardliners, *les durs,* are described as being in continual conflict with the more moderate politicians, *les modérés* (Birenbaum and Bastien 1989). The hardliners represent those frontistes who have been unwilling to moderate the harsh rhetoric that served to separate the Front from the political mainstream; their ideological perspective is more in keeping with the traditional rhetoric of the French far right. The moderates, on the other hand, have tended to downplay the overt xenophobia of the hardliners and have extended the political discussion to include criticism of both European monetary union and governmental control of the economy. Much has been written about this supposed split in the party, but the actual divisions go beyond a simple generational conflict between the hardliners/old-timers and the moderates/new arrivals. Simmons (1996) argues that there are four distinct leadership subgroups within the party's hierarchy, but also claims that there is great fluidity among the subjective labels he identifies. In reality, concrete empirical observations about the leaders' tenure in the party, previous political experience, and family background help to clarify this cloudy picture without sacrificing the descriptive attraction of Simmons's fluid categories. Such concrete observations define the leadership paths in terms of three distinct subgroups within the elite of the National Front: (1) the old guard or the founding members, (2) the showcase elite or *élites vitrinés,* and (3) the newer, younger politicians.

The Founding Members
The ideological core of the National Front is characterized by a number of respondents who share an extensive history of far right political involvement. This group includes nine founding members of the Front whose political and personal ties to Le Pen predate the creation of the party. "I was already with Jean-Marie Le Pen at the founding of the Front National des combattants," states a former National Assembly deputy whose friendship with Le Pen began in 1957. Many of the membres fondateurs claim similar long-standing personal relationships with Le Pen.

Table 6.2   Comparison of Front's Three Leadership Groups

	Founders	*Notables*	New recruits
Number of respondents	9	13	7
Average age	56	53	32
Average self-placement on 10-point ideology scale	9.4	8.3	9.7
Average placement of father on 10-point ideology scale	8.3	6.8	7.6
Percentage stating politics was discussed often during youth	89	83	57
Percentage with postbaccalaureate education	67	92	57
Percentage with previous party experience	89	69	57
Percentage who are members of Political Bureau	66	23	28

Source: Author's interviews with the National Front leadership.

They have supported Le Pen and his political activities for many years, their fidelity to the far right is complete, they believe, with all their hearts, in the political message espoused by the National Front. Furthermore, they place themselves firmly on the far right of the ideology scale, with an average self-placement score of 9.4 on a 10-point scale, with 10 representing the farthest far right point.

These founders share a set of political experiences that transcends the contemporary successes and failures of the extreme right. In addition, they share many early socialization experiences. Four of the founders say their fathers were members of Action Française, the dominant extreme right movement during the interwar period. Overall, 77 percent of the founders state that their fathers were members of political parties, compared with 31 percent for the *notables*. None of the new recruits mention that their fathers were actively involved in politics. Compared to the other two leadership subgroups, the founding members were reared in extremely conservative environments; as a group, these political elites place their fathers at the far right end of the political ideology scale, giving them a collective 8.3 ranking. The founding members claim that the discussion of political events was central to their family life, with 89 percent stating that politics was discussed often during their childhood. The data reveal that this subgroup of the Front's leadership is highly

Table 6.3 Previous Party and Organizational Affiliations of National Front Elite

POLITICAL PARTIES

Alliance Républicaine	Rally for the Republic
Comité Tixier-Vignancour	Rally of the French People
National Center for Independents	Restauration Nationale
New Forces Party	Union for French Democracy
Parti Républicain	Union for the Defense of the Republic
Poujadist movement	Union for the New Republic

MILITANT ORGANIZATIONS

Action Française

Occident

Ordre Nouveau

Veterans' National Front

CONSERVATIVE THINK TANKS

Club de l'Horloge

Comités d'Action Républicaine

Renaissance Circle

Source: Interviews with the National Front leadership.

politicized and that they were inculcated with the values of the far right at an extremely early age. Table 6.2 provides a summary of these various characteristics in a comparative framework.

The nine founding members interviewed were actively engaged in politics before joining the National Front, participating in many of the extreme right organizations of the post–World War II era. Eight of the nine respondents in this group were members of other political parties prior to joining the Front; the list of their previous political affiliations reads like a veritable litany of organizations on the extreme right, extending from the Poujadists to the National Front (see Table 6.3). Two of the nine founders trace their political awakening to the Poujadist legislative campaign of 1956; these two individuals held positions of responsibility in the Poujadist movement and have been actively involved in movements of the far right since that time. They are two of Le Pen's closest advisors and occupy influential positions in the National Front.

Another important mobilizing event for the founding members was the Algerian crisis. It not only signaled the end of the Fourth Republic, it destroyed an uneasy peace between the mainstream right and the far right. Although initially hopeful about de Gaulle's return to power, the far right viewed his decision to grant Algeria its independence an act of treason; it was at this point that the far right broke definitely with Gaullism. Individuals with political views anchored on the far right continue to harbor suspicions of the traditional conservative parties because of de Gaulle's "betrayal." These strong pro-nationalist currents have been resurrected in the National Front.

Two of the Front's charter members served lengthy prison terms because of their involvement in the OAS. The role played by the veterans of the OAS has already been discussed in detail in chapter 1. The image of the Front as a collection of hardened, war-weary veterans clinging to France's inglorious past is obviously rooted in reality. These two charter members create an ideological thread that directly links the National Front to the Algerian crisis, a moment in French history that many other French citizens would like to forget.

The 1965 Tixier-Vignancour presidential campaign also served as an important political springboard for many of the founding members. Le Pen served as Tixier-Vignancour's campaign manager, and it was during this period that he cemented many of the friendships and alliances that later helped him to create the National Front. One Front leader claims, "Basically, the Front is made up of the remnants of the Tixier-Vignancour battles," and another charter member points out, "A lot of marriages got their start during the Tixier[-Vignancour] campaign." The figures attest to the truth of their comments: six of the nine founding members were actively involved in the Tixier-Vignancour presidential effort. Their experiences working in that campaign served to solidify their commitment to one another as well as to the causes of the far right. When the debacle of the Tixier-Vignancour campaign resulted in a split in the far right, two of the Front's founding members broke with Le Pen for a short period in the late sixties and joined Tixier-Vignancour in the creation of the Alliance Républicaine. The creation of the Front in 1972 united, at least momentarily, the core of the far right in France.

This group of founding members holds great power within the party's hierarchy: they dominated the Political Bureau from 1972 until 1990, and six of the nine individuals in this group served on the twenty-person Political Bureau. They are Le Pen's closest advisors and his most trusted friends.

The Notables

A second group of influential decision makers in the National Front possess an extensive array of political experiences on the right of the political spectrum, but hesitated to be associated publicly with either the organization or some of the more hardline members of Le Pen's party until the 1984 European elections. This second group is comprised of the showcase elite, or the *notables*. Thirteen of the respondents joined the Front through this *notabilisation* of the organization. *Notables* have high-level name recognition, they are well-known within their local communities, and many have previously held political office at the local and national levels. The *notables* own the most land, may have a title, and are leaders within their communities (Ehrmann and Schain 1992).

It is important to note that French politics, especially at the local level, is still a very personal affair. Any political party in France must have a stable of widely recognized candidates to attract voters as well as new recruits. Moreover, the importance of *notables,* according to this Front leader, is magnified in the case of a new political party like the National Front:

> The obstacles: that was often the lack of men—the Front just didn't have any stars. What has hindered the Front since the beginning is the fact that it did not have enough *notables*. There must be *notables*. A new party doesn't have *notables* because the *notables* have no desire to join. Any new party is obliged to take in those who come, while the *notables* who tie a party to a region or a department are somewhat mistrustful.

To be blunt, the motivations of the *notables* seem mixed. Many claim to have joined the party and campaigned for office out of loyalty to their old friend, Jean-Marie Le Pen. But for some, it is quite obviously a friendship of convenience. Clearly, they could have joined the party earlier and provided needed support to Le Pen, but the political risks were much higher prior to the 1984 European elections. The combination of the 1984 success and the party's dire need of new and more respectable candidates for the 1986 legislative elections created a fortuitous mix of political circumstances. Le Pen's personal invitation to head the party's district-level lists was all the persuasion these reluctant *notables* needed to overcome their aversion to joining the Front. For those who had previously been on the fence, 1986 provided an unprecedented political opportunity.

Although the *notables'* motives appear somewhat ambiguous, the Front's underlying concern was obvious: to capitalize on its 1984 European success. To accomplish his goals, Le Pen made a concerted effort to attract *notables* to the party. The *notables* would help the party legitimize its new political position and give it added credibility in future elections. Recruiting name candidates was an exceedingly complex undertaking; the reciprocity inherent in the Front's recruitment processes is most apparent in the party's attempts to attract *notables* to its proportional lists for the 1986 legislative elections. It is at this juncture that we see a marked convergence between the needs of the party and the interest of the *notables*. This process of recruiting *notables* from outside the party had a tentative beginning during the campaign for the 1984 European elections. The Front included twenty-nine nonparty members on its campaign slate for the 1984 elections. This initiative to broaden the party's base included such *notables* as Olivier l'Ormesson and the Duchess of Magenta, Marguerite de MacMahon.

The difficulty of Le Pen's task was compounded by the Front's historically poor electoral showings during the 1970s and early 1980s. Moreover, the Front's negative image was not an inviting proposition to aspiring politicians. In 1984, Le Pen and his movement were viewed as a threat to democracy by large segments of the French citizenry. Weak electoral performances combined with an exceedingly negative image severely hampered Le Pen's recruitment initiatives. Prior to the notabilisation of the party, the Front's recruitment efforts had been confined to the ranks of the defunct Poujadist movement, the remains of the banned OAS, malcontents from the Tixier-Vignancour campaign, and opportunists from the neomilitaristic Ordre Nouveau. The Front's political agenda appealed to the alienated and the disaffected, who were not viewed as part of the French political mainstream. Thus, the people who did join were viewed as political marginals by those outside the party and even by some of the *notables* being recruited by Le Pen. Although clearly a supporter of the far right, this respondent discussed his misgivings about joining the party during this notabilisation process:

> There was absolutely no political hope, absolutely no hope of being elected. There were a lot of people who were socially a little strange, who were a little crazy, who were a little original, people who just weren't at ease in society. [People] who didn't have bal-

anced personalities, therefore it was necessarily a fringe movement.

After the initial local successes in Dreux, Aulnay-sur-Bois, the twentieth arrondissement in Paris, and the completely unexpected 1984 European election results, Le Pen made a concerted effort to attract the *notables* to his movement. One *notable* describes Le Pen's search in this way: "There was a continual effort which paralleled Le Pen's preoccupation to seek out individuals who were people of conviction, but balanced, and who had the moral and intellectual capacity to wage this political battle." These *notables* were added to the Front's slate of candidates in the 1986 legislative elections to help legitimize this important electoral effort. One respondent points out that he did not actually join the Front until "two weeks before the elections." Another *notable* is quick to mention that he is still not "officially" a member of the Front, preferring to maintain his association with the Centre National des Indépendants. Another seasoned politician on the traditional right and a former deputy to the National Assembly provides a good example of the self-interested *notable*. He claims the Front's inability to attract votes deterred him from placing his political future in the hands of a weak and fledgling party. "I didn't join before 1985 because when a party is not effective or important it serves no purpose. With no elected officials, no audience, it serves no purpose. I waited for a real party."

The people who joined the National Front in this manner share a number of important characteristics. First, they have higher levels of education than the members of the other two leadership subgroups, with 92 percent of the *notables* having continued their education past the baccalaureate, compared to 67 and 57 percent for the founders and new recruits, respectively. Two of the respondents in this group attended the prestigious Ecole Normale d'Administration. Second, the *notables* do not exhibit the ideological zeal of either the founding members or the new recruits. As a group, they are the least extreme in their ideological stance, with an average score of 8.3 on the 10-point political ideology scale. Although 83 percent of the respondents in this group claim politics was discussed often when they were young, only four of the thirteen respondents mention that their fathers were actively involved in a political party. Third, although they may have long been sympathetic to the goals of the far right, they tended to participate in more mainstream political movements. Nine of the thirteen *notables* were members of other political parties before joining the National Front, and the range of previous political affiliations spans the entire right side of the political spectrum. One respondent began his political career in the youth organization of Action Française, but his experience is atypical of the other respondents in this group, who tend to have participated in the more traditional conservative movements. Those *notables* mentioning a previous political affiliation name such mainstream political parties as the Union of Democrats (UDR), Union for the New Republic (UNR), UDF, and RPR. Local politics was a primary concern for four of the respondents in this group, who had served as mayors of their cities. Three of these individuals were experienced in national elections; they were National Assembly deputies prior to joining the Front. Two had held ministerial positions in previous conservative administrations. Four of the *notables* have no previous political party affiliation in the traditional sense. Surprisingly, these political neophytes indicate a collective disdain for political parties. For example, one respondent says, "I didn't believe in political activity." Prior to joining the Front, they preferred to participate in politics in different ways. This alternative form of political participation involved membership in a variety of professional unions and cultural organizations. As a group, the politically experienced and inexperienced *notables* participated in a vast network of social, cultural, and professional organizations. Their extensive extrapolitical ties provided the National Front access to an entirely untapped political marketplace.

The *notables* rose to prominence rapidly within the party. All of the respondents in this group held major positions at the highest level of the organization's hierarchy, but their admission to the Political Bureau was limited until that body was expanded to include thirty members. Le Pen controls the gate to positions of power in the party, and he opens and closes it as he sees fit (Putnam 1976). As if to harness the power of these new and influential party members, only three of the *notables* were granted membership to the twenty-person Political Bureau; Le Pen is thus able to keep tight control of the movement by restricting membership in the Political Bureau to his oldest and closest allies. Obviously, the recruitment of these well-known political figures was for electoral and cosmetic reasons; their names were placed at the top of the district-level proportional representation lists in the 1986 legislative election. Ten of the thirteen respondents in this group were members of the Front's parliamentary group from 1986 to 1988. The Front's ability to recruit nationally known individuals was an important part of its effort to sanitize its tarnished political reputation. Their mere presence on the ballot served as an affirmation of the Front's newly acquired respectability.

The New Recruits

The third important group that emerges from the sample comprises seven younger and less experienced political entrepreneurs. The new recruits, much like the founding members, joined the party without being personally recruited by Le Pen. These individuals are dedicated to the Front and evidence a true devotion to Le Pen.

The average age for these respondents is thirty-two, making them significantly younger than the leaders in the other two subsets of the sample. These individuals are also less educated than the respondents of the other two leadership groups, with only 57 percent having continued their education past the baccalaureate.

Perhaps what is most interesting about this third group of Front leaders is the small role politics played in their early socialization. No one in this group reports that his or her father was a member of a political party. In addition, only slightly more than half claim politics was a frequent topic of conversation during their childhood. One new recruit is rather typical in this regard; claiming to be from a "nonpolitical family," he nevertheless has been interested and involved in politics since the age of fourteen. Surprisingly, considering the low level of early political socialization, this group is on average more conservative than the other two leadership subgroups, with a self-placement score on the 10-point ideology scale of 9.7. Although all the elite subgroups report being more conservative than their fathers, it is the new recruits who have shifted furthest from their fathers' political ideology scores. The new recruits are indeed the political zealots of the National Front. Their youth, ideological enthusiasm, and complete devotion to the party and its president provide a mirror to the Front's future.

The political experience of the new recruits varies tremendously. Four of these individuals had participated in other political parties or movements. One respondent had been elected to a municipal council under the RPR banner but had become disillusioned with the Gaullist organization. Another respondent in this group had participated in the outlawed Occident before joining the National Front, and a third had been previously active in the PFN. This former PFN activist contends that his

decision to join the Front was "completely natural." Having been actively involved in the PFN, he stressed that joining the Front was just
the next step in his political awakening. His experience is characteristic of these young political entrepreneurs. When asked to explain why
he joined the National Front he responds, "The doctrine . . . I didn't
choose with respect to the other parties. I didn't ask myself the question,
'Should I join the RPR or the National Front?' I had the notion from very
early on that I was a nationalist." After five years of membership in the
RPR, another respondent and a former municipal councillor decided to
join the Front because she felt its economic policies were more compat-
ible with her own ideas than what she had seen in the RPR. She describes
her personal political growth in the following manner:

> I joined the RPR when the left came to power. . . . In 1985, the last
> trimester of 1985, I realized that the RPR was moving backwards in
> all areas, notably about an issue that was particularly important to
> me, the monopoly of the unions. At that point I decided to quit
> the RPR and join the National Front. . . . [It was] their determina-
> tion, and their defense of moral values and their economic poli-
> cies . . . I find, to an extent, in the policies of the National Front,
> Thatcher-like policies which interest me a lot.

This leadership subgroup also includes individuals who are participating in politics for the first time; membership in the National Front was
the first political experience for three of the seven new recruits. For this
political entrepreneur, joining the Front meant making a decision about
one's future: "I believe that it was first the fact that I did not want to
remain a spectator. If I had remained a spectator, I would have become
someone who lets things get done by others. I wanted to take my des-
tiny in my own hands."

Only two of the respondents in this group represented the Front in
elected forums. One was a deputy in the Front's 1986 parliamentary
group, and the other had been elected to serve on one of the regional
councils. All of the new recruits actively campaigned for office in the
1988 legislative contest.

Although only two of the respondents in this group had gained admission to the Political Bureau, all occupied positions of importance
in the party hierarchy. Membership in the Front provides these young
political entrepreneurs with great opportunities for quick political advancement within the confines of the organization's hierarchy. These

new recruits have infused the party with new energy, and they in turn have been rewarded with positions of importance.

Pathways to Power

A number of important observations can be derived from this analysis of the National Front elite. First, immediately following its rapid growth in the mid-1980s, the National Front provided its elite recruits with extensive political mobility opportunities. New recruits, whether *notables* or young political entrepreneurs, rapidly advanced up the rungs of the party structure. This is evident from two perspectives. It is initially apparent when we consider the respondents' previous political experience: 34 percent had never before participated in partisan politics, but they now hold key leadership positions in the National Front. A second perspective is length of membership. The political mobility opportunities are most evident with respect to the new recruits; they have less experience, both political and real-world, as well as fewer social contacts than the *notables,* but they have been given the opportunity to occupy principal leadership positions within the party. Of the twenty-nine respondents, over 70 percent joined the Front after the 1984 European elections. This underscores their rapid ascension to power within the party. Furthermore, we noted the differences in the social origins of the Front's political elite as compared to the political elite of the RPR and the UDF. Even with the inclusion of the *notables,* the Front's first generation of political leaders includes a broader cross-section of French society than do the other conservative parties. This is perhaps an important factor in the party's future electoral viability, and it may provide at least a partial explanation for the party's increasingly heterogeneous support at the mass level.

Second, we need to consider the locus of power within the National Front. At first glance, the permeability of the Front's organizational hierarchy seems high; as a new political party, the Front was in constant need of potential candidates, activists, and militants. At times, the Front had been reduced to placing ads in local newspapers to attract enough candidates to complete its electoral slates. Once recruited, the party quickly placed these individuals in leadership positions. Although advancement to the highest positions, those on the Political Bureau, is possible, these were for the longest time reserved for Le Pen's personal friends and confidants, the founding members. This leads us to conclude that political power in the National Front is first and foremost predicated on the personal relationship the power seeker shares with the party's president. Le Pen, acting as the gatekeeper, offers his blessing to only a select few; those who reach the pinnacle of power within the party serve on the Political Bureau. As we observed, the recruitment path followed by the founding members provided the most direct route to Front leadership.

Since 1986, there have been a number of defections by leaders who were originally recruited through the notabilisation process of the mid 1980s. Most prominent among these defections are Pascal Arrighi, François Bachelot, Yann Briant, Edouard Frédéric-Dupont, and Jacques Peyrat. Obviously, such defections create image and staffing problems for the Front. To remain electorally attractive, Le Pen was forced to continue recruiting *notables* and promoting them into the party's upper echelons. This was not always appreciated by the founders, who, along with the new recruits, voiced their opposition to this policy. Jean-Pierre Stirbois, before his death in 1988, openly criticized this strategy (Birenbaum 1992b).

Political recruitment in the National Front requires a delicate balance. Le Pen, the primary factor in the recruitment process, must remain constantly sensitive to the demands of the party's three leadership subgroups. In many respects, the Front's political future depends on its ability to successfully steer aspiring politicians through its recruitment channels.

A Growing Organization

Over the past twenty-five years, the Front has evolved from a marginal party operating on the fringes of French politics into a deeply anchored, well-structured political machine. As the party continued to grow, its appetite for candidates also expanded, but increasingly the party has proven able to satisfy its personnel needs from within its own ranks of militants and members. The regional and cantonal elections of 1992 and 1998 highlighted this trend, and it was further confirmed in the 1993 and 1997 legislative elections.

As the only thriving political force in an essentially stagnant political system, the Front serves as a model of party organization and discipline. Even after a quarter-century as the party's leader, Le Pen's control over the organization remains absolute. The organization that has emerged

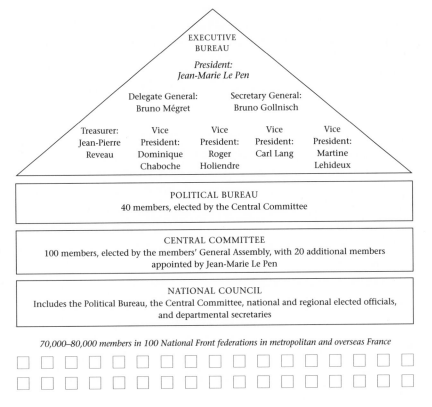

Figure 6.1   Internal Organization of the National Front

to propagate *lepénisme* is a hierarchically structured edifice that controls decision making in a top-down manner reminiscent of democratic centralism within old-style Communist Parties. The party's pyramid structure is outlined in Figure 6.1.

The Executive Bureau rests at the apex of the party's organizational hierarchy. This eight-person organ, which serves as the party's inner sanctum, draws its members from the Political Bureau. Although an executive bureau has been a constant power center within the party, its structure was enlarged and codified in the aftermath of the Party's Ninth Congress held in 1994. The current membership of the Executive Bureau includes Secretary-General Bruno Gollnisch; Delegate-General Bruno Mégret; the Front's four vice presidents, Dominique Chaboche, Roger Holeindre, Martine Lehideux, and Carl Lang; the party's treasurer, Jean-Pierre Reveau; and of course the party's president, Jean-Marie Le

Pen. In his capacity as president, Le Pen chairs the Executive Bureau and determines its membership. As a decision-making body, it meets on a more regular basis than the Political Bureau, averaging at least one meeting per week. It is charged with the day-to-day operations of the party. In certain respects, the Executive Bureau serves as the Front's government, or perhaps it can be best described as the personal *cabinet* of Jean-Marie Le Pen. The current composition of this important policymaking organ includes individuals who have followed the three separate recruitment pathways to power within the organization. Chaboche, Holeindre, Lehideux, and Reveau are charter members of the Front. Their long-standing personal relationships with Le Pen and their enduring commitment to the far right's agenda further enhance their standing in the ephemeral universe that is the French far right. Mégret and Gollnisch represent the tide of *notables* who were recruited in the mid-1980s. Lang, on the other hand, embodies the third category of frontiste, the rising political entrepreneur.

As a founding member of the Front, Dominique Chaboche has held many influential positions within the party. Like many frontistes, Chaboche began his political career in the youth arm of the Poujadist movement. A Political Bureau member since the party's creation, Chaboche began his tenure as vice president in 1978; prior to becoming vice president, he served as secretary-general, beginning in 1974. Currently, Chaboche has taken a special interest in the Front's international relations and has spent a considerable amount of time traveling abroad as the party's primary foreign emissary, his energies directed at establishing and maintaining the Front's ties with far right parties and politicians in other countries. Chaboche served in the National Assembly from 1986 to 1988 and currently holds two elected positions: he is a regional councillor and a municipal councillor in Rouen. As of this writing, Chaboche is sixty years old.

Roger Holeindre, affectionately known as Popeye within the party, has been a key member of the Front since its creation in 1972 and has been actively involved in nationalist circles his entire adult life. A military veteran of both the Vietnamese and Algerian liberation wars, his political attitudes were clearly shaped by France's devastating losses in these two failed campaigns. As a member of the ultraviolent OAS, he was deeply involved in the underground warfare that rocked the French nation in the early 1960s; he actually spent a number of years in prison for his extremist politics. Elected to the National Assembly in 1986, Holeindre acquired a patina of respectability after years of extreme right activism. In 1984, he created the Cercle National des Combattants, which serves as the center of the Front's nationalist wing, with Holeindre as its de facto leader. Warrior at sixteen, OAS partisan in his midthirties, Holeindre epitomizes the ancien combattant image that has been so difficult for the Front to shake. He is revered and loved by the party faithful, but *les arrivistes,* like Mégret and Jean-Yves Le Gallou, would probably like to see him retire. At sixty-nine years of age, Holeindre remains politically active; he is a regional councillor in the Île-de-France region and also serves as a municipal councillor in the city of Sevran.

Martine Lehideux is the highest ranking woman in the National Front. As founding members of the Front, she and her late husband, André Dufraisse, have undertaken many important functions within the party; politics is clearly a family affair for this couple.[2] Lehideux first became politically active during the Hungarian Revolution of 1956; in the aftermath of that aborted revolution she became a committed anti-Communist and has, in turn, remained committed to the causes of the French far right. She was particularly active during the Algerian crisis, participating in the organization Secours Français (French assistance), which served as a sort of support group for the returning pieds-noirs and aided political prisoners created by the OAS debacle (Birenbaum 1992b). Her husband served on the Political Bureau for many years and was the founding secretary-general of the Fédération Nationale Entreprise Moderne et Libertés (National federation for modern and free enterprise), one of the Front's key satellite organizations. Like her husband, Lehideux possesses considerable administrative skills. As the founding president of Cercle National des Femmes d'Europe (National circle for European women), she created an organization that combines her personal interests in the European Union and demography. She is fiercely anti-abortion and has aligned her organization with such pro-life groups as Laissez-les vivre (Let them live) and SOS–Tout petits (SOS–Little ones). She served two terms in the European Parliament and currently serves as a regional councillor and municipal councillor for the twentieth arrondissement of Paris. At sixty-four years of age, Lehideux is a close contemporary of Le Pen and has often been described as one of his staunchest supporters.

Jean-Pierre Reveau, like Chaboche, served in the National Assembly from 1986 until 1988 as a member of the Front's Rassemblement National. Of the seven individuals on the Executive Bureau, Reveau, who is sixty-five years of age, has the lowest public profile. Although he is not well-known outside far right circles, he is a close confidant of Le Pen and as the party's chief financial officer exercises considerable power in the Front's hierarchy. Reveau's relationship with Le Pen began during the Algerian crisis; they were members of the Front National des Combattants. Although a fierce partisan of Algérie française, Reveau managed to stay out of prison during the tumult created by the Algerian crisis. As a charter member of the Front, he was only tangentially involved in the party's day-to-day activities prior to becoming more actively engaged in 1984, when he abandoned his professional activities and assumed a more prominent role in the party's organization. Reveau currently holds two elected positions; he is a municipal councillor in Paris and serves on the regional council for the Île-de-France.

The presence of five charter members in the Executive Bureau underscores their enduring influence within the party's organizational hierarchy. In 1988, when the Political Bureau included only twenty members, the party was clearly dominated by the oil-and-water mix of old-style nationalists, *solidaristes,* and Catholic fundamentalists. As the Political Bureau expanded to include forty members, it eventually opened its doors to those outside the original leadership cadre. Generational replacement will eventually lead to a diminution of the charter members' influence, as the newly arrived *notables* and the young entrepreneurs replace the older cohort within the ranks of the Political Bureau.

Bruno Mégret and Bruno Gollnisch are products of the notabilisation process the party experienced during the mid-1980s.[3] Gollnisch joined the Front in 1983, followed by Mégret in 1987.[4] Their rise through the party's ranks is a function of their *notable* status as well as their exceptional educational backgrounds and previous political and professional experiences. Their decision to join the fledgling Front lent it an air of legitimacy and respectability at a very crucial point in the party's development.

Gollnisch's rapid promotion through the Front's ranks began in 1983, when he accepted the eighty-first position on the party's candidate slate for the 1984 European Parliament elections. He was elected to his current post of secretary-general in 1995; prior to this he served under Mégret in the National Delegation as the national delegate for international relations. As secretary-general, he is primarily responsible for the party's day-to-day operations as well as promoting and maintaining the Paris-based party's ties to its many local federations. Gollnisch served in the National Assembly from 1986 until 1988 and currently represents the Front in three elected capacities; he serves in the European Parliament and as a regional councillor from Rhône Alpes and a municipal councillor in Lyon. He holds a doctorate and is a professor at the Faculté de Lyon, where he has taught courses in Japanese studies as well as international law. At forty-seven years of age, Gollnisch represents a subset of the *notables* who made their professional mark outside the political world prior to joining the Front.

Mégret's rise through the party's ranks has been absolutely meteoric. His first major internal political coup was being named the director of Le Pen's 1988 presidential campaign; he reprised that role in the 1995 presidential contest. Educated at the prestigious Ecole Nationale des Ponts et Chaussées and at the University of California at Berkeley, Mégret began his professional life as an engineer, but quickly migrated to politics. Prior to joining the Front in 1985, he was considered a rising star in the RPR, where he was attached to the government from 1979 to 1981. Although trained as an engineer, Mégret has become the Front's most prolific political theoretician and strategist. His penchant for writing philosophical tracts began when he joined the Club de l'Horloge in 1975.[5] In 1982, he founded the Comités d'Action Républicaine and eventually made his way to the Front when he joined its Rassemblement National in anticipation of the 1986 legislative elections. He began his tenure as the party's delegate-general in 1988, assuming primary responsibility for the training of the party's candidate corps; he has also taken on the responsibility of mapping out its political agenda. If the Front succeeds in negotiating future electoral alliances with the mainstream right, it will be thanks to Mégret, who is viewed as one of the most likely frontistes to craft such an agreement. Such a turn of events would not sit well with the party's hard-core nationalists, who are more interested in ideological purity than political expedience. At forty-eight years of age, Mégret is often mentioned as the natural heir to Le Pen, although he possesses very little of Le Pen's natural charisma and crowd-pleasing geniality; moreover, he is viewed by many as a sterile intellectual and technocrat, and within party circles he is referred to as "the little Goebbels." In recent years, he has made an effort to overcome his overtly technocratic image, perhaps in an attempt to ensure that the succession is in his favor. Ironically, it is the image of the aloof technocrat that has often been the target of the Front's most vitriolic rhetoric when attacking mainstream politicians; it will prove most ironic if Mégret were eventually named to succeed Le Pen, given that he represents, in so many ways, what the National Front has ridiculed about the "Gang of Four."

Carl Lang represents the third category of frontiste, the young political entrepreneur. Although he is too young to have been a founding member of the Front, Lang has nonetheless spent his entire adulthood in the Front's fold, prompting Roland Gaucher, former editor of the Front's newspaper, to remark that Lang was a "pure product of the party" (in Birenbaum 1992b, 160). He joined the movement in 1977 at the tender age of twenty. Initially, he played an active part in the Front's youth wing, Le Front National de la Jeunesse, and subsequently rose to prominence in the power vacuum created by Jean-Pierre Stirbois's untimely death. As secretary-general from 1988 to 1995, Lang is credited with continuing Stirbois's work of modernizing the organizational apparatus of the party. He also successfully manipulated the process so that many Stirbois loyalists were replaced with people whose first loyalty was to Jean-Marie Le Pen. At forty years of age, Lang represents the rising political entrepreneur class—those young politicos who have spent their entire adult lives in the National Front. As one of three vice presidents, Lang's primary portfolio concerns itself with social issues. He currently serves in the European Parliament and also represents the Front as a regional councillor from Nord-Pas-de-Calais.

The most important organizational entities after the Executive Bureau are the parallel structures of the National Secretariat and the National Delegation, led by Bruno Gollnisch and Bruno Mégret, respectively (see Figure 6.2). In 1992, the Secretariat included six positions, three of which were controlled by charter members of the Front; the current composition of the Secretariat includes eight positions and demonstrates the increasing influence of the Front's young political entrepreneurs. Most notable among this group are Martial Bild, Franck Timmermans, and Jean-François Jalkh, all of whom have spent their entire adult lives in the Front's organization. All of these men are under forty-five years of age. The National Delegation under the leadership of Bruno Mégret has also restructured itself in the past five years. Most notable is the promotion of Philippe Olivier to national delegate for training, replacing Bernard Antony, the Front's most well-known and controversial Catholic fundamentalist; the removal of Antony from this position lends further evidence to Mégret's continual effort to solidify his position within the party. Prior to the most recent changes in these two offices, two frontistes, Jean-François Jalkh and Jean-Yves Le Gallou, held positions in

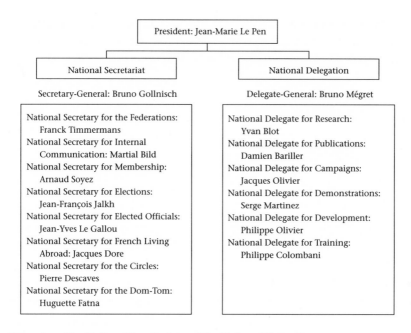

Figure 6.2   The National Secretariat and the National Delegation

both the National Secretariat and the National Delegation offices; with the Front's continued maturation, this practice has ended. These structures remain male-dominated, with only one woman, Hugette Fatna, serving in the General Secretariat as national secretary for France's overseas territories.

According to the Front's own literature, the forty-member Political Bureau represents the party's government. Its members are selected by Le Pen and it was through his initiative that it was first enlarged from twenty to thirty members after the 1988 elections, and then from thirty to forty members in 1994. The Political Bureau's most significant powers reside in its ability to appoint the party's departmental and regional secretaries.

The Political Bureau provides an excellent window onto the Front's political evolution over the past twenty-five years. Much has been made of the many personality conflicts, ideological disputes, and situational fissures that exist within the National Front (Birenbaum 1992b; Camus 1992), but compared to either the Socialist Party or the RPR and the UDF, the Front's primary leadership cadre, as evidenced by the membership of its Political Bureau, has remained remarkably stable (see Appendix 2).

Given the notoriously factious history of the French far right, no one could have expected that this odd mix of solidaristes, protonationalists, Algérie française partisans, Catholic fundamentalists, royalists, and *Horlogers* would be capable of working together in an efficient manner for any extended period of time. Of the twenty-member 1988 Political Bureau, only three people are missing from its ranks in 1990; two of these, Yann Piat and François Bachelot, left the party of their own accord, and the third, Jean-Pierre Stirbois, died in a car accident in 1988.[6] The current composition of the Political Bureau follows the same pattern: 73 percent of the 1990 body is still within its ranks. The deaths of Pierre Sergent and André Dufraisse explain their absence from the list, and the semiretirement of others accounts for some of the new promotions. With the Front's continued expansion, there has been a concomitant movement to increase the size of the Political Bureau; this has in turn provided more opportunities for the rising political entrepreneur class as well as the *notables* who joined the party in the mid-1980s. Essentially, the Front has been able to mitigate internal crises and become more inclusive as it has grown in size.

The 120-member Central Committee nominally serves as the National Front's parliament. It is, relatively speaking, the most democratic institution within the Front by virtue of the fact that it is the only organ of the party that is actually elected by the Front's rank and file. Even then, only 100 of its members are actually elected, with the president having the power to appoint an additional 20 members to the body. The Central Committee provides a democratic veneer for the constitution of the party's Political Bureau, as it has the authority to approve the slate of candidates provided by Le Pen. But it must accept or reject the entire slate; it does not have the power to delete and replace Le Pen's nominations. None of Le Pen's nominations have ever been rejected.

The National Council meets two or three times a year. It is composed of the members of the Central Committee, the Political Bureau, the elected national and regional officials, departmental secretaries, and others nominated in view of their service to the party. It meets to consider the broad outlines of the party's agenda that are essentially predetermined by the Executive and Political Bureaus.

The "Circles" and Beyond

In the past fifteen years, the Front's leadership cadre has created a veritable universe of ancillary organizations that revolve around the party's primary structures (see Figure 6.3). These satellite organizations represent an array of particular interests and social groups; they also cross-cut the dominant socioeconomic cleavages that have historically structured the French political debate. This vast network of particular interests ranges from students to the retired, from the unemployed to businesspeople, and from the repatriated French to those living abroad. Increasingly sophisticated in its recruitment techniques, the Front has successfully anchored itself in the vast social milieu that is contemporary France. Unlike the Socialists, who are linked to the government sector, or the RPR, with its ties to business, the National Front has reached out to welcome all of France *français* into its extended political family.

One of the oldest and most important satellite organizations is the Front National de la Jeunesse (FNJ), the youth wing of the party, created in 1974. Carl Lang served as the FNJ national director for many years and was eventually succeeded by Martial Bild in the mid-1980s. Bild, now a member of the Political Bureau and the national secretary for internal communication, began his political career in the PFN but migrated to the Front in 1980. At age thirty-six, Bild is a seasoned political veteran who has faithfully served the Front for many years; a rising star in the party, he ran a strong campaign in the 1997 legislative elections. The current national director of FNJ is Samuel Maréchal, a municipal councillor and member of the Political Bureau. The fact that two past directors as well as the current director of FNJ all serve on the Political Bureau is an indication of the trust the party places in the organization; moreover, it highlights the point that the directorship of FNJ serves as a direct gateway to increased power in the party as well as a seat on the powerful Political Bureau.

The FNJ has analogues in the other French political parties. It serves as a social as well as a doctrinal proving ground for the party's youngest militants, those aged sixteen to twenty-four; it runs summer candidate training courses as well as other workshops throughout the year. Maréchal claims that the FNJ has 15,000 active members. Its essential mission is to prepare the Front's youngest cadre for participation in the party proper. Its presence in French universities and high schools across the country further extends its influence among France's younger frontistes.

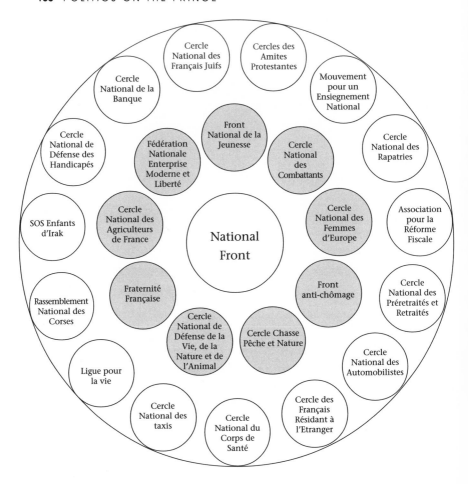

Figure 6.3 The Circles and Associations of the National Front
Source: National Front's home page at http://www.front-nat.fr; Birenbaum 1992b; and various Front publications.
Note: Those circles highlighted in gray are discussed in the text.

Entreprise Moderne et Libertés (EML) was created by the late André Dufraisse in 1984 and was an essential element of the party's initial electoral success because it linked the party to the business world and provided needed funds before the advent of generous public financing legislation. Jean-Michel Dubois, a Political Bureau member, serves as the EML president. Dubois is also the secretary-general of SOS–Enfants d'Irak (SOS–Children of Iraq), which was created in the aftermath of the Gulf war to aid the Iraqi children threatened by the international embargo.

EML characterizes itself as a sort of National Front Chamber of Commerce, where businesspeople can come together to profit from each other's experience. It claims to "understand perfectly the problems that French businesses face on a daily basis."[7]

The party's rhetorical shift away from free market economics prompted the creation of a host of social service type organizations that presume to "aid" the *French* underclass. Front Anti-Chômage (Front against unemployment) and Fraternité Française (French brotherhood) are two of the most notable examples of these organizations. According to the Front's own literature, Front Anti-Chômage was created "to help unemployed *French* men and women find a new job," and Fraternité Française is dedicated "to coming to the aid of *French* men and women who are distressed or in need." In another move in this direction, the Front opened a Paris soup kitchen in November 1996, ostensibly to help the unemployed but actually to further its recruitment efforts within the sector of society that the French now called the *exclus*. Presumably, the Front believes that social work will help its recruitment efforts. In keeping with this shift to appear as a kinder, gentler Front, the party has even created two separate environmental organizations; Cercle Chasse Pêche Nature (Hunting, fishing, and nature circle) is directed at the conservation-minded, and Cercle National de la Défense de la Vie, de la Nature et de l'Animal (National Circle for the Defense of Life, Nature, and Animals) has a more clearly environmentalist ring to it.

In recent years, the Front has made great progress in expanding its influence in the trade unions. It has been especially successful in recruiting within the ranks of the police; the Front's police union is now the fourth largest in the country. The party has also found success by creating its own union for prison workers and is beginning to make significant inroads in this sector of the workforce.

The Front continues to create additional satellite organizations that address what the party's leaders see as unmet needs, but many of these are ephemeral organizations with minuscule memberships and an inactive agenda. Nevertheless, the most important ones, like FNJ, EML, and the Cercle National des Combattants, serve important functions within the party and are important additional linkage mechanisms that bind the party to its growing mass-level support.

L'Après Le Pen

Since the Front celebrated its twenty-fifth anniversary in 1997, the party, its leaders, militants, supporters, and its enemies have been fixated on the question What is going to happen after Le Pen? Jean-Marie Le Pen's decision to sit out the 1997 legislative election turned the heat on this discussion, but although the succession question is loudly debated in the French media, the issue remains muted within the party itself. As we have noted in previous chapters, the role Le Pen has played at each stage of the party's development has been crucial; in addition, his ability to rein in all the factious elements that make up the French far right has been instrumental in the party's ability to endure. *L'Après Le Pen* debate revolves around not only the issue of the eventual successor but whether that person will be able to build upon Le Pen's legacy and keep the factious far right united.

Along with the obvious choices of les deux Bruno, there has been talk that Marie-France Stirbois is in the running to succeed Le Pen. Stirbois's exclusion from the Executive Bureau may limit her future somewhat, but she remains strongly linked to the party's rank and file because of their devotion to her dead husband, Jean-Pierre Stirbois, the party's former secretary-general. Yet, although she has a large following within the party, it seems unlikely that a woman would be named to succeed Le Pen. Gollnisch and Mégret are the more likely candidates. Although Gollnisch did not join the Front until early 1983, he nevertheless flirted with far right politics during his student days and possesses stronger personal ties to the nationalist wing of the far right than does Mégret. Such experience makes Gollnisch more appealing to some subgroups within the Front. Mégret, a relatively late convert to the politics of the far right, has done much to solidify his far right credentials since joining the Front. Although Mégret's politics (his willingness to work with the mainstream right) are relatively expedient, his rhetoric has become increasingly hostile. Because both men are excellent students of history and know only too well how weak a fractured far right can be, it does not appear that either will sacrifice the party for his individual ambitions. Beyond les deux Bruno there are many young and highly experienced far right partisans who actually have longer far right résumés than either Mégret or Gollnisch.

One thing seems certain: once Le Pen retires or is eventually pushed aside, the reins of leadership will pass to a new generation of frontistes.

Le Pen's cohort, those frontistes who trace their political experiences all the way back to Action Française and through the Poujadist era and the Tixier-Vignancour presidential campaign, are now fast approaching their seventies and eighties; they have no choice but to step aside and offer what they have built to a new generation of nationalists. The edifice that is the contemporary National Front is growing and vital and will continue to play a role in French politics long after the old *routiers* have been laid to rest.

VOTING FOR THE

NATIONAL FRONT

Toutes les couches sociales votent le Front national.

—National Front Central Committee member[1]

Voting in France can be a difficult and labor-intensive enterprise. For example, from 1984 to 1990, the French were called to vote in more than five national-level elections conducted under a multiplicity of electoral frameworks and regulated by a perplexing maze of electoral rules and regulations. European Parliament elections in 1984 began this especially charged electoral cycle. The first regional council elections coincided with legislative elections in 1986. These were quickly followed by presidential elections in 1988 that precipitated President François Mitterrand's hasty decision to dissolve the National Assembly and hold legislative elections again in the summer of 1988, thereby reconstituting the legislature after only two years in office. The third direct European Parliament elections, in 1989, brought this seemingly never-ending election cycle to a close. But the dawn of the new decade did not stem the tide of electoral currents: from 1990 to 1997, there were municipal contests, regional and cantonal elections, two legislative elections, European Parliament elections, and the prize of the presidency in the spring of 1995. Regional and cantonal elections in the spring of 1998 brought this electoral cycle to a close.

Such a rapid series of elections is exacting for parties, candidates, and voters alike. The difficulty of preparing for such an arduous election cycle is even more complex when a party has only recently begun to operate on the national political stage. The inherent complexity of such a process is further exacerbated when the rules are changed by political incumbents seeking to facilitate their own electoral advantage. This was the case in the 1986 legislative elections that were conducted under a modified proportional representation system according to the desire of President Mitterrand. The two-round single-member majority system was reestablished as soon as the center right coalition regained power; thus, the 1988 National Assembly elections reverted to the traditional electoral system of the Fifth Republic. The National Front, urged on by its president, contested each election with renewed vigor; moreover, as the party began to anchor itself in the lucrative arena of local politics, it became more competitive and better able to attract greater numbers of better qualified candidates. According to this membre fondateur, "We were always running for something because Jean-Marie Le Pen wanted the people in the Front to contest every election."

As a new party only beginning to make political progress, the National Front faced an interesting set of challenges through this rapid-fire series of elections at the end of the 1980s. Navigating through multiple elections operating under a wide variety of electoral formats in quick succession was in some respects the party's least imposing challenge. The National Front had to attract candidates to fill its electoral slates, and, most important, it had to convince supporters to vote for those candidates.

Casting a ballot for the French National Front means different things to different people. For some, it is tantamount to admitting that at one's core lies a strong streak of racism and bigotry; for others, it implies an affinity for a resurgence of Poujadism and the extremism inherent in the OAS crisis; still others characterize it as a simple manifestation of what has been explained and thus easily dismissed as the omnipresent French protest vote. French academics have been especially quick to characterize the Front's support as merely a reflection of the historically significant protest vote (Mayer and Perrineau 1992); additional analyses characterize the Front's recent development as a new form of French populism (Taggart 1995). As is so often the case, the reality is more complex than any of these explanations. But whatever the explanation, the visceral reaction generated by the National Front underscores deep-seated fissures in French public opinion. In April 1995, fully 77 percent of the French public held a poor opinion of the National Front, and 80 percent declared that Jean-Marie Le Pen should not be allowed to play any role in the country's political future (Dupoirier 1996). No other political party and no other political figure engenders the same level of political animus as the French National Front and its president.

Although the National Front is clearly a polarizing phenomenon in the contemporary arena of French politics, its negative ratings should not be viewed in isolation. In the summer of 1997, as France prepared for its fifth shift in the governing majority in slightly more than ten years, the country's morale was clearly on a downward spiral. This pessimistic mood is demonstrated by the fact that the legislative majority has changed hands in all five elections since 1981. Politicians of the left and the right are viewed with disfavor and distrust; moreover, they are found severely wanting because of their continued inability to address the country's economic crises. In addition, the country continues to reject the politics practiced by the system's mainstream parties, as evidenced by their declining share of the vote. In 1981, the parties of government—the Socialists (and their allies), the RPR, and the UDF—accounted for 77.6 percent of the vote; by 1997, their share had decreased to 57 percent. Politics in France has become a desultory affair. Protest voting has now manifested itself throughout the system. In sanctioning the governing majority in the previous five legislative elections, the French continue to vote *against* the incumbents, while failing to vote *for* anything. The dramatic shifts in the National Assembly elections underscore this point. On the other hand, the evidence increasingly demonstrates that the Front's voters are actually choosing to vote *for* something—a new alternative—rather than only voting *sortir les sortants* (to throw the bums out).

The negative reaction produced by the Front's political progress over the past decade has tended to eclipse the fact that the party has made significant electoral gains. Moreover, it is the only thriving political movement in an increasingly stagnant political party system. Public opinion polls conducted at regular intervals throughout the first half of this decade highlight time and time again that fully 30 percent of French citizens agree with the Front's stand on the major issues of its political platform. Of that 30 percent, nearly half voted for Le Pen in the first round of the 1995 presidential election. This represented an improvement of almost 200,000 votes over his record-setting 1988 presidential performance, when he amassed 4,375,894 votes in the first round of that electoral contest. Le Pen's personal charisma has started to rub off on the Front's political candidates in the legislative, regional, and municipal arenas. The Front posted its highest score ever in the regional elections of 1992, and its performance in the 1997 National Assembly elections set the record for legislative contests. Although the Front seated only one deputy in the National Assembly in the 1997 elections, it has made significant inroads at the municipal and regional levels. In the 1992 regional elections, the Front succeeded in placing 239 of its candidates on regional councils throughout France; in the 1995 municipal contest, the Front made significant gains by electing 1,075 of its candidates. The Front also succeeded in capturing three mayoral posts in these elections: Jean-Marie Le Chevallier in Toulon, Daniel Simonpieri in Marignane, and Jacques Bompard in Orange. Another city was added to this list in 1997 when Catherine Mégret, the wife of Delegate-General Bruno Mégret, was elected mayor of Vitrolles.[2] With four mayoralties, over a thousand municipal councillors, and representation on nearly all the regional councils, the party's investments in local-level politics had clearly begun to pay off. Uncovering the origins of this support is an important step in understanding the role the National Front plays in contemporary French partisan politics.

The First National Success

In the 1981 legislative elections, the French far right managed to attract only .4 percent of the electorate. Its poor electoral showing in those elections as well as its lackluster performance throughout its early history provided little warning for its unprecedented electoral showing in the 1984 European elections. Simply put, the Front experienced a dramatic surge in mass-level support between the 1981 National Assembly elections and the 1984 European contest. Over 11 percent of the electorate cast their ballots for the Front's slate of candidates in the 1984 elections. When a party emerges so suddenly and with such remarkable political force, one is required to ask Where did these people come from? Analyses of the National Front's breakthrough vote highlight the diverse origins of the party's 1984 electorate.

Exit polls taken after the 1984 European contest indicate that the Front's voters came from all political camps. A quarter of the Front's 1984 electorate had not been old enough to vote or had abstained in the first round of the 1981 presidential election, providing early confirmation of the Front's youth appeal. Another quarter came from the left, with a vast majority of these voters having supported Mitterrand in the 1981 presidential election. Although Socialist voters were willing to support the Front, the Communist left had not yet been seduced by the party's populist rhetoric. In 1984, only 3 percent of the Front's supporters had voted for Communist candidate Georges Marchais or for the other candidates representing the extreme left parties. The mainstream right parties provided the bulk of the Front's supporters in the 1984 contest; over 50 percent of the new party's electorate had voted for mainstream right presidential candidates in the 1981 election (Ysmal 1989a). Overall, the Front's mass-level support in the 1984 election was decidedly middle class, almost bourgeois in its origins. Many observers argued that the support was a reaction to the left's arrival to power in 1981. Over the next decade, the composition of the Front's electorate would change significantly, but before these changes are described in detail, it is appropriate to uncover the Front's political strongholds— namely, where in France the Front's message has proven most attractive.

Geographic Concentration of the National Front's Mass-Level Support

Not only is it important to know who the Le Pen voters are, it is also important to know where they are. The geographic distribution of the National Front's vote is distinct from that of previous far right movements; it does not correspond to either the 1956 Poujadist vote or the 1962 vote on the Evian Accords (Bréchon 1995). There are some similarities between the Front's political strongholds and the 1965 presidential vote for Jean-Louis Tixier-Vignancour, but the Front's influence has extended well beyond the narrow range of the 1965 vote to include areas that were immune to Tixier-Vignancour's message.

Early discussions of the Front's vote attempted to link it to the Poujadist movement. Although the Front has been successful in remobilizing many people who had been active in Poujade's antitax revolt, its appeal has grown well beyond Poujade's strongholds. The geographic differences between Poujade's vote and the Front's are striking: Poujade's areas of strength were especially located in rural France, with large concentrations in the Massif Central; the Front, on the other hand, has not had great success attracting the rural vote. Linking the Front's early vote to Poujade was probably wishful thinking, in that many hoped the Front would disappear from the political scene as quickly as the Poujadists did in the late 1950s. At first, the Front was described as a flash party in the mode of the Poujadists, and many political pundits believed the Front's success in the 1984 European Parliament elections would not translate to other less favorable electoral frameworks.

Tixier-Vignancour's vote, on the other hand, was strongest in the

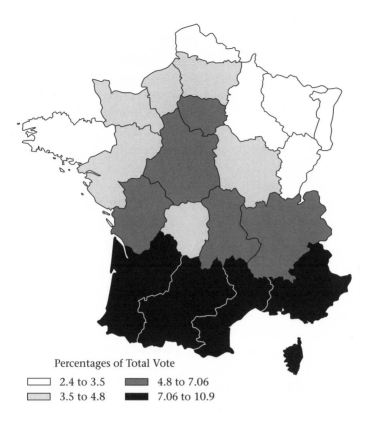

Percentages of Total Vote

☐ 2.4 to 3.5		■ 4.8 to 7.06	
☐ 3.5 to 4.8		■ 7.06 to 10.9	

Figure 7.1 1965 Tixier-Vignancour Presidential Vote, by Region

southernmost tier of France (see Figure 7.1). From east to west across
the southern sector of France, Tixier-Vignancour performed quite well,
with an average vote well above his national score of 5.3 percent. The
large pieds noirs population in southern France was drawn to the Tixier-
Vignancour campaign; his success there demonstrated the continued
resonance of Tixier-Vignancour's anti-Gaullist rhetoric and the nostalgic appeal of the Algérie française lament. In contrast, the industrial
north was particularly immune to Tixier-Vignancour's appeal. In the
contemporary arena, the National Front has now succeeded in recaptur-
ing much of this vote. This provides a partial explanation for the party's
continued strength in the Var, Alpes-Maritimes, and Bouches-du-Rhône
regions, but it also has been able to extend well beyond the confines of
the 1965 Tixier-Vignancour vote. Simply put, the Front's strength does

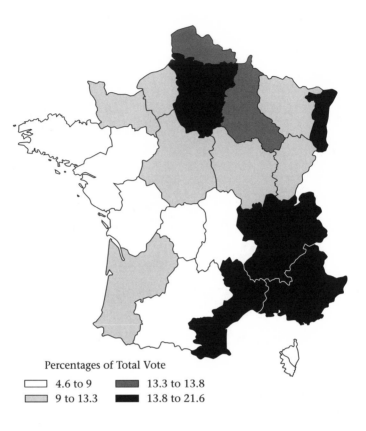

Figure 7.2   National Front First-Round Score in the 1993 Legislative Elections, by Region

not correspond to the Poujadist vote, and it has significantly broadened its support beyond what Tixier-Vignancour received in the 1965 presidential elections.

The National Front's geographic concentration is a unique addition to French political cartography. The distinctive nature of the Front's geographic strongholds is also illustrated by the fact that the Front has increased its electoral presence in areas where both the left and the right once held political sway. The political progress of the National Front and its ability to anchor itself in the French political landscape has led some observers to argue that its increasing electoral strength "seems more social than political" (Perrineau 1989). Figure 7.2 shows the geographic distribution of the Front's vote in the 1997 legislative election.

Although in recent years the Front has become a party of truly national dimensions, there are certain areas of the country that are more susceptible to the Front's message than others. The Front's electoral strength is concentrated around the Île-de-France—the Paris basin—as well as along an arc that runs first from west to east and then from north to south and finally east to west along the northern, eastern, and southern borders of metropolitan France. The Mediterranean coast and the Nord, Alsace, Moselle, the Rhône-Alpes, and the Alpes-Maritimes are Front strongholds. If one closely examines these geographic strongholds, it becomes readily apparent that the party has made significant gains in the country's northeastern, eastern, and southern borders. The Front's supporters increasingly seem to be hovering on the frontiers, as if protecting their compatriots from an onslaught of foreign invaders. It is also interesting to note that these borderlands are experiencing the greatest upheavals because of the continuing process of integration, and, in another odd twist of history, many of these frontiers are relatively new to the geographic and political fold that is modern France (Mayer 1997).

Urban France is more likely to find appeal in the National Front's message; rural France and the long western coastline have not yet become enamored of the party's political rhetoric. Areas of high population density, suffering from the social ills of economic dislocation, declining industrial capacity, unemployment, and the insecurity that comes with the anomie of everyday urban life find solace in the Front's parallel messages of anger and hope. Anger abruptly anchors the Front's message by emphasizing what has already been lost and by pointing out what is currently being taken away, and hope in a grander France and a better future softens the message and provides its music. The inherent twist in the Front's message is that the future is framed by retrieving the once glorious past. But the burdens of urban life are not the only indicators of National Front strength; at the level of the individual departments, the Front's electoral strength also corresponds to areas with high concentrations of North African immigrants, although this correlation tends to diminish when the level of analysis is smaller than the department. Mayer (1987) argues that people who live near immigrants, who come in contact with them on a daily basis, are less likely to support the Front. In addition, analyses of Le Pen's performance in the 1995 presidential election uncovered a new piece of the puzzle of the Front's geographic strongholds. Le Pen's political strength was clearly corre-

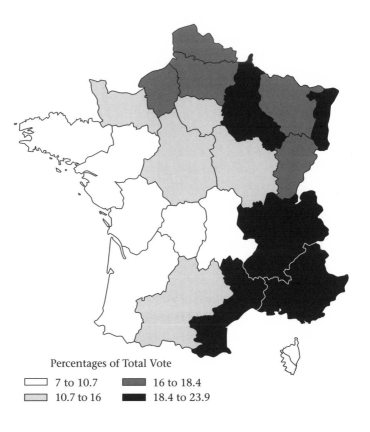

Percentages of Total Vote

☐ 7 to 10.7   ▨ 16 to 18.4
▨ 10.7 to 16   ■ 18.4 to 23.9

Figure 7.3   National Front First-Round Score in the 1997 Legislative Elections, by Region

lated with high concentrations of working-class men and women (Jaffré 1996). Perrineau (1995) labeled this phenomenon *gaucho-lepénisme* (left-leaning lepénisme).

In the 1997 legislative elections, the Front solidified the gains it had made in the 1995 presidential contest and improved on its 1993 legislative score by more than two percentage points. The Front's 1997 performance confirmed the party's continued implantation and the nationalization of its electoral base. In all but four of France's ninety-five departments, the National Front improved on its 1993 legislative score. Having reached a plateau of between 20 and 30 percent in most of southern France, the Front's most significant advances in 1997 were in the northeast. In Alsace, where the party's convention delegates received a hostile welcome in March 1997, the party added 6.3 percentage points to its 1993 score; in the Champagne-Ardenne and Lorraine regions, the Front improved on its 1993 score by 5.6 percent and 5.1 percent, respectively. Figure 7.3 provides the complete details of the Front's electoral growth from 1993 to 1997.

The Loyal Voters

The National Front's voters are a loyal lot. From one election to the next, from the first round of an election to the second, and even when in competition with other far right candidates, the Front's mass-level supporters remain extraordinarily loyal to their party. During the first few years of the Front's political evolution, a proportion of the voters would desert the party before the next election and return to their previous political affiliations, but they would in turn inevitably be replaced by an even larger group of new arrivals. Although the Front's vote was initially somewhat unstable, its political progression was explained by a slight but constant increase in its core support. This early instability in the Front's vote has now been replaced by a fierce loyalty that no other contemporary political party can match.

In contrast to the supporters of the other political parties, the Front's loyalists appear to be the most politically mobilized; for example, 71 percent of the Front's voters had made up their minds for months prior to the 1993 elections, compared to 60 percent of the total voting public. This same pattern of early mobilization was again apparent in the 1995 presidential elections, when exit polls indicated that Le Pen's supporters had made up their minds earlier than those who eventually voted for other parties. And the pattern was again confirmed in the 1997 legislative elections: the Front's voters made up their minds sooner than their counterparts in the other parties, and once their minds were made up, they were less likely to change them. Here is evidence that Front voters are not simply casting a protest ballot; they are choosing to vote *for* something.

This high level of early political mobilization is matched by a high degree of voter loyalty between elections. Fully 91 percent of those who voted for the Front in the 1992 regional elections cast their ballots for the Front once again in the 1993 legislative contest (Mayer and Rey 1993). This represents the highest level of party loyalty of all the French political parties. Voter loyalty was equally impressive from the 1988 presidential elections to those held in 1995, as 80 percent of those who voted for Le Pen in the first round of the 1995 race had voted for him in 1988.

Another way to examine voter loyalty is to consider the transfer of votes from one round of an election to the next. The elections held in the spring of 1992 provide an interesting case study of this phenomenon. The spring of 1992 brought the French back to the ballot booths for two elections; the regional elections and the first round of the cantonal elections took place on March 22, 1992, and the second round of the cantonal elections followed a week later. Exit polls indicate that 62 percent of the voting public expressed their intentions through a straight party ticket, and the voters most likely to cast their ballots in this manner were the supporters of the National Front, 82 percent of whom cast a straight party ticket from the regional vote to the cantonal vote (Laurent and Wallon-Leducq 1992). When the vote from the runoff elections of the following weekend is factored in, the Front's voters emerge as the most loyal and the most stable compared to the other political parties.

Finally, the Front's voter loyalty is also demonstrated by the hegemony the party has established over the other movements of the French far right. Historically, the political viability of the French far right has suffered from the constant infighting among the many movements on the far right fringe of French politics (the frères ennemis phenomenon identified earlier). In the 1993 legislative elections, the PFN and the Alliance Populaire ran competing slates of candidates. These far right foes of the Front often targeted electoral districts where the Front had an excellent chance of standing in the second round and even of winning the election. Their challenge to the Front's hegemony over the far right vote was without political payoff because in the 1993 legislative elections the Front received 98.9 percent of the votes cast in support of far right candidates (Mayer and Rey 1993). The Front reconfirmed its hegemony over the universe of the French far right when it amassed 99 percent of the far right vote in the 1997 legislative elections. This level of loyalty to a single far right movement is unprecedented in French politics, in which the history of the far right is replete with internecine conflicts between like-minded movements. This difference between the far right's past and the Front's present is that Jean-Marie Le Pen has succeeded in unifying the disparate elements of the French far right; moreover, he has enlarged upon the base that he inherited and expanded the movement beyond what was once its natural constituency. Today the French far right's influence extends well beyond the disaffected of the Poujadist movement and the disheartened veterans of the OAS crisis. Many people currently active in the National Front have no memory of or little practical experience in these historical far right movements; fully one-third of those who voted for National Front candidates in the 1997 legislative elections were under thirty-four years of age. Only the French Greens can claim a younger electorate, but that electorate represents only 42 percent of the Front's almost 4 million voters.

The National Front Continues to Grow

The National Front is the only contemporary French political force to have increased its mass-based membership over the span of the past decade. Because of this gradual but constant growth in party membership and vote share, the National Front is now without question the third most powerful political force in the Fifth Republic. In the 1997 legislative elections, the Front surpassed the UDF as the second largest force on the right; in metropolitan France, the Front collected 3,773,901 votes compared to 3,684,937 for the UDF, a significant development in an era characterized by a decline in all forms of conventional political participation. Over the past fifteen years, French citizens are not only voting less, they have also begun to abandon the mainstream political parties in large numbers; public opinion polls have also registered an increased disillusionment and dissatisfaction with the political parties as well as the men and women who lead them. According to a SOFRES poll conducted in 1992, 70 percent of respondents said they did not feel well represented by even one political party, and 71 percent said they did not feel well represented by even one political leader (Ysmal 1994).

Given this sorry state of French political life, it is all the more surprising that the Front has been able to continue its electoral advance. Yet this development is even more compelling when one considers the negative publicity that the Front routinely receives from the mainstream media.[3] In fact, over the past ten years, the membership rolls of the Front have swelled with new recruits—both at the mass and elite levels—while the other mass-based parties, the Communists, Socialists, and the RPR, have experienced significant and dramatic declines in membership. No longer is the Front required to place classified advertisements to attract candidates in order to complete its electoral slates; the party claims that over 80,000 members have paid the 260 francs (about $50) to join the party.[4]

Other mass-based political parties are suffering from a decline in interest as well as membership; of the major mass-based parties, the French Communist Party (PCF) has experienced the most dramatic drop in party members. Estimated at more than 500,000 in 1978, the PCF can today claim slightly more than 200,000 members—a decline of more than 50 percent. The rate of decline for the other two mass-based parties, although not as dramatic, is nevertheless significant. Surprisingly, given its crushing victory over the ruling Socialists in the 1993 legislative elections, the RPR has also undergone a 30 percent decline in members over roughly the same period. The Socialist Party has not been immune to this trend, going from 200,000 declared members in the early 1980s to approximately 150,000 in the 1990s (Ysmal 1989a; Charlot 1992). The Socialist victory in the 1997 legislative elections does not constitute a reversal of its decline, given that its score of 25.7 percent is far from the 37.6 percent it received in the afterglow election following Mitterrand's presidential victory.

In contrast, the National Front's membership, according to very conservative estimates, has increased sevenfold since 1985. Estimated at 10,000 in 1985, the Front has perhaps as many as 70,000 members today. Moreover, it attracts political activists who are resolutely devoted to the party's political mission. The Front's ability to mobilize its supporters is in stark contrast to the other parties, who are losing members and often are unable to generate any appreciable enthusiasm from them. Clearly, the party is poised to continue to have an impact on French politics as well as the policy debate.

The National Front's Electorate Identified

Writing after the 1988 legislative elections, Colette Ysmal maintained that, "If there are in France communist, socialist, centrist and conservative voters, there is not (or at least not yet) a core of extreme-right voters who can be identified over a series of elections" (1989a, 290). Although this was arguably the case in 1988, the many electoral contests that have occurred since that date have underscored two important points about the Front's electorate. The first important development since 1988 is that the Front's electoral support continued a slight but constant increase throughout the first half of the 1990s: the 1992 regional elections marked an improvement of four percentage points over the 1986 contest, and the same pattern is true for the legislative elections in 1993, when the Front improved on its 1988 score by three points and continued to increase its support in the 1997 contest. Le Pen himself added 200,000 voters between the 1988 and 1995 presidential elections. From the late 1980s throughout the 1990s, the Front's support at each electoral level has continued to increase.

In addition to this gradual increase in support, the supporters have become more clearly identifiable. This second development became especially clear when the Front's support among working-class men and women became more pronounced than its links to areas with large concentrations of immigrants (Jaffré 1996). Table 7.1 presents a complete picture of the Front's electorate.

This long-term view of the Front's electorate not only gives us several snapshots of the party's sources of strength within the body politic, it also provides us the opportunity to evaluate the changes in that strength over time. The National Front of 1984 is not the National Front of 1995 nor of 1997. The Front's support in 1984 was much more typically right than either right-wing or populist.

The presidential election of 1988 provides the first glimpse of significant change in the Front's electorate. Le Pen, with his clowning and speech-making skills, reached into the working classes and pulled 19 percent of them to the polls. Neither an Enarque (a graduate of the Ecole National d'Administration, a school that has served as the source for the vast majority of the country's leading politicians and high-ranking civil servants) nor an insider, but always able to speak perfect French, Le Pen appealed across all socioeconomic boundaries and in no category did his support fall below double digits. This obvious heterogeneity of the Front's vote would become a hallmark of the party's strength in future elections. As elections were contested and results counted, the Front's share of the professional vote began to decline, but it remained steady or improved among the workers. The increasingly populist tone of the party's electorate is the key to its ability to survive under electoral systems that are constructed to highlight its weaknesses and banish it into electoral oblivion.

The Front's long-term future is contingent, in part, on its eventual success in the legislative arena. Le Pen may have dreams of the presidency, but it is in legislative elections that the mettle of the party will be tested and pronounced sound for the next contest. An analysis of the four legislative contests since 1981 provides a complete picture of the party's changing support.

Table 7.1 Evolution of the Vote for French National Front, in Percentages

	European elections 1984	Legislative elections 1986	Presidential elections 1988	Legislative elections 1988	European elections 1989	Regional council elections 1992	Legislative elections 1993	European elections 1994	Presidential elections 1995	Legislative elections 1997
Total National Front Vote	11.0	10.0	14.5	10.0	12.0	14.0	13.0	10.5	15.5	15.0
Sex										
Male	14.0	11.0	18.0	12.0	14.0	15.0	15.0	12.0	19.0	18.0
Female	8.0	9.0	11.0	7.0	10.0	13.0	13.0	9.0	12.0	12.0
Age										
18–24	10.0	14.0	16.0	15.0	9.0	19.0	18.0	10.0	18.0	16.0
25–34	11.0	10.0	17.0	9.0	8.0	15.0	10.0	15.0	18.0	19.0
35–49	12.0	11.0	17.0	8.0	12.0	10.0	13.0	10.0	15.0	15.0
50–64	12.0	9.0	11.0	10.0	15.0	15.0	13.0	12.0	17.0	15.0
65+	10.0	6.0	12.0	10.0	12.0	15.0	13.0	7.0	9.0	12.0
Occupation										
Farmers	10.0	17.0	13.0	3.0	3.0	9.0	13.0	7.0	16.0	4.0
Shopkeepers/Craftsmen	17.0	16.0	27.0	6.0	18.0	7.0	15.0	10.0	13.0	26.0
Executives/Professionals	14.0	6.0	19.0	10.0	11.0	7.0	6.0	6.0	6.0	4.0
Middle management	15.0	9.0	12.0	6.0	7.0	11.0	8.0	5.0	14.0	11.0
White collar	—	12.0	13.0	8.0	11.0	15.0	18.0	20.0	24.0	17.0
Workers	8.0	11.0	19.0	19.0	15.0	15.0	18.0	17.0	23.0	24.0
Religion										
Practicing Catholic	14.0	7.0	7.0	5.0	15.0	16.0	12.0	8.0	10.0	7.0
Irregularly practicing Catholic	6.0	8.0	16.0	10.0	12.0	12.0	12.0	6.0	12.0	12.0
Nonpracticing Catholic	13.0	12.0	17.0	11.0	12.0	15.0	13.0	13.0	18.0	18.0
No religion	5.0	7.0	9.0	9.0	10.0	8.0	15.0	11.0	14.0	17.0

Sources: Mayer and Rey 1993; Grunberg 1995; Jaffré 1996

Three compelling points become clear when the evolution of the Front's vote from 1986 to 1997 is examined in greater detail: the National Front has become somewhat more attractive to women, its share of the youth vote has increased, and it is now attracting a significant share of the country's working classes. Early analyses of the Front's bases of support clearly revealed that the party suffered from a significant gender gap (Blondel and Lacroix 1989; Mayer and Perrineau 1989). At the outset, the Front was decidedly a male-dominated enterprise at both the mass and elite levels. In the aftermath of the 1986 legislative elections, the party's late secretary-general, Jean-Pierre Stirbois, recognized the need to extend the Front's support among women: "We must convince women and senior citizens, who are perhaps more reticent when it comes to us than men and the young people, that today's choices are fundamental societal choices for the future of their children and their grandchildren" (1988, 168). This follows in the tradition of such previous far right movements as the Croix de Guerre, the OAS, and Occident. The interwar Croix de Guerre and the OAS were heavily populated with veterans, and Occident was dominated by young male militant activists; this testosterone-heavy image of previous far right movements was resurrected with the creation of the Front in 1972. As we have noted, a number of the Front's key founding members were directly linked to the OAS crisis; these men share a military past that defined, especially during the early years, the image of the National Front. The ancien combattant image of the Front was certainly unattractive to women and made it difficult to recruit them.

In addition to the image problem, the Front's emphasis on traditional values conveys undercurrents that are decidedly retrograde in their lack of support for feminist ideals. The party's commitment to a maternal salary equivalent to the minimum wage connotes an image of barefoot and pregnant women slaving over a hot stove as they care for a passel of *French* children. This gender gap became even more entrenched in the 1988 National Assembly elections, when 14 percent of male voters but only 7 percent of female voters cast their ballots for a Front legislative candidate. From 1984 until the regional elections of 1992, the Front continued to be handicapped by this significant gap. Then, in the 1992 regional elections, a decline in the gender gap was noted and subsequently confirmed in the 1993 National Assembly elections. By 1993 the gap had all but disappeared, and men and women were now voting for the Front in near equal numbers. In these elections, the percentage of women vot-

Table 7.2   Evolution of the Vote for French National Front in Legislative Elections, in Percentages

	1986	1988	1993	1997	Change 1986–1997
Total National Front vote	10.0	10.0	13.0	15.0	+5.0
Sex					
Male	11.0	12.0	15.0	18.0	+7.0
Female	9.0	7.0	13.0	12.0	+3.0
Age					
18–24	14.0	15.0	18.0	16.0	+2.0
25–34	10.0	9.0	10.0	19.0	+9.0
35–49	11.0	8.0	13.0	15.0	+4.0
50–64	9.0	10.0	13.0	15.0	+6.0
65+	6.0	10.0	13.0	15.0	+9.0
Occupation					
Farmers	17.0	3.0	13.0	4.0	−13.0
Shopkeepers/Craftsmen/ Business Owners	16.0	6.0	15.0	26.0	+10.0
Executives/Professionals	6.0	10.0	6.0	4.0	−2.0
Middle Management	9.0	6.0	8.0	11.0	+2.0
White Collar	12.0	8.0	18.0	17.0	+5.0
Workers	11.0	19.0	18.0	24.0	+13.0
Religion					
Practicing Catholic	9.0	9.0	12.0	7.0	−2.0
Irregularly practicing Catholic	11.0	13.0	12.0	12.0	+1.0
Nonpracticing Catholic	10.0	13.0	13.0	18.0	+8.0
No religion	6.0	—	15.0	17.0	+11.0

ing for the Front rose to 13, an increase of six percentage points over the 1988 legislative contest. In 1993, women found the option of voting for the National Front far more appealing than they ever had. In a span of five years, the gender gap had decreased by four points, though it was to rise again once the results were tabulated for the 1997 legislative elections (see Table 7.2).

With 239 regional councillors, the Front has become a very real presence in local politics. This work at the local level and the party's efforts at constituency service provide partial explanations for this shift in the women's vote. For example, Front activists visit crime victims in many areas of the country. An additional explanation may be found in the Front's continual exploitation of the corruption scandals that have plagued the system's major political parties, the Socialists, the RPR, and the UDF. One of the Front's more pithy campaign slogans of the 1993 legislative elections squarely addressed this issue: "Mains propres, tête haute" (Clean hands, head held high). The Front's attempts to discredit the entrenched political class may have helped to bring some women to the Front's electoral camp.

Another important shift in the party's mass-level support involves the increasing number of young voters who are now casting their ballots for the National Front. In 1986, 14 percent of the 18 to 24-year-olds and 10 percent of the 25- to 34-year-olds voted for the Front; by 1993, this figure had risen to 18 percent of the under-24-year-old vote. In that election, the Front attracted a greater percentage of the 18- to 24-year-old vote than the center right and even the Entente Ecologiste. Of all the political forces, only the Socialist Party was as attractive to the youth vote as the National Front. Moreover, the Front's support from those aged 25 to 34 held steady at 10 percent.

Although the Front's share of the youth voted declined by two percentage points from 1993 to 1997, it is in the next age cohort where we see important gains. In 1993, the Front received only 10 percent of the votes cast by 25- to 34-year-olds, but by 1997 this had climbed to 19 percent of that age group. The youth vote is often viewed as quite volatile, but data indicate that this interpretation does not hold for the National Front. Clearly, many voters who cast their first ballot for the Front in 1986 have stayed with the party as they have matured.

The Front's ability to attract the youth vote and to gain its loyalty provide important clues to the party's ability to sustain itself even within the discriminatory electoral framework of the National Assembly elections. The Front's resolve to create a "France for the French" appeals to the economic insecurity felt by this sector of the population. That slogan revolves around two primary political issues: the Front's continuing diatribes against immigration and its anti-Maastricht rhetoric. With respect to the former, the Front has continued to blame the country's immigrant population for the society's decade-long experience with double-digit unemployment. This plays quite well among French youth, who suffer from much higher unemployment levels than the general population; in some areas of the country, youth unemployment reaches 20 percent. The Front has also argued extensively against the continued integrative efforts of the European Union. Specifically, it has been decidedly anti-Maastricht. The party's rhetoric on this issue stresses the fact that "Today, France's identity is threatened by the world vision of the political establishment."[5] The core of its anti-Brussels message emphasizes, "A French France in a European Europe."[6] The Front's legitimacy on this issue has been enhanced by the behavior of the system's mainstream political parties, where dissension in the ranks has served to legitimize the National Front's opposition to Maastricht.

Perhaps the most important development in the evolution of the Front's electorate over this series of four legislative elections is the fact that the Front has made inroads into the voter pool that had once been reserved for the parties of the left. As this former National Assembly deputy says, "Jean-Marie Le Pen is the only man on the right capable of winning over the voters on the left—most especially those in the Communist Party." Another frontiste expresses the same idea, but in a more colorful way: "Le Pen is taking the cheese right out of their mouths. He's taking their cheese and their bread right out of their mouths."

In the 1997 legislative election, the Front's share of voters who were either employees or manual laborers surpassed the share held by the Communist Party. The Front attracted 17 percent of the latter and 24 percent of the former compared to 6 and 15 percent, respectively, for the Communist Party (*Revue Française de Science Politique* 1997). Except for a 1 percent drop in the 1988 legislative elections, the Front has continually increased its share of the working-class vote. In the 1995 presidential elections, the Front actually surpassed the Socialist Party as the first choice of France's working classes—a stunning achievement in the development of French partisan politics. Le Pen's heightened popularity among the working class led Pascal Perrineau to comment, "For the first time in its history, a current of the French far right has a true popular foundation" (1995, 248). The populist character of the Front's vote is important not only because of who these people are but because of how they vote when the Front is absent from the contest. In second-round ballots where there is no Front candidate, an increasing number of the Front's first-round vote has either sat out the contest or has voted for the left rather than the right. In early elections, the center right could depend on at least 50 percent of the Front's first-round support, but this has continued to decrease as the Front's electorate has become increasingly populist. In the 1997 legislative elections, the marginally resurgent Socialist Party garnered a greater share of the working-class vote than

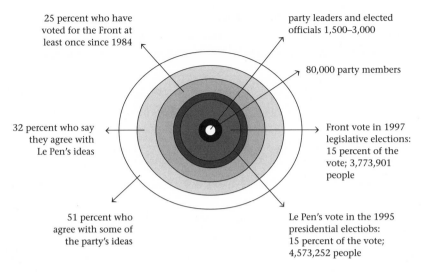

25 percent who have
voted for the Front at
least once since 1984

party leaders and elected
officials 1,500–3,000

80,000 party members

32 percent who say
they agree with
Le Pen's ideas

Front vote in 1997
legislative elections:
15 percent of the
vote; 3,773,901
people

51 percent who
agree with some of
the party's ideas

Le Pen's vote in the 1995
presidential electiobs:
15 percent of the vote;
4,573,252 people

Figure 7.4   Actual and Potential Universe of National Front Supporters
Source: Adapted from Mayer and Perrineau 1993.

did the Front, but it remained nevertheless strongly anchored among the workers and the unemployed.

As in previous elections, the Front's 1997 voters remained a heterogeneous mix of people from all sectors of French society. The social composition of the Front's mass-level support clearly cuts across the socioeconomic cleavages that for centuries had dominated the political debate in France. The Front's ability to keep the issues of immigration and insécurité at the forefront of the political agenda have perhaps led to the creation of alternative cleavage structures (Schweisguth 1994). Its ability to transcend the old, entrenched socioeconomic cleavage structure provides important information about the Front's future political viability. Unlike its far right predecessors, the Front has successfully solicited voters from almost every sector of French society; only the aging agricultural population has remained immune to the Front's political charms. As a new example of a "catch-all" party, the Front, if it is able to maintain its links to these disparate groups, may be on the verge of forcing a realignment in the French body politic. The 1997 elections marked an important step in the Front's development, for the party continued its ascent in the face of a barrage of negative publicity, and it did this without its primary attraction, Jean-Marie Le Pen.

Support for the National Front has indeed changed over time. After the first round of the 1993 legislative elections, *Le Monde* commented, "Mr. Le Pen can legitimately be indignant that with a higher vote than the Communists, he will only be able to get one or two deputies elected. He does show that henceforth he has at his disposal an electoral base that is somewhat stable and is now a durable part of French political life" (March 23, 1993). More women, young, and working-class French citizens voted for the Front in 1997 than they did in 1986. The party's overall share of the vote increased, as did its appeal to working-class men and women. Public opinion polls routinely demonstrate that the party's potential electorate extends well beyond the 15 percent who cast their ballots for the Front in the 1997 legislative elections. The Front's future support is contingent on convincing those who share similar views to take the next step and cast a vote in its favor. Figure 7.4 presents a graphic description of the Front's current and potential electorate; as we can see, the Front's influence does indeed extend well beyond its core leadership and membership.

The party's unique hold on its electorate as well as its strong support from the youth of France portend a continued presence on the French political scene. Those who originally dismissed the Front as a rerun of the Poujadist movement or as merely a reflection of the omnipresent protest vote failed to understand the deep-seated anxieties about modern life that nurtured the National Front's development. In 1984 Prime Minister Laurent Fabius said, "The Le Pen phenomenon poses real questions, but provides the wrong answers." His cautionary comments continue to ring true almost fifteen years after he first made that statement. The solidification of the Front's electoral base leads one to conclude that an increasingly significant sector of the voting public is finding the Front's answers more attractive.

THE FAR RIGHT IN

COMPARATIVE PERSPECTIVE

L'extême-droite, ce qu'on appelle l'extrême-droite, a toujours

existé. —National Front Political Bureau member[1]

The French case is not unique. The phenomenon of French "exceptionalism" is often used to describe the rather unique character of French political culture, but this explanation is neither necessary nor useful in explaining the recent resurgence of French far right extremism. Far right movements are resurfacing across Europe, and the National Front's continual growth has served as a model for these other parties. Over the past ten years, the National Front has emerged as the doyen of the far right movement in Western Europe, and by virtue of his lengthy run on the political stage, Le Pen serves as its nominal head. His fourteen-year tenure in the European Parliament has provided him with a bully pulpit from which to propagate the gospel of the far right according to Jean-Marie.

Since the Front first broke into the European Parliament in 1984, that legislative forum has functioned as the focal point for trans-European right-wing cooperation. In 1984, Le Pen, Giorgio Almirante (secretary-general of MSI), and Chrysanthos Dimitriadis (president of *Ethniki Politiki Enosis,* EPEN) created the Group of the European Right in the European Parliament, which included the Front's ten European Parliament members, five representatives of the MSI, and one lone Greek. The group was reconstituted after the 1989 European elections under a different name but without the Italians, who had balked at cooperating with the newly arrived Germans. This time Le Pen, who has a greater affinity for his German compatriots, brought the six Germans from the Republikaner Partei into his alliance and once again met the requisite criteria for the creation of a parliamentary group. Although the far right failed to coalesce into a viable parliamentary group in the aftermath of the 1994

European elections, Le Pen and the National Front continue to serve as the centerpiece of the European far right movement.

Similar to far right movements at the national level, the trans-European far right is not immune to the quarrelsome nature of its participants. As the MSI transmogrified into the newly named Alleanza Nazionale, it attempted to recast itself as a postfascist party and has consciously chosen to distance itself from the National Front; meanwhile, the recently arrived Austrians remain skeptical about aligning themselves with Le Pen's group too quickly.

In the early spring of 1997, an unfolding story in Strasbourg made the front pages of all the major national dailies. Although the city serves as one of the part-time hosts to the European Parliament, it found itself in the glare of the media spotlight for another reason: the National Front had come to town. The Front held its 1997 convention in the picturesque city, an event that prompted the leaders of Europe's far right to trek to France and join in the festivities. Many of the most prominent European far right personalities were invited to speak at the Front's Party Congress, among them Ricardo Saenz de Ynestrillas, president of the Spanish Alianza Unidad Nacional; Frank Vanhecke, president of the Flemish Vlaams Blok; and a former German Republikaner representative to the European Parliament, Hans-Gunter Schodruch. Other countries represented in Strasbourg were Finland, Greece, Hungary, Italy, Romania, Slovakia, the Czech Republic, Serbia, and Croatia. For three days at the end of March—right at the Easter holidays—Strasbourg became a veritable United Nations of proto-nationalists.

In the past fifteen years, far right movements, often harkening back to the dark days of World War II, have emerged in many European countries. From Sweden to Italy and from Belgium to Austria, it seems that no European state is immune to the provocative rhetoric of the far right. Beyond the borders of the fifteen-member European Union, resurgent nationalism in the guise of far right political parties has emerged in Russia, Poland, and Romania. It is fair to say that the inflammatory political rhetoric espoused by the far right has succeeded in capturing the imagination of people across the European continent. Moreover, if Patrick Buchanan and David Duke are thrown into the mix, the message of the far right is also playing to large audiences across the Atlantic. In fact, the resurgent far right is politically mobilized from "the Urals to the Ozarks."

Austria

Jörg Haider, leader of Austria's Freedom Party, received his early political training from his parents, who were enthusiastic Nazis during World War II. As the leader of the Freedom Party, Haider has spent his career on the fringes of what is politically acceptable. His vehement attacks on immigrants and homosexuals are in stark contrast to his laudatory comments about Hitler's Third Reich. Like Le Pen in France, Haider is a polarizing figure in contemporary Austrian politics, and also like Le Pen, Haider's rhetorical excesses have gotten him into trouble. Although elected provincial governor of Carinthia in 1989, he was forced to resign for making comments that appeared favorable to Hitler.

Haider has successfully exploited the country's trenchant xenophobia, proving to be an equal opportunity hatemonger by attacking third world immigrants with as much force as those from the conflict-ridden former Yugoslavia. In 1993, his charisma and persuasive powers helped him to collect almost 800,000 signatures on a petition to end immigration. Austria, a country that walked a political tightrope during the cold war, has been especially sensitive to the political and economic instability that is so prevalent in the former Soviet satellites, and Haider has effectively stoked his country's anxieties about the rapid pace of change in the East.

He has also borrowed more than one page from the National Front's campaign strategy. In the early 1980s, the Freedom Party was a declining political force that could barely muster 5 percent of the vote; prior to Haider's election as the party's president, it appeared to be drifting toward political oblivion. Before Haider took control of the Freedom Party, it was viewed as a minor mainstream party on the right; in fact, it had been serving as a junior partner in a governing coalition with the Socialist Party prior to Haider's assuming the party's reigns of power. Then, elected to lead the party in 1986, he immediately took steps to move it further to the right. Like Le Pen in France, Haider has successfully capitalized on the public's disgust with a political class mired in scandal and cronyism. Scandals, political and financial, have caused a dramatic drop in the public's confidence in their elected officials, and Austria, like France and Italy, has been particularly hard hit by the corruption of its political class. The Freedom Party's slogan for the 1996 European elections was "Election Day is Pay Day." This slogan, like so much of Haider's rhetoric, parallels the National Front's ever popular "Sortons les sortants" (Let's throw the bums out).

Another of Haider's favorite sayings is, "There are 140,000 unemployed Austrians and 180,000 foreigners." Except for the difference in the numbers, Le Pen has been saying the same thing in France for over a decade. Haider's anticorruption message and his continual refrain on immigration secured the election of forty party members to the national legislature in 1995; this reflected the support of 1,060,175 Austrians, which translated into 21.9 percent of the vote. Although the Freedom Party actually increased its total vote when compared to the previous election, it received a lower percentage overall and thus lost two seats in the legislature. Haider's rising tide of support is evidenced at all levels of the political contest. In 1994, the party performed well in local contests, receiving 33 percent of the vote in Carinthia and 22 percent in Vienna (Laqueur 1996).

In October 1996, the Freedom Party attracted 27.6 percent of the vote in a special election for Austria's European Parliament deputies. This remarkable showing placed Haider's party on a nearly equal footing with the system's two major parties, the Social Democrats and the People's Party, which received respectively 29.1 percent and 29.6 percent of the total vote. Its impressive performance in this election translated into six European Parliament deputies. Thus, with nearly 30 percent of the total vote, albeit in a minor election, Haider became the most popular far right politician in Europe (Lee 1997).

In Austria as in another recent EU member, Sweden, there appears to be an anti-EU backlash that Haider has been most adept at exploiting. As in France, fears related to the austerity measures demanded by monetary union have played well to a skeptical Austrian population that was late to join the EU in the first place. Haider also shares Le Pen's affinity for off-the-cuff remarks that highlight his extremist tendencies. Both of these politicians may want their tasteless comments to appear spontaneous, but in reality they are quite calculating in their dealings with the media. The handsome, youthful Haider has successfully crafted an image of a matinee idol that obscures his links to Austria's historically accommodative relationship with fascism. Walter Laqueur argues that Austria was "never properly de-Nazified" after World War II and that this has continued to create a climate favorable to parties and politicians of Haider's ilk (1996, 117).

Belgium

The president of the most influential far right organization in Belgium, the Vlaams Blok, is Frank Vanhecke, but the country's answer to Jean-Marie Le Pen is Filip Dewinter. It would be an oversight to dismiss Dewinter as just a younger version of Le Pen; he is, in fact, that and much more. The Vlaams Blok party, of which Dewinter is a prominent member, appeals to Flemish-speaking Belgium on two separate fronts: the party's fierce attacks on Belgium's immigrant population is clearly reminiscent of the French National Front and the Austrian Freedom Party, but it has also successfully exploited the ethnic divisions that mandate Belgium's unique governmental structure. Dewinter's party slyly stresses Flemish nationalism in place of the Belgian variety. Belgium's distinctive federal arrangement has never been completely successful in mitigating the intense ethnic rivalries that exist between the country's two dominant subcultures, the Walloons in the south and the Flemish in the north. Central to the party's political appeal is a dissolution of the Belgian nation as it stands today. Bruno Mégret, delegate-general of the French National Front, has said that he and his colleagues in the Front would welcome the Walloons if Belgium ever did succumb to the secessionist pressures of the increasingly strident Vlaams Blok. Liberating the Flemish people from economically stagnant Wallonia is central to Dewinter's political agenda.

Like the National Front, Vlaams Blok experienced rapid growth in the 1980s. This was especially true in local elections in Antwerp, where the Belgian far right collects nearly 30 percent of the vote. Although still a minor political party presence, the Belgian far right has succeeded in gaining representation at the federal, regional, and municipal levels as well as in the European Parliament. The party received 12 percent of the votes in the most recent elections to the Flemish Regional Council, which translated into fifteen seats in the 124-member body. On the national level, Vlaams Blok is represented in both houses of government; it received just under 8 percent in the 1995 elections and seated eleven deputies in the lower house and three in the Senate. The party's presence in the national legislature has made it increasingly difficult for this fragile party system to create working coalitions (Husbands 1992).

Dewinter and his Vlaams Blok party have copied much of their political repertoire from the National Front. In many ways, Dewinter tries to emulate Le Pen and his party. One of Vlaams Blok's primary campaign slogans, "Our Own People First," is clearly reminiscent of the Front's "Les Français d'abord" (French first). Political agendas have also been borrowed from the Front; for example, Bruno Mégret's fifty-item list about French citizenship has become a seventy-point plan under Dewinter.[2] In Belgium, as in France, immigrants from North and Central Africa are viewed suspiciously, and Dewinter and the Vlaams Blok have effectively exploited the religious, racial, and ethnic divisions that separate Belgium's immigrants from its native population. According to Dewinter, "We must stop the Islamic invasion. It's very difficult to accept somebody over here who believes in Islam. I think it's, in fact, impossible to assimilate in our country if you are of Islamic belief" (Crouch 1996, 41).

Germany

No matter how earnestly Germany tries to address its far right problem, there remains a small minority fascinated by the vestiges of the country's Nazi past. The fall of the Berlin Wall in 1989 and the resultant reunification of East and West has not proved to be as easily accomplished as the optimistic Helmut Kohl had originally envisaged. Rising taxes to pay for the process and a deep-seated mistrust between the residents of the East and West have spawned an increase in political discontent. The most extremist elements of the German far right exploited this uncertainty and engineered a reign of terror in Germany that lasted from 1991 to 1993. As violence continued to erupt, the more mainstream forces of the far right saw their influence decrease as the most radical groups, composed of neo-Nazi youths and skinheads, attacked foreign workers, asylum seekers, and gypsies. The most active cells of neo-Nazis emerged in old East Germany, where economic dislocation and unemployment were increasing as fast as the pace of social and political change. Roger Eatwell reports, "[D]uring 1992 alone there were over 2,500 attacks on foreigners across Germany, 697 cases of arson, and 17 people were left dead" (1995, 293). Eventually, the violence began to subside; the government invoked Article 21 of the Basic Law and by 1995 had unilaterally banned ten different extremist organizations. These extraordinary events were unique to Germany and completely overshadowed the presence of such far right political parties as the Republikaner.

The Republikaner Partei actually traces its roots to the Christian Social Union (CSU); its founders are refugees from that more mainstream political party. Franz Handlos, Ekkehard Voigt, and Franz Schonhüber created the party in 1983 to provide an alternative to the more overtly fascist Deutsche Volksunion (DVU). From the start, they wanted this new electoral initiative to develop an image of a legitimate partisan option that would replicate the burgeoning successes of the Italian MSI and the French National Front. Handlos and Voigt were both former members of the Bundestag under the CSU banner, but Schonhüber was a card-carrying Nazi as well as a former member of the Waffen SS.

Of the many far right political parties in Germany, the Republikaner has received the most media attention. After a fallow period following its creation, the Republikaner made an impressive showing in a series of elections in 1989, amassing 7.5 percent of the vote in elections to the Berlin parliament and 7.1 percent of the vote in the European Parliament elections of the same year. Germany's far right entered the European Parliament with a contingent of six deputies who promptly aligned themselves with the French National Front.

The party rapidly saw its brief electoral influence diminish. Given the increase in instability due to reunification and the resurgent extremist violence, it is interesting that the party was unable to profit electorally. Although marginally successful in a few local elections, the party has been unable to break the 5 percent threshold for election to the Bundestag, and in 1994 lost its representation in the European Parliament. Compared to France, the German far right movement has remained weak and organizationally underdeveloped. Personal rivalries among its leaders and the inability to find a German equivalent of Le Pen have kept the German movement disunited and increasingly electorally impotent. In some respects, its pronounced weakness in the more legitimate political arena has probably influenced some of its most radical supporters to express their political discontent in more violent ways (Koopmans 1996).

Italy

The Italian contribution to the European far right movement, although chronologically older than its counterparts in other countries, is currently undergoing an important transformation that may render it an even more significant player in the chaotic world of Italian national politics. Although Ignazi and Ysmal (1992) argue that the MSI is more influenced by the "fascist tradition" than its French counterpart, its most recent history accents its attempts to break with that tradition and refashion for itself a new image as a mainstream party capable of governing.

Created in 1946, the MSI was without a doubt tightly linked to the Italian fascist tradition. Its primary leaders, Giorgio Pini and Giorgio Almirante, had held positions of minor influence in the Social Republic (Eatwell 1995). For the next thirty years, the MSI achieved marginal electoral success and was represented at the local and national levels of Italian politics. This Italian version of the far right has always participated in the electoral arena, but breakaway fringe elements engaged in violent acts of terrorism throughout the 1970s. As noted in chapter 2, it was the relative electoral success of the MSI that inspired the French Ordre Nouveau to embark on the electoral path by creating the National Front.

Today, Gianfranco Fini is Italy's preeminent right-wing politician, a member of the MSI since he was only seventeen years old. At forty-five years of age, he has revitalized and refashioned the stagnant MSI during his twenty-eight-year tenure as an activist. Under Fini's leadership, the party has attempted and nearly completed a total transformation. He has successfully exploited the Italians' exasperation with their more mainstream politicians as well as their disappointment with the poorly functioning Italian democracy. In a 1992 poll, 88 percent of Italians expressed dissatisfaction with the way democracy works in their country (Wilson 1994). Mainstream parties of the left and right found themselves facing an increasingly hostile electorate, eager to sample other partisan options. Such low levels of legitimacy for the system and its mainstream parties have allowed Fini to advocate his cause more successfully; he is, in fact, the most popular politician in the country. Political instability in the system's dominant parties during the early 1990s created new opportunities for the MSI. Bull and Newell claim that the rapid pace of change in Italian politics constituted "a meltdown of the post-war party system" (1995, 77).

Fini watched and appreciated the opportunity this chaos afforded him, and in January 1994 rechristened the MSI the National Alliance. Prior to the official name change, Fini had worked tirelessly to consolidate his power in the party and began the process of transforming the organization into a more respectable right-wing alternative. In the 1993 municipal elections, the party came very close to taking control in two of Italy's largest cities; Fini himself was nearly elected mayor of Rome.[3] This unexpected success hastened the party's "transformation." Media magnet Silvio Berlusconi's invitation to participate in an electoral alli-

ance in the south placed a patina of respectability on the newly energized National Alliance (Ignazi 1996). In the 1994 elections, the "new"
MSI received more than 13 percent of the vote, which represented its best
performance in the party's forty-eight-year history. As a member of Berlusconi's victorious Freedom Alliance, Fini's group seated 107 deputies
in the legislature and placed five of its compatriots in Berlusconi's cabinet. Although that government lasted only a short time, the National
Alliance's participation in the cabinet served as a sort of political audi-
tion, preparing it for future political opportunities. More recently, Berlusconi's legal problems have created a serious void on the right of the
Italian political spectrum, and Gianfranco Fini is poised to replace him
as the new leader of the loosely structured Freedom Alliance.

National elections were held again in 1996 and the National Alliance
further solidified its growing strength by capturing 15 percent of the
vote and becoming without a doubt the third largest party in the system. Prior to the election there was much speculation about whether
or not the National Alliance would return to the government, but the
issue proved moot when the left received enough votes overall to cobble
together a governing majority. Although the National Alliance was prevented from rejoining the government, it remains incredibly popular and has accomplished something that Jean-Marie Le Pen and the
National Front have been unable to do: it became, if only for a short
time, a party of government.

This short review of four of Western Europe's more significant far right
movements is far from exhaustive. In each of these countries there are in
fact other movements or parties that also claim to represent the far right.
For example, in Belgium there is also a Front National that represents
the Walloon version of the far right. In Austria, the Patriotic Extraparlia-
mentary Opposition competes with Haider's Freedom Party for space on
the far right. And in Germany, we find the Deutsche Volksunion as well
as the Nationaldemokratische Partei Deutschland. Far right movements
and political parties have appeared with increasing speed in the past decade; there are active movements in Denmark, Finland, and the Netherlands as well as Norway and Greece.[4] Eastern Europe and the breakaway
republics of the former Soviet Union have also experienced a resurgence
of far right proto-nationalist politics. The risk of radicalization is especially acute in these countries because of the rapid pace of political,
social, and economic change.

Fascist? Neofascist? Extremist? Radical? Populist? Right-Wing?

The seemingly simple act of classifying these many movements and parties has instead proven extremely difficult. The large body of literature that has developed in response to the increased importance of these various political groupings has been unable to provide clear definitions and terms to organize our understanding of these movements and their place in the politics of late-twentieth-century advanced industrial societies. Often, the author's political biases become too readily apparent on the page as he or she attempts to "classify" the movements of the far right. Milza (1987) declines to label Le Pen and the National Front fascist, but Mayer and Perrineau's seminal volume on the party's early development advocates "attacking the evil at the roots" (1989, 353). Husbands (1992) seems to agree with Mayer and Perrineau and explicitly labels the Front neofascist. Harris, on the other hand, argues, "[I]t seems quite likely that it does more harm than good to compare the FN with fascist and Nazi parties" (1994, 69). A recent English-language study of the Front claims that it "poses a serious threat to democracy" (Simmons 1996, 258), but Safran (1993) puts a different spin on the issue when discussing the Reaganite agenda of the Front and seems to imply that it is but another variation of Poujadism. Kitschelt (1997), in his important cross-national study of the reemergence of far right politics, dismisses the popular bases for the Front's support and labels the Front a radical right movement partly because of its strong pro-market policies.[5] Taggart (1995), emphasizing a different aspect of the party's character, argues that the National Front represents a new populist party, which he claims is distinct from a neofascist party.

With the multiplicity of voices writing about the Front and the variety of labels they use to describe it, definitional clarity has been, not surprisingly, somewhat elusive. Scholars and pundits have had difficulty affixing an appropriate ideological label to the party because they tend to treat it as a static entity. The Front's singular ability to adapt to the ever changing political landscape has been an important element of its political and electoral development. The party's early years as an ad hoc mixture of nationalists, student militants, and Catholic fundamentalists gave way to an infusion of free market advocates in the 1980s, who in turn saw their influence decline as the party's core leadership realized the political potential of protectionism within the country's working-class constituencies.

In this study of the National Front, I have consciously eschewed the phrase extreme right when describing the party, instead cautiously employing the less inflammatory label far right to characterize the people and agenda of the National Front. This distinction is subtle but most important. One member of the Front's leadership cadre whose own political experience dates back to Action Française provides an interesting and rather self-critical perspective on this definitional dilemma:

> They say that Jean-Marie Le Pen and the National Front are the extreme right. It's not true. Those who are saying that are liars, the great majority of them are liars. The extreme right—I know it because that's from whence I come. The extreme right is essentially characterized by two things. First, by its rejection of universal suffrage. The National Front has always accepted the verdict of the ballot box. Second, by its reliance on violence, notably to seize power—it's necessary to seize power by any means. Action Française did it by any and all means, even by the gutters and most especially by violence. Jean-Marie Le Pen has personally been the victim of such violence. We are going to gain power by democratic means, by elections.

This respondent's experience encompasses the entire spectrum of far right political behavior in France, and because of that experience he offers a rather unique perspective on the Front and its place in the pantheon of French far right movements.

In the past, the French and, for that matter, the European extreme right joyously embraced violence to further their miscreant agendas. These movements, especially in France, refused to endorse the democratic path, more often than not actively opposing it; they did not participate in the electoral process and rarely accepted the legitimacy of the duly elected authorities. In addition, previous extreme right movements refused to accept the legitimacy of the status quo's political institutions. In fact, throughout much of the twentieth century, the French extreme right acted as if postrevolutionary France was but a long nightmare that would be easily ended once they seized power.

Unlike its ideological ancestors—the OAS, Occident, and Ordre Nouveau—the Front has consistently refrained from violence. Granted, violent episodes have occurred near or at Front rallies and demonstrations, but there is no credible evidence that these horrific acts were either endorsed or committed by the Front's leaders.[6] Unlike the extreme right movements of the past, there is no evidence that the Front's leaders are advocating the violent overthrow of the Fifth Republic, nor are they advocating that their supporters do harm to minority populations or political opponents. Does their rhetoric at times perhaps incite their less enlightened supporters to violence? We can only answer in the affirmative, but we must also point out that the Front's most injudicious behavior has had its consequences at the ballot box as well as in the courts. And in a democracy, this is how it should be. When the Front has gone too far, when its rhetoric has been too destructive, it has been sanctioned by the voters. By operating within the parameters of democracy, Le Pen and his party have subjected themselves to the harsh judgments of that democracy. Clearly, the party has been punished at the ballot box and will continue to be unless it convincingly moderates its most hateful rhetoric.

Whatever label one chooses to describe this panoply of political parties and movements, it is perhaps most important to understand the multiplicity of causes that led to the resurgence of such movements in France and in Europe as a whole. Certain scholars have attempted to explain the reemergence of these so-called populist/neofascist movements by linking them to a resurgence of "ethnic nationalism" (Smith 1995). In many respects this is true, but it is a qualitatively different nationalism than what Europe and the world experienced in past centuries. Rather than being an offensive nationalism that is engaged in extending geographic boundaries, amassing colonies, and exporting one's cultural heritage to those newly acquired territories, this new form of nationalism is fundamentally defensive in nature. The current scenario does not involve conquest or war; rather, it focuses on the fact that many citizens believe, whether justifiably or not, that their national heritage, culture, and language—in essence, the core of their national identity—is threatened from within the borders of their own country.

This defensive nationalism manifests itself in a variety of ways, but the pathology of this trans-European sociocultural phenomenon is increasingly evident at all levels of the political debate. In Germany, skinheads attack and kill asylum seekers, while Chancellor Kohl lends credence to their racist rhetoric by launching a national debate about the country's historically liberal asylum policies. In France, young extremists participating at the tail end of a National Front demonstration attack and cause the drowning death of a young Frenchman of North African descent, while the mainstream conservatives rework the country's immigration laws three times within ten years. Such political actions and reactions are direct consequences of this defensive nationalist posture, which is related to the changing notion of national political identity. What was once viewed as an immutable social construct—one's claim to being either French, German, or Austrian—is now called into question by the demographic transformations of a declining birthrate in juxtaposition to decades of liberal immigration policies.

In France, the national identity question has an ever increasing power to provoke debate, dissension, and even violence. The infamous *foulard* episode of 1989 illustrates to what extent the French political elite, of both the left and the right, are unable or unwilling to accommodate the growing Islamic presence within its borders. Two young Islamic girls unintentionally provoked a national crisis when they attended school in traditional Muslim dress; their desire to cover their heads, as is appropriate to their faith, prompted their school principal to expel them. The ensuing debate shook the foundations of France's secular society. René Rémond, the eminent scholar of the French right, commented on the foulard affair in his book, *Politics Is No Longer What It Used to Be.* He argued that "The secular left [the authorities in power] hesitates to apply restrictions on foreign religions that it imposes without any misgivings on those devout French men and women who practice the faith that is an essential part of France's cultural heritage" (1993, 184). An almost manic dedication to the separation of church and state has served as an elemental aspect of postrevolutionary France. The emergence of Islam as the second largest religion in the country will eventually force France to redefine itself and its commitment to secularism.

Unlike the mainstream parties, the National Front has taken a stance on this issue and refuses to equivocate. Simply put, the Front has drawn a line in the sand. National Front Vice President Martine Lehideux, in a brochure dessiminated by her Cercle National des Femmes d'Europe, typifies the far right's views on this issue: "We all reject, with an equal determination, that France and Europe are going to become multiracial and plural-cultural societies as desired by the leftist parties and those of the false right."

Other countries are also experiencing similar versions of this national identity crisis. In Belgium, the dual nature of this issue continues to frustrate the system's leading politicians. Vlaams Blok rejects not only the immigrant population but also the French-speaking Walloons. Germany appears to be experiencing a problem parallel to that in Belgium, as reunification has profoundly altered the concept of what it means to be German. The processes related to reunification, and they are many, have forced Germans to question their national identity in ways never imagined. These multiple processes of reunification involve changes at all levels of the society. Compounding the issue is the presence of millions of Turkish guest-workers who feel more German than Turkish but are summarily rejected by German law. Even the heretofore homogeneous societies of Scandinavia are grappling with the serious question of what it means to be Finnish or Swedish or Norwegian.

Although simplified and overexploited by the parties of the far right, immigration phobia is only one part of the national identity question; there are in actuality two other issues at play. The second is in essence the result of legal immigration. Millions of Asians, North Africans, Pakistanis, Turks, and Indians now legally call Europe home. Europe's borders could slam shut tomorrow and all clandestine immigration be immediately halted, but Europe will still need to address its national identity crisis through the prism of an emerging multicultural society. This is an exceedingly difficult challenge that the governments of these countries have refused to confront, and in turning a blind eye to this issue, they have compounded the problem because those citizens who are not "typically" European have been excluded from and neglected by the dominant political culture.

The third issue in the national identity crisis is related to the rapid pace of European integration. At the outset, the processes of integration were wholeheartedly endorsed by a European citizenry grown weary after decades of bloodshed and conflict. Public opinion polls routinely demonstrated unqualified support for the European enterprise, but as the peoples of Europe stand on the threshold of actually becoming European they have begun to question the necessity of cognitively integrating their own national identities with an apparently unformed European one. A shared consciousness of what it means to be European has not yet been identified; until it is, the inherent conflict between being French and being European cannot be resolved.

These issues of national identity are central to the rhetoric of the far right and provide the frame for a clearer picture of far right political activism. But it is what we find within that frame—the colors and images of the picture, so to speak—that explain the renewed vigor and durability of these far right movements. Simply put, Europe is anxious about its future, and this anxiousness is reflected in many areas. The continued unemployment crisis that has baffled European policymakers for more than a decade is an essential element of this unease as well as an important component in the electoral appeal of far right movements (Jackman and Volpert 1996). Lashing out at immigrant populations is clearly misguided but easily understood given the double-digit unemployment that a country such as France has faced for more than ten years. The irony of the anti-immigrant rhetoric is that, according to demographers, most of Western Europe will soon need large numbers of workers to help support the aging baby boomers, and given the low levels of fertility in all European countries except Ireland, these workers will once again need to be imported. The economic dislocation and feelings of worthlessness that result from long-term unemployment are prime targets for far right politicians, so it comes as no surprise that the National Front currently attracts a greater share of the unemployed vote than any other party. Successive administrations, of the left and the right, have proven incapable of addressing the problem. Lionel Jospin's political honeymoon was abruptly halted in the winter of 1998 when his own left-wing supporters took to the streets and expressed their dissatisfaction with the government's slow response to the unemployment situation.

The apparent inability of the mature social welfare state to provide for future generations is another factor that engenders anxiety. Europeans are being asked to accept cutbacks and in some cases to forfeit social welfare benefits that they have taken for granted for decades. Declining unemployment compensation, increased medical costs, fewer vacations, and less job security are factors that also promote unease and trepidation about the future. Cradle-to-grave care—taken for granted by Europe's rich populations—must now be modified to meet the demands of impending monetary union and prepare these countries for the massive numbers of retirees that will soon flood the social welfare rolls. These necessary modifications in the social safety net necessitate sacrifices that Europe's citizens seem unwilling to make.

Separate from the national identity crisis is that Europeans are also worried about the future of the European Union. Between 1990 and 1995, support for the EU declined in eleven of the twelve member states. The greatest decline in support was reported in Belgium, where it dropped from 69 percent in 1990 to 50 percent in 1994, but double-digit declines were also reported in Greece, Italy, Germany, and France

(Grunberg 1995). In addition, support for the EU in Austria and Sweden, two of the three newest members, is notoriously low, evidenced by the rash of anti-EU parties and politicians that these new member states elected to represent them in Strasbourg. The support in the centers of policymaking for increased integration is not matched in the homes of the average European citizen.

The academic debate about increased horizontal or vertical integration of the EU is not just an issue for Eurocrats; whether the EU should widen its membership or deepen its substantive hold on policymaking is also of paramount importance for Europe's citizens. And these citizens are beginning to question the very foundations of increased integration. Denmark's very public unease over the Maastricht treaty, Austria's election of anti-European parliamentarians to Strasbourg, the unprecedented popularity of anti-Maastricht politicians in France, and the United Kingdom's continued euro skepticism are manifestations of these anxieties; moreover, if monetary union should become stalled or prove unworkable, they could signal a new period of euro sclerosis. The need to accelerate the pace of monetary union is difficult for citizens to accept when so many of the countries are unable to maintain order within their own financial houses. Political leaders across Europe have advocated further integration by presenting it as a panacea to the intractable domestic problems facing most of the member states. But the citizens of Europe no longer accept such a facile explanation, and the electoral support for anti-Maastricht politicians highlights the citizenry's rejection of accelerated integration.

Another reason for the rising support for these far right parties centers on the voters' rejection of the current political elites. In Austria, Belgium, France, and Italy the voters have lost confidence in the entrenched political class. Scandals of all kinds have revealed a political class that has clearly lost touch with its constituents. Betz underscores this point when he argues that there is "a marked increase in public disaffection and disenchantment with the established political parties, the political class, and the political system in general. At no point of time in postwar West European history has the level of political distrust and cynicism been so profound, pronounced, and widespread as in the 1980s" (1994, 167). Since Betz published his seminal study on the radical right, the public's opinion of its political class has continued to decline. The tragic blood scandals in France, corruption in Austria and Italy, and salacious stories about Belgian elites have further contributed to the European public's rejection of its political leaders. It is no coincidence that as constituents continue to be disappointed by their mainstream politicians, they have increasingly turned to those who have long operated outside the tainted mainstream.

Finally, it is important to note that European voters have been looking for alternatives to the mainstream political parties for more than two decades. The once dominant frozen cleavage structures first identified by Lipset and Rokkan (1967) began to melt in the aftermath of the tumultuous 1960s, a decline that fostered the development of political alternatives on the left and the right. New political parties have emerged in most European countries. Green parties have been regularly contesting elections and seating representatives in a wide variety of electoral outlets for the past two decades. These "new left" parties have perhaps accelerated the development of "new right" parties, but to describe, as some have done, the emergence of the new right as merely a backlash to the new left is a simplification of a much more complex process of sociopolitical change (Minkenberg 1997; Weinberg 1997).

The most interesting development in the parties of the new right is that they clearly cut across the once dominant cleavage structures; the old left-right economic paradigm has given way to a new political debate. The populist character of the major far right movements is undeniable: although such movements as the Austrian Freedom Party, the Belgian Vlaams Blok, and the French National Front attract voters from across the political and socioeconomic spectrum, they now claim significant support in Europe's working-class neighborhoods. Over the past ten years, all of these movements have seen their share of the working-class vote continue to rise from one election to the next. The shift of working-class voters from the Communist and Socialist Parties to political parties of the far right is probably the single most important development in postindustrial politics since Inglehart (1977) first identified the new left. Although often dismissed as merely a reaction to the new left, these resurgent far right movements are more than mere reactions to the politics of postmaterialism.

In recent years the politics of the far right have become central to the political debate in most advanced industrialized democracies. In the mid-1980s, after years of political oblivion, the French National Front emerged as the first true postfascist far right party to challenge the political status quo. Ignazi actually maintains that the Front "is the prototype of post-industrial extreme-right parties" (1997, 57). As the Front has extended its political influence, first domestically and now internationally, it has been joined in its crusade by a wide range of far right political actors. Like the National Front, these political parties continue to develop their support in their domestic arenas, and they are also reaching out to their far right cohorts in other countries. Some of these parties, like Jörge Haider's Freedom Party and Gianfranco Fini's newly labeled National Alliance, have enjoyed successes that on certain levels have eclipsed the National Front. But, although Fini's and Haider's parties can claim greater parliamentary representation, Le Pen and the National Front remain the vanguard of the European far right movement. Le Pen, for example, has emerged as a major celebrity on the far right speakers circuit, having visited a host of far right leaders in both Western and Eastern Europe. His visits to the former Communist countries are especially problematic because of the anxiety he can exploit in these rapidly changing countries; the economic and social dislocation that has accompanied the dual transition from one-party command economies to democratic free markets has created a fertile recruiting ground for politicians plying the rhetoric of the far right.

This resurgent far right has proven incredibly adept at exploiting the technological revolution that began with the mass-marketing campaigns for the personal computer. These movements are technically proficient and continue to extend their reach by exploiting the resources of the World Wide Web. They maintain their own home pages on the Web and communicate with one another via e-mail (Ebatra 1997). The National Front was one of the first French political parties to create a Web page, and it currently maintains one of the most complete and complex Web sites among European political parties, providing a complete overview of the party's agenda, history, and organization while maintaining direct links to friends and foes alike. Its apparent appreciation for the advanced technology of the late twentieth century is another indication that this party, although linked to the past, is clearly preparing for the future.

These technically adept and politically proficient far right movements have made inroads throughout the advanced industrialized world. The fact that they appear with such force and frequency in democratic systems reflects both the strengths and the weaknesses of these systems. Representative democracies continue to thrive and even multiply in the face of the far right's demagogic rhetoric; this is an important element of their strength. On a more cautionary note, the popular appeal of these movements underscores the vacuum of leadership that exists in many advanced industrialized democracies. The system is sound, but the incumbents have been found wanting.

❑ ❑ ❑ CONCLUSION

Je crois que le Front National,

pour le moment, est parfaitement placé pour élargir son

audience. — National Front vice president[1]

It is customary at this point in a study of this type
to comment that the National Front is now at a crossroads in its development, but such an assertion would be an overstatement of the current
political reality facing this increasingly influential political party. The
Front's exceptional first-round performance in the 1997 legislative elections did in fact signal another significant step in the party's quest for
political legitimacy. Those results reconfirmed its performance in the
1995 presidential elections by preserving Le Pen's 15 percent share of
the popular vote. This was indeed an important accomplishment because it was the first time the party's candidates had proven capable of
replicating the truly impressive vote totals their leader had amassed in
the previous two presidential contests. After the 1997 elections, the parliamentary party was, for the first time in its history, on an equal footing with its perennial presidential candidate. Simply put, the National
Front, *as a political party,* had finally emerged from the long shadow cast
by Le Pen's leadership.

Armed with an increasingly experienced cadre of candidates, the Front
successfully capitalized on its growing party infrastructure to supplant
the UDF as the third largest political force in France. Although the far
right Front seated but one deputy in the National Assembly, its strong
performance rankled and even frightened the seemingly somnolent
mainstream right. The 1998 regional elections scheduled for the spring
of 1998 will further test the electability of the party's expanding candidate base. However, it will face its next crucial challenge when Jean-
Marie Le Pen, who has been so essential to the party's development,
either decides to step down or is pushed aside. At that point the party
will surely find itself at a decisive crossroads.

The Front's development from a minor groupuscule on the far right
fringe of French politics into a solidly anchored, mass-based political

party is central to the evolution of the French Fifth Republic. Given the party's solid base of support in contemporary French politics, the Republic's ability to withstand the challenges posed by the far right fringe is an important note of political stability in an increasingly factious party system.

The elements that contributed to the party's creation, electoral breakthrough, and ultimate durability have served as the focus of this study. The party's initial toehold in the drama that is French politics was inextricably linked to two important factors. First, the Front managed to unify the expansive issue base that historically defined the desperately disparate ideological heritage of the French far right. Le Pen successfully folded the many currents that make up the far right into a seemingly coherent philosophy: lepénisme. By capitalizing on the cleavage structure that separated the far right from the political mainstream, Le Pen melded together the amorphous philosophies that have for centuries represented French far right thinking. This was indeed an important political accomplishment. Second, he managed to unite the many colorful characters who have populated the far right fringe. By the sheer force of his charismatic personality, he unilaterally bridged the gaps that for so long divided these frères ennemis, whose petty politics and personal rivalries had rendered them politically impotent. Violence-prone student militants, disaffected Algerian war veterans, Catholic fundamentalists, pieds noirs, and royalists joined together under Le Pen's leadership to create the National Front. They were followed years later by disillusioned center rightists from the RPR, independents from the Centre National des Indépendants, and solidaristes of the Jean-Pierre Stirbois variety. Other prominent figures had previously tried to unite the factious elements of the French far right, and they had all failed miserably. Because the far right is characterized by a multiplicity of voices, attempts at unity have often resulted in electoral disappointments at the very minimum and internecine warfare at the most extreme. Rare is the individual who is able to bring together the myriad interests on the far right into a cohesive whole; whoever attempts this monumental task must effectively articulate the diverse interests that purport to speak for the many crosswired circuits of the far right. French history is crowded with a failed army of pseudo-leaders who have claimed to represent the many movements of the far right. Until Le Pen, no one had actually achieved success.

Charles Maurras was never successful in leading the far right movement that he nurtured so judiciously. He was the intellectual mainstay of the far right but never its unchallenged leader. Neither Georges Valois, nor Pierre Taittinger, nor Colonel de La Rocque were ever successful in becoming the undisputed leader of the far right. Their organizations, memberships, and agendas overlapped too closely to create room for compromise; mediation with one of the other competing organizations would have promoted the extinction of the mediator. In some respects, Marshal Pétain was partially successful because he succeeded in promulgating public policies that actually advanced far right ideals. His reign as the undisputed leader of the far right was brief and marred by the tragedies of war. For a few fleeting moments many important themes of the far right were advanced as legitimate public policies, but the wartime practice of such contentious policies exiled the collaborationist far right to the political sidelines for decades. Pierre Poujade and Jean-Louis Tixier-Vignancour reached the top of the far right pyramid for brief periods in the 1950s and 1960s, respectively, but they were unable to maintain their positions. Omnipresent during both of their short reigns, Le Pen played the dutiful foot soldier to both men and patiently awaited his turn at the top. Le Pen's political apprenticeships under Poujade and Tixier-Vignancour served him well as he bided his time, polished his oratorical skills, and cemented the relationships that would serve as the foundation for his successful bid for power on the far right fringe.

With more than forty years of political experience, Le Pen has successfully navigated his way through the morass of conflicts and personalities that predominate on the far right fringe of French politics. He has somehow withstood all challenges from other contenders and has emerged as the most successful leader in the far right's inglorious history. Furthermore, he possesses a remarkable ability to rise phoenixlike from near disaster. He has survived constant and perhaps warranted media assaults, an assassination attempt that left his Paris apartment building a bombed-out shell, numerous lawsuits and trials, a humiliating public divorce, and stunning electoral defeats.[2] As a political survivor, Le Pen holds a truly unique position in contemporary French politics.

As we have observed in our analysis of the interview data and documentary sources, Le Pen's contribution to the Front is unrivaled; for example, one of the founding members claimed, "Jean-Marie Le Pen is the cement of the National Front." The devotion many of the respondents express toward him underscores the importance they attach to his leadership; during the interviews, the respondents repeatedly stressed his dominant position in the party. When pressed to consider the future of the party without Le Pen, many quickly responded by saying "The party would cease to exist." This was undoubtedly true in the late 1980s; as a new party, the Front was singularly dependent on Le Pen's leadership skills. This follows a rather general pattern for parties of the far right; historically, such parties have tended to coalesce around authoritarian leaders, and in our discussion of the Austrian, Belgian/Flemish, and Italian contemporary far right we noted similar patterns of charismatic leadership.

Two of the leadership subgroups, the founding members and the new recruits, are overwhelmingly positive in praising Le Pen's leadership. This new recruit, for example, describes Le Pen's role in the following manner:

> It's a charismatic role. Before being charismatic, it's a role of drawing together the latent feelings of the French. He's the megaphone, someone who succeeds in expressing in a very clear and very strong manner what people are feeling, but either don't know how or don't have the courage to express themselves.

The tone approaches the reverential as this founding member and Front vice president examines Le Pen's lasting impact on the party. As one of the party's charter members, this respondent's relationship with Le Pen dates to the Poujade era, and as evidenced by the comments, her devotion to the leader of the National Front is complete:

> He is the president of the National Front. He is an extraordinary political leader. A man of faith, of courage, of determination. . . . He has an extraordinary vision of the future . . . without a doubt one of the greatest men of the times.

Surprisingly, given the unflinching loyalty most respondents display toward Le Pen, there does exist an alternative perspective. Although few in number and expressed only within the ranks of the *notables,* some respondents are critical of Le Pen's leadership. They are careful in their choice of words, and more than one respondent asked for extra assurance that their comments would be kept confidential before they expressed any criticism of Le Pen. For example, one former National Assembly deputy contends "that he [Le Pen] should not be involved with everything, just the essential." This is rather mild in tone and substance, but one of his colleagues, another *notable,* is more direct and maintains that an important obstacle to the party's future development is "the authoritarianism of Jean-Marie Le Pen, who still refuses to share his authority." He goes on to say, "A party will not become a great party without working as a team." Although this is clearly a minority view, the pace of defections during the late 1980s and 1990s lends credence to these sentiments. Moreover, the Front has been abandoned by many of its most high-profile political *notables*, those individuals who were so aggressively recruited in the early 1980s; the most publicized and potentially damaging defections were Olivier d'Ormesson, Pascal Arrighi, and François Bachelot. D'Ormesson, one of the first moderates to align himself with Le Pen's movement, was elected to the European Parliament in the 1984 election; he defected in 1987 after Le Pen's "detail" remark about the Nazi death camps. Arrighi, a politically popular *notable* who actually received almost 100 votes for National Assembly vice president in 1986, resigned from the Front in the political firestorm that followed Le Pen's vulgar pun on the name of Michel Durafour.[3] Bachelot, known throughout France as Dr. SIDA because of his public pronouncements that AIDS sufferers and HIV-positive citizens should be quarantined from the general population in *sidatoriums*, also quit the party at the same time as Arrighi.[4] Other *notables* such as Pierre Ceyrac and Charles de Chambrun eventually followed suit and abandoned the party in the 1990s.

At each stage of the political party life cycle—creation, electoral breakthrough, and durability—Le Pen's leadership has proven crucial to the party's continued success. The elite interviews as well as the historical record clearly illustrate the centrality of Le Pen's leadership throughout the development process. As the Front cautiously awaits Le Pen's inevitable retirement from the political arena, it will increasingly come to depend on other factors besides leadership to maintain its position as a permanent fixture in the French political landscape. With Bruno Mégret apparently poised to replace Le Pen in the near future, the party, for so long merely a vehicle for Le Pen's personal political ambitions, will need to rely more heavily on its national organizational structure and its increasingly tight links to the nation's mass electorate. In his capacity as delegate-general for the past decade, Mégret, who is viewed as a political strategist and technician rather than a rabble-rousing charismatic street fighter, has successfully created a political machine that clearly can challenge the system's more mainstream parties.

The common description of the Front as a one-man, one-issue political operation has been outdated for some years. In the aftermath of the 1988 legislative elections, the Front's political elite recognized that they needed to reenergize their party by undertaking an organizational makeover and by recruiting more and stronger candidates. The central feature of the Front's development throughout the 1990s has been a focused and disciplined effort to expand the party's potential pool of candidates, activists, and voters. During the past decade, the Front has erected a sturdy party organization that has become a truly national political presence buttressed by a devoted, nearly fanatical following of voters, activists, and local-level political elites.

In our model of political party development, we emphasized the crucial role played by such political factors as the level of mass commitment and party organization in the party's evolution; at the third stage of the party life cycle, durability, the historical record as well as the interview responses provided by the Front elite clearly demonstrate the unique importance of these two factors. The party leadership's single-minded focus on creating an organizational base capable of solidifying the Front's position in the French party system was detailed in chapters 4 and 6, and the Front's growing attraction to the French electorate was the focus of chapter 7.

Although leadership, party organization, and mass commitment are central to understanding the Front's dynamic evolution, they do not act alone. Another important element of the Front's political development has been its relationships with the system's other political parties. The proportional representation system used in the European Parliament elections was essential in facilitating the Front's first major success at the ballot box, but the behavior of the system's more mainstream parties has also influenced the Front's political development. Remarkably, the traditional parties of both the left and the right have contributed to the sociopolitical legitimatization of the National Front. Whether it was Mitterrand's decision to use district-level proportional voting in the 1986 National Assembly elections or the center right's feckless attempts at usurping the Front's primary issue base, the system's mainstream parties have, without a doubt, been complicit in the Front's early development, electoral success, and durability.

The most recent legislative elections further illustrate the extent to which the Front's political fate is inextricably linked to that of the center right. Immediately after the 1997 legislative elections, a chorus of political pundits proclaimed that the National Front had become the arbiter of French elections (Jaffré 1997; Ponceyri 1997). The insurgent Front did indeed play an important role in defeating Alain Juppé's center right governing coalition; with its 15 percent share of the first-round vote and 131 second-round candidates, the Front strongly influenced the election's outcome. Its energetic performance in those elections was a major embarrassment to the mainstream center right; moreover, it acutely demonstrated that the incumbents had no coherent strategy for dealing with the rising National Front.

The 1997 legislative contest highlights the center right's inability to grasp the gravity of its current political predicament. Although in recent years it has adamantly refused to entertain the possibility of reciprocal withdrawal agreements with the Front, it continues to shamelessly court the Front's voters between the first and second rounds of balloting.[5] As noted in previous chapters, this behavior occurred in the 1995 presidential elections and was repeated in the 1997 legislative elections. Its arguably noble stance of refusing to negotiate with the insurgent frontistes has cost it dearly at the ballot box. Except for its blatantly transparent and rather desperate appeals to the Front's voters, the center right has been unable to develop and implement a coherent strategy to counter the National Front's rising tide of support. Since the Front's electoral breakthrough in 1984, the center right has instead employed a variety of tactics in its dealings with Le Pen's party. This plethora of conflicting strategies has included cutting deals with the Front, as in the 1984 municipal elections in Dreux and the 1988 legislative elections, objectifying the far right and its leaders as the devil incarnate, disingenuously adopting much of the Front's most distasteful rhetoric, and even implementing some of its proposals with respect to immigration legislation. The singular most important criticism of its strategy of multiple and conflicting approaches is that it has confused the voters; moreover, it has left them ideologically adrift, wondering exactly where the center right stands with respect to its relationship with the far right National Front.

In 1993, when the mainstream right faced a declining Socialist Party engaged in a dramatic free fall at the ballot box, it had the political strength and flexibility to ignore the Front's growing influence. But in 1997, when the Socialist Party had regained its electoral vitality, the RPR-UDF alliance desperately needed to rethink its strategy vis-à-vis the National Front. Its inability to communicate with its electorate in a unified voice contributed to President Jacques Chirac's humiliating public rejection and to his party's massive legislative losses. The advent of a third period of cohabitation has forced the mainstream right to reevaluate its electoral strategy with respect to the National Front. Further complicating the issue is that the Front's voters are now, after years of neglect and even outright abuse, much more likely to reject the mainstream right in the second round of balloting: because the mainstream right has so effectively alienated a core of the Front's electorate, it can no longer count on their support in the decisive second round (Ysmal 1995; Mayer 1997).

The center right is also seriously disadvantaged by Chirac's decline and the lack of a credible leadership alternative on the right. The marginalization of Chirac that began in the aftermath of the 1997 legislative elections has continued to the present. The summary rejection of Chirac's chosen heir, Alain Juppé, and the rapid rise of Philippe Séguin have further rendered Chirac rather inconsequential within his own party, a movement that he nurtured for more than twenty years. Séguin, allied with Charles Pasqua, in February of 1998 engineered a mutinous attempt to rename Chirac's party—an overt rebuke of Chirac's leadership.[6]

Chirac's personal strategy toward the Front has vacillated greatly during his political career. Most often he has chosen to ignore it, but when necessary, as in the 1995 presidential election, he has used surrogates to court the Front's voters. On occasion, he has also adopted the rhetoric of the Front in an attempt to usurp their monopoly of the immigration issue.[7] But the dominant strategy has been to attack the Front as a collection of extremists who have more in common with Hitler's Brownshirts than with the political realities of the late twentieth century.

Chirac's wavering influence within Gaullist circles is also appropriately illustrated by the increasing public discussion of possible future electoral alliances with the Front. In July 1997, supporters of the RPR and the UDF were given the opportunity to express their opinions regarding a possible electoral alliance with the National Front. In a national survey of 962 voting-age citizens, 30 percent of RPR supporters and 19 percent of UDF supporters favored either a local- or national-level alliance with the Front. In the immediate aftermath of the disastrous 1997 legislative elections, a chorus of disgruntled UDF and RPR local-level elites began to register their dissatisfaction with the leadership cadres of the two mainstream center right parties. In September 1997, Jean-Luc Chapon, UDF mayor of Uzès, openly criticized his party's verbal attacks on the Front: "The Léotard-Juppé stance of demonizing the National

Front was very wrong. Today, it's just out of date" (in *Libération,* September 20, 1997). During an October 1997 strategy session of RPR activists in the department of Seine-Saint-Denis, those attending the meeting were asked whether their party should enter into an alliance with the Front; 95 of the 115 activists present supported such an alliance (Barbier and Rosso 1997). If the national leaders of the center right fail to address the concerns of their activists, the departmental and local-level leaders may enter into individual electoral accords with the National Front.

The center right's inability to develop and maintain a clear position on its relationship with the Front has also promoted dissension within its own leadership ranks. In the Picardie region, northwest of the Île-de-France, the incumbent UDF president, Charles Baur, openly flirted with the National Front's voters prior to the regional elections, and thus opened himself to criticism from his own party members. François-Michel Gonnot, the UDF vice president, argues, "He [Baur] has a very flexible position on the National Front and he is leaving all possibilities open." The National Front, for its part, carefully courted the center right in the months prior to the regional elections. For example, Pierre Descaves, former National Assembly deputy and the Front's candidate for the Picardie presidency, sounded almost solicitous as he campaigned for the same position as Baur: "I have never attacked him. He's a true democrat, a courteous man who respects all elected officials" (in *Libération,* February 18, 1998).

The mainstream right of French politics, ranging from the amorphous UDF to the hardliners of the RPR, is increasingly threatened by the National Front. Unable or perhaps unwilling to finalize a political marriage that has been too long in the offing, the center right remains mired in a stagnant and conflict-ridden long-term engagement that has increasingly left its supporters standing at the altar. Moreover, the traditional right has turned into a sort of Hydra, expressing its political aspirations through a multiplicity of talking heads, whereas the Front's authoritarian administration is able to present itself as a more cohesive and thus better-organized political option. Two of the mainstream right's primary leaders, Philippe Séguin, the newly elected leader of the RPR, and François Léotard, the titular head of the UDF, continue to exacerbate the right's primary problem: its inability to come to grips with the National Front. Léotard is more committed than ever to demonize the National Front, but Séguin feels that continuing such a practice is counterproductive; he argues that such an approach will only further alienate the Front's 4 million voters and further weaken the mainstream right.

In the fall of 1997, the Front successfully contested a cantonal by-election in Mulhouse, a city in the Haut-Rhin department, where it posted impressive gains in that year's legislative elections. Its successful candidate, Gérard Freulet, is a former National Assembly deputy who has long labored to enhance his profile and the profile of his party.[8] In the end, the center right's greatest threat is no longer from Jean-Marie Le Pen, but from the many hundreds of locally based frontistes like Freulet who have spent years sowing the fields of political discontent left unattended by the mainstream political parties. These homegrown *notables* provide the Front with a vast support network in the all-important arena of French local politics.

In the build-up to the March 1998 regional elections, it became painfully obvious that the regional and local leaders of the mainstream right were prepared to ignore their party leaders' edict against working with the National Front. The Paris-based UDF and RPR parties were still reeling from their humiliating defeat in the 1997 elections, and another setback of similar proportions would further call into question the political viability of France's mainstream right. Although the control of the country's twenty-two regional councils hung in the balance, the parties' leadership remained steadfast in demanding that their local chieftains refrain from working with the Front. Early polls indicated that the center right, which presided over twenty of the twenty-two regional councils, would lose control in as many as ten of them. The only way for the center right to prevent another leftist rout in the regional elections was to initiate discussions with the National Front; although anathema to most of its leadership, this was viewed as an increasingly viable option to the mainstream right's local activists, as well as its rank and file.

The results of the regional elections highlighted the increased political power of the National Front and further solidified its position in the French party system. While improving its 1992 score by a mere one percent, the Front nevertheless continued to increase its share of the vote. The party has now captured 15 percent of the vote in three different electoral contexts: the 1995 presidential race, the 1997 legislative elections, and the 1998 regional contests.

The results of the regional elections underscore the fact that the Front has clearly become a party of national dimensions; it has succeeded in gaining representation on all of the mainland's regional councils.

The party's success in the regional councils also emphasized its areas of strength in the following regions: Nord-Pas-de-Calais with 15.3 percent and eighteen regional councillors, Picardie with 18.5 percent and eleven councillors, Alsace with 20.6 percent and 13 regional councillors, Rhônes-Alpes with 19.0 percent and thirty-five councillors, and Provence-Côte-d'Azur with 26.5 percent and thirty-seven councillors.

With 275 regional councillors across mainland France, the Front has continued to flourish in the lucrative arena of subnational politics; moreover, its influence extends well beyond the simple import of its vote totals. In Bourgogne, Centre, Languedoc-Roussillon, Picardie, and Rhône-Alpes the Front succeeded in seducing the local leaders of the mainstream right into an electoral agreement, thereby guaranteeing right-wing presidencies in those regions. Surprisingly, the five center rightists who were elected presidents of these regions were all members of the UDF. Their rogue attitudes vis-à-vis their party's leadership provoked the Paris-based federation to demand their immediate suspension. The political fallout from the regional elections provided Prime Minister Lionel Jospin with an excellent opportunity to denounce the right's willingness to compromise with the far right Front. This in turn prompted President Chirac to address the nation through a televised speech wherein he denounced the Front as "racist and xenophobic" and openly criticized those in his own party who were considering working with the Front (in *Le Monde,* May 25, 1998). Although Chirac's RPR will survive the crisis of conscience created by the regional council elections, the organizationally fragile UDF may be the first victim of Bruno Mégret's plan to position the Front as the one and true voice of the French right.

Our study of the evolution of the far right in France reveals that the object of its derision may change from one political generation to the next, but what remains constant is that the far right is deeply anchored in the society's political culture. Whether attacking Jews in the financial industry, Socialists in the Catholic Church, Communists in the bureaucracy, or, as is done currently, American cultural imperialists, North Africans on public assistance, and Eurocrats in Brussels, the far right fringe remains a powerful force in French politics; there seems to be a constant appetite for its brand of politics.

The ideological foundation of the French far right is not wedded to one single philosophy. It is an amalgamation of many different but closely related ideological tenets, which have been expressed most successfully by far right political movements. The ideas that have been important to the French far right encompass a number of complementary yet competing perspectives that find their contemporary expression in the French National Front. Monarchism, anti-Semitism, nationalism, and xenophobia have been integral to the message of the far right for generations. Combining these historical themes with more modern anxieties about a changing Europe, the need to radically modify the welfare state, and public mistrust of mainstream politicians has created fertile ground for the politicians of the far right. As purveyors of pessimism and fear, the French far right has maintained a narrow niche on the fringes of French politics for decades, and within the past ten years it has successfully broadened its mass appeal by exploiting French fears of the postindustrial society.

The ties that bind the French far right revolve around a complex web of ideological perspectives. The far right is in many ways like a bad penny; it continually shows up at inopportune times. In 1983, Petitfils summarily concluded that the far right "no longer existed as a political force" (1983, 362). The experiences of Dreux and the 1984 European elections immediately following the publication of his book obviously proved him wrong; since those early electoral breakthroughs the Front now commands the support of 15 percent of the electorate.

The current representative of the far right, the National Front, may attempt to distance itself from its ideological ancestors, but the links are too strong, the shared personnel too numerous, and the rhetoric too reminiscent of a time long past for the contemporary French far right to repudiate completely its ideological antecedents. The links within the ideological universe of the French far right are at times undeniably attenuated, but they are also omnipresent. What separates the contemporary far right from its historical predecessors is its ability to endure and ultimately become a stable presence in the French political landscape. Because of its durability, the National Front, as the contemporary manifestation of the French far right, is truly unique in the annals of history. When the Front was created in 1972, no one, not even its core leadership cadre, was confident of its future. More than ten years later, when the party latched onto the immigration issue and rode that to Strasbourg and representation in the European Parliament, most observers felt Le Pen's boisterous Parliament deputies would fade from view as rapidly as the Poujadists of the 1950s. Still again, in 1986, after François Mitterrand had cynically altered the electoral system and opened the portals of the National Assembly to thirty-five frontistes, everyone knew their time in the legislature was controlled by the center right, who quickly readopted the previous electoral framework, thereby pushing the Front out the back door by the end of the next electoral cycle. The Front suffered serious setbacks in the aftermath of losing its 1986–1988 legislative contingent, and still it endured.

A number of important factors have contributed to the party's survival. First, the party's cadre of elites understood early on the importance of Le Pen's leadership to their political enterprise; they supported him and suffered through his racist and anti-Semitic rhetorical excesses, all the while profiting from his thirst for the limelight and his maniacal devotion to the Front. Second, they eventually created a mature party structure that began to develop an organizational life separate from Le Pen; with its newfound institutional maturity, the party extended its reach within the electorate and successfully seated its candidates at nearly all levels of the political contest. Third, although the party has always been viewed as the pariah of French politics, the imminent retirement of Le Pen has enabled those in the polite circles of French politics to begin serious discussions about alliances and interparty cooperation that will build upon the tentative steps taken by the renegade rightists in the aftermath of the regional council elections. Bruno Mégret, Le Pen's most likely successor as well as a refugee from the RPR, relishes these developments and believes the Front is poised to usurp his former party's position as the dominant force on the right of the political spectrum. The Front's delegate-general may be overly optimistic about his party's political future, but it is true that the Front has known no better days than the present. In 1988, one of Le Pen's closest confidants said, "I believe that the National Front is, at this moment, perfectly situated to enlarge its audience." These comments are perhaps more applicable today than they were even a decade ago. Ominously, the future does indeed belong to the National Front.

□   □   □   AFTERWORD

Le vieux n'est pas mort.[1]

—Jean-Marie Le Pen

C'est une diva qui est un train de rater sa sortie.[2]

—Bruno Mégret

Only days before this manuscript was to go to press, the leadership of the National Front entered into a fratricidal war that may ultimately lead to its political suicide. Unable, or perhaps just unwilling, to savor its relative successes in the 1997 legislative elections and the 1998 regional contests, the National Front did what the far right has always done: it decided to eat its own. Turning a blind eye to the harsh lessons of history, the French far right split into two nearly equal political movements—the National Front, still under the stewardship of Jean-Marie Le Pen, and the National Front–National Movement, led by former National Front general delegate Bruno Mégret.

Although internal conflicts had been brewing for some time, even astute political observers of the French far right like Jean-Yves Camus believed that Mégret would once again back down and politely swallow the verbal onslaughts of Jean-Marie Le Pen. Even as the crisis continued to mount, Camus argued that "[Mégret's] not going to give up at 49, time is on his side. That's why he will try to calm things down and wait for an opportunity" (*France-Soir,* December 8, 1998). But this time Le Pen had pushed Mégret too far.

Mégret's patience with Le Pen's snide and at times vicious verbal assaults was legendary within the movement. He and the other leaders at the top of the National Front's organizational pyramid suffered gallantly through the many years of Le Pen's rhetorical excesses, brushes with the law, and political missteps, which include a litany of ridiculous, sometimes criminal acts. While Le Pen's behavior served to anchor him and his party in the more populist sectors of French society, it may have hindered their progress with more mainstream voters, thus making it difficult for the Front to surpass the artificial threshold of 15 percent of the vote. In the last few years, Le Pen's proclivity for political gaffes and blunders seems to have increased. His decision to revisit the "detail" remark during a 1997 visit to Munich underscored his anti-Semitic excesses, prompting German authorities to ask the European Parliament to strip him of his immunity; he now faces charges in Germany related to that country's strong anti-Holocaust denial laws. Also in 1997, during the middle of the hastily called legislative campaign, Le Pen's public pronouncements in favor of a leftist National Assembly forced his general delegate and general secretary to disavow his rash remarks in an attempt at damage control. During the same legislative contest, Le Pen further exasperated the party's more staid supporters when he became embroiled in a highly publicized street brawl as he was campaigning with his daughter Marie-Caroline. Found guilty of assault in the attack on his daughter's Socialist opponent, Le Pen is awaiting a decision on his most recent appeal in that case.

Faced with the possibility of losing his civil rights, and thus being forced to abandon his political aspirations, Le Pen proffered his wife, Jany, as his possible successor in the upcoming European elections.[3] Mégret immediately and formally stated his disapproval, but the question was rendered moot when Le Pen was granted the right to campaign for the European Parliament as he awaited word on his appeal.

Le Pen's increasingly public excesses must have been especially excruciating for Bruno Mégret, whose air and attitude are antithetical to those exhibited by Le Pen. Le Pen's antipathy toward Mégret is not, in fact, related to policy disagreements but to their lack of personal rapport and their differences in style—this personality conflict is central to the discord that led to the extraordinary party conference held in Marignane, January 23–24, 1999. Repeatedly mocked for his aloof manner and his palpable discomfort in public settings, Mégret has rebuffed rumors of homosexuality (he married late in life), smiled wanly at Le Pen's jokes about his short stature, and suffered an endless series of indignities at the hands of the man he has always addressed with the French formal *vous* rather than the more familiar *tu*.

But as Mégret grew in stature among both the party's activists and its mass level supporters, Le Pen's fear of being supplanted increased. Le Pen has always been acutely alert to real—and imagined—threats to his supremacy, and his past behavior reflects a continuous effort to mitigate the power of potential challengers. In 1987, Le Pen exuberantly welcomed Mégret into the higher echelons of the party's hierarchy when he named him director of his presidential campaign. Given Mégret's short tenure in the party, this was viewed as not only a slight but also a warning to the late Jean-Pierre Stirbois. However, Mégret's success as general delegate prompted Le Pen to counter his growing influence by naming Bruno Gollnisch, a longtime Le Pen loyalist, to the post of general secretary. Gollnisch was also accorded a staff structure parallel to that of Mégret, in a none-too-subtle attempt on Le Pen's part to signal that the question of succession was not by any means settled. As it became clear that Mégret, not Gollnisch, was increasingly touted as Le Pen's natural successor, Le Pen undertook additional moves to signal his displeasure with such developments. In 1998, he chose Jean-Claude Martinez, an avowed enemy of Mégret, to head his shadow government, ultimately selecting Martinez as the party's campaign manager for the 1999 European Parliament elections.

As we have noted, the series of miscalculations that led to Mégret's dismissal and ultimately to the creation of a competing National Front began well before the political fireworks that exploded during the 1998 Christmas season. The 1997 Strasbourg Party congress clearly highlighted the rise of not only Bruno Mégret but also that of a cadre of his closest supporters. Mégret, on the heels of the political victory that he engineered for his wife in Vitrolles, received more votes than any other person during the elections for the party's Central Committee. And, perhaps more significantly, four of the other top ten vote-getters for Central Committee positions were well-known Mégret loyalists, another clear sign of the general delegate's growing power within party circles.[4]

The combination of Le Pen's continued political gaffes and Mégret's increasing popularity led to a rather public battle over the party's list for the upcoming European Parliament elections. With Le Pen back in the race, it was a given that he would head the list, but the question circulating among party activists in the fall of 1998 concerned Mégret's placement on that list. On November 27, 1998, a document alleged to be a draft of the party's list for the upcoming European Parliament elections was circulated within Front circles. Three thinks were striking about the list: (1) the appearance in the number two spot of Charles de Gaulle, the general's grandson who in 1995 had been elected a member of the de Villiers list; (2) the placement of Bruno Mégret in the tenth spot; and (3) the fact that only one other Mégret loyalist, Yvan Blot, was on the list of fifteen. Conspicuously absent from the list was Jean-Yves Le Gallou, an incumbent deputy, president of the Front's Ile-de-France regional group, national secretary for elections, and a close Mégret ally. The provenance of the list remains in doubt, with Le Pen's inner circle denying responsibility for both its creation and circulation.

Following soon after the conflict generated by the debate over the European Parliament list, Le Pen unilaterally decided to dismiss from paid positions within the party two of Mégret's trusted co-workers, Nathalie Debaille and Hubert Fayard, both well-regarded frontistes. Debaille, a Central Committee member and close personal assistant of Mégret, as well as a longtime party member in good standing, was fired from her party job on Le Pen's orders during the first week of December. Her removal and that of Hubert Fayard, *premier adjoint* to Mayor Cathérine Mégret, were seen as clear signs that Le Pen had finally decided to publicly resist Mégret's rising influence, although Le Pen's people defended this action as a belt-tightening move and even threatened more dismissals.

On December 5, 1998, only days after their dismissal, Debaille and Fayard decided to attend the National Council meeting, defying Le Pen in a highly visible manner. When Fayard tried to enter through the main door, he was blocked by the Front's security service; Debaille proved more savvy than her comrade and entered the meeting hall by a side entrance. Her somewhat tardy arrival precipitated waves of applause and generated an immediate controversy—Le Pen was being openly confronted by a woman. Her presence, and the support it garnered, threw the usually irrepressible Le Pen off his mark, causing him to demand that Debaille be forcibly removed from the meeting: "We will begin when the uninvited have left." In a further act of defiance, Debaille stayed long enough to sing the Marseillaise, then promptly departed to another round of applause. Upon exiting, she met with reporters in the street and stated, "On the very day that I was fired, in order to save money, four people—two of them from Samuel Maréchal's [Le Pen's son-in-law and one of his strongest supporters] family—were hired. This is aimed directly at Bruno Mégret. It's the predicted purge, the *démégretisation* has begun" (*Libération,* December 7, 1998).

The meeting continued, but Le Pen was never really able to gain complete control of the proceedings. This was the first time that his authority had been so publicly challenged, and it produced a tremendous outcry on both sides of the debate. One longtime far-right activist, Roger Holeindre, who had experienced all of the fratricidal conflicts of the French far right dating back to the 1950s, prophetically took to the microphone to plead for unity, but too much damage had already been done.

The emergency meeting of the party's political bureau that followed failed to resolve the many conflicts, and by Monday, December 7, 1998, Le Pen's authority was under direct attack. Serge Martinez, a high-ranking party leader who had held such posts as director of personnel, national secretary, and elected regional councillor from Languedoc-Roussillon, called for a party congress. His was an unlikely voice to be raised against Le Pen, given that he had been a close protégé of Le Pen and had never had particularly close relations with Mégret. Eventually there was a chorus of frontistes demanding a special congress and loudest among these were Bruno Mégret's closest confidants: Jean-Claude Bardet, Yvan Blot, Jean-Yves Le Gallou, Fernand Le Rachinel, Daniel Simonpieri, and Franck Timmermans.

Events surrounding the brewing crisis took a decidedly melodramatic turn in the middle of December, when the private affairs of Le Pen's family came to the fore. In some respects, the Front's schism began to mirror the story of a family divided. The father of three daughters, Le Pen has always known how to exploit his family in a way that partially mitigates his hard edge and pugnacious personality. Photos of Le Pen *en famille* serve as important reminders that he is a loving husband and a doting father who practices what he preaches with respect to his own nuclear *French* family. His three daughters—Marie-Caroline, Yann, and Marine—took on even greater symbolic importance in the Le Pen mythology following his very public and humiliating divorce from their mother, Pierette. Siding with their father, they chose to seek their political and economic fortunes within the extended family that is the National Front. But the image of a unified family was subsequently shattered when Marie-Caroline, Le Pen's eldest daughter and arguably the most politically active over the longest period of time, entered the political melee on the side of the Mégret contingent. The creation of a second National Front forced Le Pen's daughters to choose between their father and their political futures, but the difficulty was magnified for Marie-Caroline, because her lover and the father of her unborn child is Philippe Olivier, one of the many Mégret loyalists expelled from the party in the December purge of the *mégretistes*. In an act of familial betrayal, Marie-Caroline Le Pen signed the petition for a special party congress.

Eventually, Mégret added his voice to the chorus demanding the unscheduled meeting. He was not rash in this decision, as he was fully cognizant of his large base of support within the ranks of party operatives and elected officials. In addition, knowing Le Pen as well as he did, he understood the consequences of calling such a congress: expulsion from the party that he and his cohorts had helped to build. And that is precisely what happened. As calls for the special congress reverberated across the hexagon during the month of December, Mégret's public pronouncements became more aggressive, and in January, with just days remaining before the special congress, he was publicly attacking Le Pen: "Whether it's the Munich detail, Mrs. Trautmann's decapitated head, his [Le Pen's] pronouncements in favor of Mr. Jospin that totally served to dissuade the disaffected RPR and UDF voters from joining us, or yet again his support for Bernard Tapie . . . all of this has prevented the FN from being able to escape this ghetto of 15 percent of the vote" (*Agence France Presse*, January 17, 1998). Known for his cautious behavior, Mégret made those comments only after he had a complete picture of his standing within the party, with sixty-two of the party's 102 departmental secretaries adding their names to the petition and the additional support of 141 of the Front's 275 regional councillors. Moreover, Mégret's backers were spread out across the country: eleven of the twelve regional councillors in the important Alsace region, eighteen out of thirty-six councillors in the Ile-de-France region, and twenty-two of thirty-five councillors in the Rhône-Alpes region. In advocating the call for the Marignane congress, Mégret knew he had reliable support in all of France's twenty-one regions (*Le Monde*, January 12, 1999).

Although the Front's charter specifically grants 20 percent of the membership the right to call for a special party congress, Le Pen refused to entertain the idea, stating that he was not about to make "a pilgrimage to Lilliput" (*Le Monde*, January 25, 1999). During the early stages of the crisis, Bruno Gollnisch, who remained loyal to Le Pen, did go on record saying that the autocratic Le Pen would respect the wishes of his party members: "If one-fifth of the membership desires a convention, Jean-Marie Le Pen will respect the statute even if it were to be political suicide" (*Libération*, December 11, 1998). But when it came time to receive the petition signed by thousands of dues-paying Front members, the Le Pen loyalists at party headquarters refused to open the door.

In many respects, the actual convention was rather anticlimactic. The approximately twenty-five hundred attendees elected Bruno Mégret as president of the new party, which they named National Front–National Movement (FN–MN). They also attended to the business of party building in an orderly and cooperative fashion, paying particular attention to highlighting the differences between their new movement and that of the old National Front, now known as the National Front for French Unity (FNUF). According to early reports, the FN–MN will be much more democratic than the old National Front. The new Central Committee will be larger, and the new president, Mégret, will have less power to appoint members to that body. Mégret's movement will also divide the party's finances in a more equitable manner, thereby creating a reservoir of good will between the party's headquarters and its local federations. This democratization of the far right represents an important effort on the part of Mégret and his allies to demonstrate to mainstream rightist parties that the FN–MN is a movement with which they can do business. Mégret has always argued for a *rassemblement national,* and now that he has successfully purged the demonized Le Pen from the ranks of his party, he will clearly strive to further sanitize this new movement. A far right party *sans* Jean-Marie Le Pen is clearly more palatable to the mainstream right.

The future of these two movements and the roles they may play in the French party system represent an important unknown at this time. Even though all reports indicate that Le Pen is robust for his age, it is a factor that weighs heavily on his weakened party's future. Le Pen has purged his party of its most efficient organizers, and the combined talents of Bruno Mégret, Jean-Yves Le Gallou, and Serge Martinez will be sorely missed. These were the "idea" men of the National Front, the most prolific in writing and defining the Front's philosophical orientation. Le Pen's vicious attacks on party activists who demanded the special congress also served to diminish his support within the National Front's security service, the Département Protection-Sécurité (DPS). Bernard Courcelle, director of the DPS, reportedly submitted his resignation and defected with many of his closest co-workers to the Mégret camp. During the months of December and January, Le Pen was openly criticized by the party's newspaper, *National Hebdo,* and was under attack from a large number of the Front's ancillary organizations. Most notably, many of the party's youth organizations expressed their disappointment with Le Pen's decision. Le Pen's decision to rely more heavily on Jean-Claude Martinez and Bruno Gollnisch highlights his need for sycophants and submissive underlings; both Martinez and Gollnisch have repeatedly demonstrated their loyalty to Le Pen but have also proven to be poor administrators who lack the vision of either Mégret or Le Gallou.

As this book goes to press, momentum clearly rests with the Mégret faction, but it, too, faces serious obstacles. Early polls indicate that Mégret's brand of far-right activism faces a difficult challenge in the upcoming European Parliament elections. Three recent public opinion polls reached a similar conclusion: Le Pen has a solid hold on the hearts of the party's rank-and-file voters. In each of these surveys, Le Pen garners the support of 9 percent of the electorate, while Mégret can only count on 3 to 4 percent. With the European elections representing Mégret's first head-to-head challenge with Le Pen, Mégret's greatest source of strength is embodied by the twenty-five hundred party loyalists who abandoned their political home and threw their lot in with him. Their willingness and ability to get the vote out on election day in June will play an important role in the election's outcome. If Mégret's party is unable to surpass the five percent threshold, it will be denied representation and the public financing that comes with it. Current court battles over use of the party's name, trademark, real-estate holdings, and finances will take months to sort out, and Mégret's organization requires an infusion of cash as soon as possible.

Three scenarios seem possible as one considers the future of *two* National Fronts. Each organization could limp along through the next electoral cycle, beginning with the European Parliament elections in 1999, municipal contests in 2001, and presidential and legislative elections in 2002. But the two parties will be competing for essentially the same electorate with candidates who are in many respects interchangeable. A split in the far-right vote, which continues to hover at 15 percent, will not only fail to extend their influence but will also render the two parties impotent with respect to legislative and cantonal elections. In these elections, second-round participation depends on receiving 12.5 percent of the registered vote in the first round—next to impossible if the far-right vote remains divided.

A second scenario could find the two Fronts facing early legislative elections if President Jacques Chirac manages to further rehabilitate himself and his mainstream rightist allies in the public eye. Recent policy conflicts within the ruling Socialist cabinet, led by Prime Minister Lionel Jospin, reflect the very tentative good will that exists between Jospin and his various left-leaning cabinet ministers. Chirac may profit from the discord within both the government and his far-right flank. A divided National Front will clearly strengthen the mainstream right by reducing the number of three-way second-round contests that so bedeviled them in the 1997 legislative contest. Early elections might thus hasten the collapse of one of the far-right movements.

A third and final scenario would involve a continuation of the strategy that Mégret advanced in the 1998 regional elections. If his party reaches the 5 percent threshold in the upcoming European Parliament elections, he could use his new-found strength to enter into strategic agreements with the more conservative members of the rightist mainstream. Charles Million, former president of the Rhône-Alpes regional council, has already indicated his willingness to work with Mégret. Others who may be willing to enter into such agreements with the FN–MN include former RPR Interior Minister Charles Pasqua and Picardie regional council president Charles Baur. In many respects, the mainstream right remains more divided than ever, and this may be advantageous to Mégret's new movement.

Although the French far right has become two separate parties, there is no reason to believe that the political agendas of these volatile movements will vanish. The hot-button issues that have attracted 30 percent of French citizens to vote for the Front at least once in the last decade remain central to the political debate, which the Front has been incredibly successful at shifting in their direction during the last fifteen years. Take immigration legislation, which has been taken up by both the Socialist and the Conservative governments. Clandestine immigration is more policed than ever before, work permits are more difficult to get, and family reunification proceeds at a slower pace than ever before. Other Front issues have also become increasingly central to the political discussion. Recent increases in juvenile delinquency have played directly into the hands of Front politicians, who have argued for more police and stricter law enforcement for more than a decade. Their emphasis on *insécurité* underlies the law-and-order arguments currently taking place in the Socialist-controlled cabinet. In addition, as details of the Amsterdam Treaty are examined in the countdown to the European elections, European integration continues to be central to French political life. The issues of immigration, *insécurité*, and Europe will remain at the heart of French politics for many years, regardless of the number of far-right parties.

A divided far right is not a new phenomenon; in fact, throughout history, the French far right has been balkanized into a multiplicity of *groupuscules*. Soon after the Front's creation, for instance, a more militant faction became dissatisfied with Le Pen's leadership and abandoned the Front to form the *Parti des Forces Nouvelles,* competing for members, votes, and resources throughout the party's early years. In the early 1990s, Jean-François Touzé, membership director of the National Front, also challenged Le Pen's authority and founded the *Alliance Populaire,* a competing party that faced off against the Front in the 1993 legislative elections. Neither of these movements remains electorally viable.

Whatever the outcome to the current crisis facing the French far right, it is important to remember that the recent division is not at all surprising. What *is* surprising is that, despite all historical precedents, the National Front remained united under the leadership of one individual for almost three decades. The pattern followed by the French far right before the ascension of Le Pen had been one of dissension, distrust, and animosity. Without a doubt, Jean-Marie Le Pen is the most successful far-right leader in the history of French politics. The National Front, the party he has led since its creation, amalgamated many competing currents of French far-right thinking into a cohesive whole for more than a quarter of a century. But, because he was unwilling to anoint a successor, he has finally led his party down the same path followed by the movements that antedate the National Front—the path of division and possible marginalization. While this most recent development in the factious history of the far right may not represent a positive step for the millions of French people who have voted for the National Front, it clearly represents an unanticipated "Christmas gift" for the French mainstream right in particular and for French democracy in general.

Elected and Party Positions Held by Respondents in 1988

PRIMARY LEADERSHIP POSITIONS

Vice president of the National Front

National secretary for the Front National de la Jeunesse

National secretary for research and argumentation

National secretary for health and social concerns

National secretary for the repatriated

National secretary for the preservation of national identity

Director of the circles

Director of the national banking circle

Director of the national European women's circle

Treasurer of the National Front

National secretary for the movement's press

National secretary for administration and finance

National secretary for the employment of French citizens

National secretary for education

National secretary for veterans

Director of the national veterans circle

Director of the national law and liberty circle

Secretary-general for Entreprises modernes et liberté

National secretary for categorical actions

National secretary for the commissions

Membership chairman

National secretary for cooperation

National secretary for the DOM-TOMS

National secretary for justice

Codirector of the European youth movement

Director of the national health circle

10 members of the Political Bureau

ANCILLARY LEADERSHIP POSITIONS

Chair of the Rhône-Alpes Federation

Chair of the Seine-et-Marne Federation

Chair of the 15th Arrondissement Paris

Foreign Policy Council

Legislative liaison for social concerns

Chair of the Nord Federation

Chair of the Paris Federation

Editor of *National Hebdo*

Vice president of the legislative group

President of the Liaison Office for Regional Councillors

President Support Committee for Le Pen's presidential campaign

Chair of the Yvelines Federation

Chair of 7th Arrondissment Paris

2 national speakers

Secretary-general of the legislative group

Director of Le Pen's presidential campaign

ELECTED POSITIONS

15 National Assembly deputies	7 regional councillors	2 European Parliament deputies
4 mayors	1 municipal councillor	

Sources: *Passeport pour la Victoire* 1987, and interviews with the National Front leadership.
Note: The primary leadership positions are listed in the order in which they appear in *Passeport pour la Victoire.*

Evolution of the National Front's Political Bureau

1988	1990	1997
Antony	Antony	Antony
Baeckeroot	*Baeckeroot*	*Baeckeroot*
Bachelot	——	——
		Bardet
		Bariller
	Bayvet	Bayvet
Bild	Bild	Bild
		Blot
		Bompard
		Brissaud
Chaboche	*Chaboche*	*Chaboche*
	de Chambrun	——
Collinot	Collinot	Collinot
		Descaves
		Dubois
Dufraisse	Dufraisse	——
Durand	Durand	——
Gaucher	Gaucher	——
	Gendron	——
Gollnisch	*Gollnisch*	*Gollnisch*
Holeindre	*Holeindre*	*Holeindre*
		Jaboulet-Vercherre
Jalkh	*Jalkh*	*Jalkh*
Jamet	Jamet	Jamet
		Lafay
	Lang	Lang
Le Chevallier	Le Chevallier	Le Chevallier
	Le Gallou	Le Gallou
	Lehideux	Lehideux
Le Pen	*Le Pen*	*Le Pen*
		Le Rachinel
		Maréchal
	Martinez, J.-C.	*Martinez, J.-C.*
		Martinez, S.
	Mégret	*Mégret*
		Milloz

Evolution of the National Front's Political Bureau—Continued

1988	1990	1997
	Monnerot	——
		Olivier
Piat	——	——
Reveau	*Reveau*	*Reveau*
		de Rostolan
Schenardi	*Schenardi*	*Schenardi*
	Sergent	——
		Sirgue
Stirbois, J.P.	——	——
	Stirbois, M.-F.	Stirbois, M.-F.
Tauran	*Tauran*	——
		Timmermans
		Varanne
		Vial
	Wagner	*Wagner*

Note: Names in boldface refer to a new promotion. Names in italics denote members of the Front's 1986–1988 National Assembly group. A long dash indicates members who have reneged or been removed.

Sources: Author's interviews; Birenbaum 1992b; National Front's home page.

Introduction

1 The National Front is a popular liberation force, a political instrument of regeneration, it is the path by which France can once again make its mark on history (Mégret 1997).

2 Catherine Mégret is the wife of Bruno Mégret, the National Front's secretary-general. Bruno Mégret was prevented from running in this by-election because of campaign irregularities in the 1995 election.

3 The Front leaders interviewed during the summer of 1988 continue to occupy the most influential positions within the party. For example, of the party's seven-member Executive Bureau, five were interviewed for this study; of the party's forty-member Political Bureau, fourteen were interviewed for this study.

4 The National Assembly shifted right in the 1986 elections, left in 1988, back to the right in 1993, and returned a large Socialist majority to power in 1997.

Chapter 1   The French Far Right: The Legacy of History

1 The National Front was legally created in 1972, but in reality it has inherited a number of tendencies that are much older.

2 All material quoted in this manner was collected by the author during face-to-face interviews with the political elite of the National Front. The interviews were conducted in and around Paris during May and June 1988. All interviews were tape-recorded and transcribed by the author. Respondents were assured their anonymity would be protected. The author is solely responsible for all translations.

3 In 1964, Le Pen created a "historical" record company, Société d'études et de relations publiques (SERP), that released recordings of nationalist songs and speeches. One of the records, *Songs of the German Revolution,* created a political firestorm during the heart of the Tixier-Vignancour presidential campaign. In August 1965, Le Pen was charged with being an apologist for war crimes, for which he eventually received a hefty fine and a suspended sentence.

4   Michel de Rostolan is currently a mamber of the Front's Political Bureau and the founding president of Cercle Renaissance, a social-political club that promotes a "renaissance of cultural, civic, moral and spiritual values." As a member of the Centre National des Indépendants, he joined the Front's Rassemblement National in anticipation of the 1986 legislative elections. Jean-François Touzé held a number of prominent positions within the Front, but defected in the early 1990s to create a competing rightist organization, Alliance Populaire. Touzé's decision to abandon the Front was prompted by his belief that it was becoming too accommodating in its rhetoric and relations with the mainstream right.

Chapter 2   The Far Right Reappears: The Creation of the National Front

1   In 1972, it was the perception of a political void, a political void on the right. . . .

2   The Front was to outlast the PFN, which eventually atrophied in the early 1980s only to reappear in 1988 and challenge the Front in both the 1988 and 1993 legislative elections.

3   Jean-Maurice Demarquet, a physician, was one of Le Pen's oldest comrades. As Lambert lay dying, Le Pen called his friend to examine him. Years later, in 1985, Lambert accused Le Pen of taking advantage of a dying man. He also confirmed the stories that Le Pen had tortured prisoners when he served in Algeria.

4   The National Front has consistently attracted as much as 15 percent of the vote in the two-round system used for electing deputies to the National Assembly, but it has been unable to ensure the elections of its candidates in the pivotal second-round contest.

5   To determine the relative and absolute importance of the various facilitators at the creation level of the political party life cycle, the Front's leaders were asked to rank, in order of importance, three responses from a list of eight. This list included four political facilitators, two institutional facilitators, and two additional factors considered to be of critical importance to the development of new political parties. The four political facilitators are leadership, behavior of the existing parties, party organization, and level of mass commitment. The two institutional factors are the electoral system and the focus of electoral competition. In addition to the aforementioned factors are the primary issue concerns of the Front's dominant cleavage structure and the media.

6   Le Pen refers to the system's dominant political parties: the Communists, Socialists, RPR, and the UDF as the "Gang of Four."

Chapter 3   Initial Success: Election Victories in 1984 and 1986

1   The problem isn't the creation, but the development.

2   In late 1989, Marie-France Stirbois, widow of Jean-Pierre Stirbois, was elected
    to the National Assembly in a by-election in Dreux. With the defection of
    Yann Piat in 1988, Marie-France Stirbois became the Front's only deputy in
    the National Assembly, where she represented the Front in the legislature
    until her narrow defeat in the 1993 legislative elections. Given the National
    Front's profound gender gap, it is ironic to note that the party's last two
    duly elected National Assembly deputies have both been women.

3   For an excellent account of the Dreux elections, see Gaspard 1995.

4   The abstention rate of 42.78 percent for the 1984 European elections illus-
    trates the relative importance the French attach to these elections. This was
    the highest abstention rate for national elections in the history of the Fifth
    Republic (Cole and Campbell 1989).

5   In all but one of the Fifth Republic's legislative elections, the two-round,
    single-member district system has been used. This type of electoral frame-
    work discriminates against minor political parties, thereby leading voters to
    cast a meaningful vote (*un vote utile*) in the first round of balloting. Euro-
    pean Parliament elections, because they use a proportional representation
    framework, render the vote utile phenomenon irrelevant.

6   In European Parliament elections, regional council elections, certain mu-
    nicipal contests, and the 1986 legislative elections, the Front has success-
    fully gained representation in the respective legislative bodies. All of these
    elections share a common feature: they use proportional representation. In
    all other National Assembly elections (save 1986) and cantonal elections,
    the Front continues to be underrepresented relative to its share of the popu-
    lar vote. Clearly, the evidence indicates that a marginal party such as the
    National Front will perform more successfully under proportional represen-
    tation frameworks.

Chapter 4   Legislative Losses and Beyond

1   The National Front must anchor itself in local politics.

2   The National Front candidates were, respectively, Jean Roussel, André Iso-
    ardo, Gabriel Domenech, Pascal Arrighi, Jean-Marie Le Pen, Ronald Per-
    domo, Bruno Mégret, Jean-Pierre Stirbois, and Yann Piat.

3   *Four* is the French word for "oven"; *crématoire* is obviously "crematory." The
    pun is not only offensive but rather senseless. Some argue that Le Pen pur-
    posely attacked a Jewish minister to bait the media and infuriate his critics
    in order to get himself and his party back into the media limelight. In late
    1997, Le Pen reopened the controversy about his flawed interpretation of

World War II history when, during a trip to Germany, he reiterated his belief that the Nazi death camps were only a historical "detail." The German authorities responded quickly by saying they were considering filing charges against Le Pen.

4 Marie-France Stirbois, widow of the revered former party secretary-general Jean-Pierre Stirbois, was elected to the National Assembly in 1989 in a by-election in Dreux. With the defection of Yann Piat, Mme Stirbois became the Front's sole representative at the national level.

5 Respectively: Majority for Another Europe, Another Policy, and Hunt-Fish.

6 In the spring of 1998, Le Pen was found guilty of assault and stripped of his civil rights. The case is currently under appeal as Le Pen awaits a final decision on his eligibility for the upcoming European Parliament elections.

7 In February 1998, the Constitutional Council invalidated Le Chevallier's election to the National Assembly because of campaign finance irregularities. The decision served to mobilize the Front's supporters and lent credence to the argument that the Front was being politically martyred by the French political class. Prior to the by-election, Le Chevallier unilaterally named his replacement on the Front's ticket: his wife Cendrine Le Chevallier, a longtime activist in her own right. Although she emerged as the top vote getter after the first round, she eventually lost the second round ballot by thirty-three votes. Thus, the Front which represents 15 percent of the voting public was once again denied access to the National Assembly.

Chapter 5   The Political Agenda of the National Front

1 For centuries, France, Europe, and Christianity fought back the Muslim invasion.

2 This slogan first appeared in the Front's campaign literature in 1978, when it read, "One million unemployed, that's one million immigrants too many." As unemployment increased, the slogan was revised, first to 2 million and then to its current form at 3 million. This slogan echoes a theme from the Nazi era: "Five hundred thousand unemployed, four hundred thousand Jews, the solution is simple" (Gourevitch 1997, 149).

3 Law-and-order issues are an important element in the Front's political agenda, and crime statistics underscore the party's prescient ability to exploit issues left unexploited by other political parties: "Between 1972 and 1985, for example, the total number of felonies and misdemeanors have increased by 133 percent; homicides by 73 percent, violent robberies by 328 percent, and burglaries by 238 percent" (Le Gall 1994, 122).

4 Stirbois was actually borrowing from an earlier work by Mégret. The following compares the two original passages, Stirbois's in 1988 and Mégret's in 1986.

Imaginer pour la France un avenir solitaire est désormais impossible. Pour éviter la dépendance et survivre, pour retrouver les valeurs communes qui ont fait la civilisation et la puissance de notre continent, nous ne pouvons nous dérober à l'impérieuse nécessité de ce temps: lier notre sort à l'Europe et être lemoteur de son devenir. (Stirbois 1988, 156)

Imaginer à la France un avenir solitaire est désormais impossible. Pour éviter la dépendance et survivre, nous ne pouvons nous dérober à l'impérieuse nécessiteé de ce temps: lier notre sort à l'Europe et penser en termes de continent. (Mégret 1986, 126)

5 Michel de Rostolan actually served as the French coordinator of Ronald Reagan's 1988 reelection bid.

Chapter 6 The Leadership and Organization of the National Front

1 It is really disparate, the revolutionary right.
2 Both spouses being actively engaged in the party's operations is a common situation for Front activists. For example, we have already mentioned the work of Jean-Pierre and Marie-France Stirbois in the town of Dreux. Christian Baeckeroot, former National Assembly deputy and Political Bureau member, is joined in his political activities by his wife, Myriam, who currently serves on the Île-de-France regional council and is a member of the party's Central Committee. Cendrine and Jean-Marie Le Chevallier represent another prominent political couple in the Front's leadership hierarchy; Jean-Marie served for many years as the director of Le Pen's office, a sort of chief of staff, and his wife has been just as active in the party's operations at the local level. Martine Lehideux and her late husband, André Dufraisse, charter members both, held a series of important positions within the party. And, as already noted, Catherine Mégret became her husband's surrogate for the mayoral election in Vitrolles.
3 Interestingly, Gollnisch and Mégret are each married to women who are not typically French. Mme Mégret is the granddaughter of Russian Jewish immigrants and Mme Gollnisch is Japanese by birth.
4 Although elected in 1986 to the National Assembly under the Front's Rassemblement National banner, Mégret did not actually join the party until 1987.
5 Mégret's major works include *Demain le Chêne,* which served as the manifesto for the Republican Action Committees. He has also published *L'Impératif du renouveau* and *La Flamme.*
6 Officially, Yann Piat was "excluded" from the party, but in her book she makes it perfectly clear that she chose to defy the party's leaders on a number of important points and in fact forced their hands.
7 This claim can be found on the National Front's web page.

Chapter 7 Voting for the National Front

1 All levels of society are voting for the National Front.
2 In another demonstration of his verbal acuity, Jean-Marie Le Pen publicly derided Bruno Mégret as the "maire-consort" of Vitrolles. Many viewed this comment as Le Pen's way of indicating that he was not yet ready to step aside for Mégret.
3 It can be argued without any difficulty that the Front has deserved its negative publicity. Le Pen's infamous "detail" remark and his pointless pun, "Durrafour-crématoire," are only two examples in a long list enumerating the party's ability to create negative media firestorms. But the essential point is that, whether deserved or not, the preponderance of the media's Front coverage has been decidedly negative. Given this fact, it is again all the more surprising that the party continues to grow.
4 All French political parties compulsively overestimate their membership. Estimates for the French National Front range from 40,000 (Camus 1992) to 50,000 (Simmons 1996). Taking into consideration the Front's increasing strength in the 1995 presidential and 1997 legislative elections, the party's actual membership most likely hovers between 70,000 and 80,000 members.
5 See the National Front's web page.
6 Ibid.

Chapter 8 The Far Right in Comparative Perspective

1 The extreme right, what one calls the extreme right, has always existed.
2 In 1991, Bruno Mégret released a fifty-item platform that served as the cornerstone of the Front's immigration proposals.
3 Fini received 46.9 percent in the second round; his party comrade, Alessandra Mussolini, the granddaughter of il Duce, received 44.4 percent of the vote in Naples.
4 For example, the Norwegian Progress Party led by Carl Igar Hagen received 15 percent of the vote in the 1997 legislative elections. This dramatic increase in its share of the vote allowed Hagen's group to seat twenty-five representatives in the national legislature. The Progress Party is now the second strongest political party in the country.
5 Kitschelt's analysis of the Front's economic agenda is time-bound and thus fails to consider the increasingly nationalistic, protectionist, and anti-EU rhetoric that has dominated the Front's political campaigns since the Maastricht treaty referendum in 1992. In short, over the past five years, the Front has become less supportive of free market ideals.
6 The episode between Le Pen and Socialist Annette Peulvast-Bergeal clearly crossed the line of civil behavior. After a series of appeals, Le Pen was ulti-

mately stripped of his electoral positions in the European Parliament and the PACA regional council. He was also barred from seeking electoral office for a year for his attack on Peulvast-Bergeal. Geoffrey Harris maintains that "FN activists were directly implicated in incendiary attacks on a cinema in Paris which was showing the controversial Martin Scorsese film *The Last Temptation of Christ*." Romain Marie, a Front European Parliament deputy and a member of the Political Bureau, was said to be the inspiration for the attack (Harris 1994, 101). Marie's fundamentalist Catholicism is, as we have demonstrated, an integral element in the development of French far right thought, but in the contemporary world of the National Front it is decidedly a minor influence and one that is actually declining in importance.

Conclusion

1 I believe that the National Front is, at this moment, perfectly situated to enlarge its audience.

2 Pierrette Le Pen, Jean-Marie's ex-wife and mother of his three adult daughters, has publicly denounced her ex-husband in a variety of media outlets. Her most infamous attack on Le Pen occurred when she posed seminude in the pages of the French edition of *Playboy*.

3 Pascal Arrighi was nominated for vice president of the National Assembly and actually received two-thirds of his support from non–National Front deputies. It was a secret ballot.

4 SIDA is the French acronym for AIDS. Bachelot, a doctor, became rather notorious for his extremist views about the treatment of AIDS.

5 French citizens vote under a complex variety of electoral formats. In parliamentary elections, a minor party's political fortunes are dependent on its ability to strike reciprocal withdrawal agreements with its larger like-minded competition. In recent years, on the left, this has ensured the survival of the French Communist Party and paved the way for the French Greens to enter the National Assembly in 1997. The mainstream right, on the other hand, has refused such accommodations with the Front.

6 Séguin's attempt to change the name of Chirac's post-Gaullist creation met with a lukewarm reception at the party's Paris conference in February 1998. The new name, Rally for France, was endorsed by 49.9 percent of the delegates attending the conference; with the vote so close, it was decided to stick with Chirac's Rally for the Republic moniker. Although this was viewed as a win for Chirac, the fact that so many of the party faithful want to break with the past is an important sign of his diminishing influence.

7 For all Chirac's apparent distaste for the rhetoric of Le Pen and the Front, he has not been above incorporating rather hateful speech into his own public discourse. In what remains the most infamous example of this behavior,

Chirac in 1991 expressed sympathy for the average French worker, who has to deal with the "noise" and "smell" created by immigrants.

8   In a face-to-face runoff with his Socialist opponent (the center right having been eliminated in the first round), Freulet received 53.6 percent of the vote.

Afterword

1   The old man isn't dead.

2   He's like a diva who is in the process of screwing up her exit.

3   The Front has developed a sort of tradition when it comes to wives substituting for their husbands. Marie-France Stirbois was elected to the National Assembly after her husband's death in a car accident. More recently, Cathérine Mégret and Cendrine Le Chevallier replaced their husbands on the ballots when they were ruled electorally ineligible. In his own defense, Le Pen argued that he was simply following in the tradition of his colleagues, most notably Bruno Mégret, who Le Pen has called the *maire-consort* of Vitrolles.

4   The top ten voters at the 1997 party congress were Bruno Mégret (3,758), Jean-Yves Le Gallou (3,439), Bruno Gollnisch (3,398), Roger Holiendre (3,381), Franck Timmermans (3,362), Jacques Bompard (3,328), Yvan Blot (3,316), Marie-France Stirbois (3,288), Carl Lang (3,287), Damien Bariller (3,166). Interestingly, Le Pen's daughter Marine was not elected to the Central Committee, but Le Pen used his power as president to find her a slot on the committee. Le Gallou, Timmermans, Blot, and Bariller are close allies of Mégret.

All translations are by the author, unless otherwise noted.

Aberbach, Joel D., Robert D. Putnam, and Bert A. Rockman. 1981. *Bureaucrats and Politicians in Western Democracies.* Cambridge, MA: Harvard University Press.

Alquier, François Fonvielle. 1984. *Une France poujadiste?* Paris: Editions Universitaires.

L'Alternative Nationale: 300 Mesures pour la renaissance de la France. 1993. National Front Publication. Paris: Editions Nationales.

Anderson, Malcolm. 1974. *Conservative Politics in France.* London: Allen and Unwin.

Azéma, Jean-Pierre. 1993. "Vichy." In *Histoire de l'extrême droite en France,* ed. Michel Winock. 191–214. Paris: Editions du Seuil.

Bachelot, François. 1986. *Ne dites pas à ma mère que je suis chez Le Pen elle me croit au RPR.* Paris: Editions Albatros.

Barbier, Christophe, and Romain Rosso. 1997. "FN: La droite piégée." *L'Express* 2–8 October 1997, p. 34.

Bardèche, Maurice. 1970. "Le fascisme dans le monde. Progrès et chances du fascisme. Le redressement national en Europe. Comment passer au fascisme. Fascisme et pseudo-fascisme." *Défense de l'Occident* (October–November): 87. Quoted in René Chiroux, *L'Extrême-droite sous la V e République.* 1974. Paris: Librairie Générale de Droit et de Jurisprudence.

Bartolini, Stefano. 1984. "Institutional Constraints and Party Competition in the French Party System." In *Party Politics in Contemporary Western Europe,* ed. Stefano Bartolini and Peter Mair. 103–27. London: Frank Cass and Company Limited.

Begeron, Francis, and Philippe Vilgier. 1985. *De Le Pen à Le Pen.* Bouère, France: Editions Dominique Martin Morin.

Betz, Hans-Georg. 1994. *Radical Right-Wing Populism in Western Europe.* New York: St Martin's Press.

Birenbaum, Guy. 1992a. "Le Front national à l'Assemblée (1986–1988)." *Politix* 20: 99–118.

————. 1992b. *Le Front national en politique*. Paris: Balland.

————. 1995. "Le Front national devant l'élection présidentielle." In *Le Vote de crise*, ed. Pascal Perrineau and Colette Ysmal. 141–56. Paris: Département d'Etudes Politique du Figaro/Presses de la Fondation Nationale des Sciences Politiques.

Birenbaum, Guy, and Bastien François. 1989. "Unité et diversité des dirigeants frontistes." In *Le Front National à découvert*, ed. Nonna Mayer and Pascal Perrineau. 83–106. Paris: Presses de la Fondation Nationale des Sciences Politiques.

Blondel, Jacqueline, and Bernard Lacroix. 1989. "Pourquoi votent-ils Front national?" In *Le Front national à découvert*, ed. Nonna Meyer and Pascal Perrineau. 150–72. Paris: Presses de la Fondation Nationale des Sciences Politiques.

Bréchon, Pierre. 1995. *La France aux urnes: Cinquante ans d'histoire électorale*. Paris: La Documentation Française.

Bréchon, Pierre, and Subrata Kumar Mitra. 1992. "The National Front in France: The Emergence of an Extreme Right Protest Movement.' *Comparative Politics* 25: 63–82.

Buffotot, Patrice. 1993. "Le Référendum sur l'union Européenne." *Modern & Contemporary France* NS1, 3: 277–87.

Bull, Martin, and James L. Newell. 1995. "Italy Changes Course? The 1994 Elections and the Victory of the Right." *Parliamentary Affairs* 48: 77–99.

Buzzi, Paul. 1991. Le Front national entre national populisme et extrêmisme de droite. *Regards sur l'actualité*, no. 169 (March): 31–43.

Camus, Jean-Yves. 1992. "Political Cultures within the Front National: The Emergence of a Counter-Ideology on the French Far Right." *Patterns of Prejudice* 26: 5–16.

Camus, Jean-Yves, and René Monzat. 1992. *Les Droites nationales et radicales en France*. Lyon: Presses Universitaires de Lyon.

Cayrol, Roland, and Jérôme Jaffré. 1980. "Party Linkages in France: Socialists, Leaders, Followers and Voters." In *Political Parties and Linkage*, ed. Kay Lawson. Cambridge, UK: Yale University Press.

Chatain, Jean. 1987. *Les Affaires de M. Le Pen*. Paris: Editions Messidor.

Charlot, Jean. 1992. The Political Parties and the Party System in France. Paris: Direction de la Presse, de l'Information et de la Communication, Ministère des Affaires Etrangères.

Charlot, Monica. 1986. "L'émergence du Front national." *Revue française de science politique* 36: 30–45.

Chebel d'Appollonia, Ariane. 1988. *L'extrême-droite en France: De Maurras à Le Pen*. Brussels: Editions Complexe.

Chiroux, René. 1974. *L'Extrême-droite sous la Ve République*. Paris: Librairie Générale de Droit et de Jurisprudence.

Chombart de Lauwe, Marie-José. 1987. *Vigilance: Vieilles traditions extrémistes et Droites Nouvelles*. Paris: Etudes et Documentation Internationales.

Cole, Alistair, and Peter Campbell. 1989. *French Electoral Systems and Elections since 1789*. Brookfield, VT: Gower.

Converse, P. E., and Dupeux, G. 1962. "Politicization of the Electorate in France and the United States." *Public Opinion Quarterly* 26: 1–23.

Criddle, Byron. 1987. "Parties in a Presidential System." In *Political Parties, Electoral Change and Structural Response*, ed. Alan Ware. 136–157. New York: Oxford University Press.

————. 1992. "Electoral Systems in France." *Parliamentary Affairs*. 45: 108–16.

Crouch, Gregory. 1996. "Three to Watch: Populists of the Hard Right." *The New York Times Magazine*, 21 April: 41–43.

Dalton, Russell J. 1984. "Patterns of Stability." In *Electoral Change in Advanced Industrial Democracies*, ed. Russell Dalton et al. 399–401. Princeton, NJ: Princeton University Press.

————. 1988. *Citizen Politics in Western Democracies*. Chatham, NJ: Chatham House Publishers.

De Rostolan, Michel. 1987. *Lettre ouverte à mon peuple qui meurt*. Paris: Editions Fernand Lanore.

Duhamel, Alain. 1993. *Les Peurs françaises*. Paris: Gallimard.

Dumont, Serge. 1983. *Les brigades noires*. Berchem, Belgium: Editions EPO.

Dumont, Serge, Joseph Lorien, and Karl Criton. 1985. *Le système Le Pen*. Brussels: Editions EPO.

Dupoirier, Élisabeth. 1996. "Popularités 1988–1995." In *SOFRES L'état de l'opinion 1996*, ed. Olivier Duhamel and Jérôme Jaffré. 49–76. Paris: Editions du Seuil.

Duprat, François. 1972. *Les mouvements d'extrême-droite en France depuis 1944*. Paris: Les Editions Albatros.

Eatwell, Roger. 1996. *Fascism: A History*. New York: Penguin Books.

Ebata, Michi. 1997. "The Internationalization of the Extreme Right." In *The Extreme Right: Freedom and Security at Risk*, ed. Aurel Braun and Stephen Scheinberg. 220–49. Boulder, CO: Westview Press.

Ehrmann, Henry W., and Martin A. Schain. 1992. *Politics in France*, 5th ed. New York: HarperCollins.

Fysh, Peter, and Jim Wolfreys. 1992. "Le Pen, the National Front and the Extreme Right in France." *Parliamentary Affairs* 45: 309–26.

Gaspard, Françoise. 1995. *A Small City in France*. Translated by Arthur Goldhammer. Cambridge, MA: Harvard University Press.

Gaxie, Daniel. 1977. "Economie des partis et rétributions du militantisme." *Revue française de science politique*.

Gourevitch, Philip. 1997. "The Unthinkable: How Far Will Jean-Marie Le Pen's National Front Movement Go?" *The New Yorker*, 28 April and 5 May: 110–49.

Grunberg, Gérard. 1995. "Les élections européennes." In *SOFRES L'état de l'opin-*

ion 1995, ed. Olivier Duhamel and Jérôme Jaffré. 81–100. Paris: Editions du Seuil.

Harmel, Robert. 1985. "On the Study of New Parties." *International Political Science Review* 6: 403–18.

Harmel, Robert, and John D. Robertson. 1985. "Formation and Success of New Parties." *International Political Science Review* 6: 501–23.

Harris, Geoffrey. 1994. *The Dark Side of Europe.* Edinburgh: Edinburgh University Press.

Hauss, Charles, and David Rayside. 1978. "The Development of New Parties in Western Democracies since 1945." In *Political Parties: Development and Decay,* ed. Louis Maisel and Joseph Cooper. 31–57. Beverly Hills, CA: Sage Publications.

Hoffmann, Stanley. 1956. *Le Mouvement poujade.* Paris: Librarie Armand Colin.

Holiendre, Roger. 1987. *Aux Larmes, citoyens!* Paris: Editions Robert Laffont.

Husbands, Christopher T. 1981. "Contemporary Right-Wing Extremism in Western European Democracies: A Review Article." *European Journal of Political Research* 9: 75–99.

———. 1992. "The Other Face of 1992: The Extreme-Right Explosion in Western Europe." *Parliamentary Affairs* 45: 267–84.

Ignazi, Piero. 1989. "Un Nouvel acteur politique." In *Le Front national à découvert,* ed. Nonna Meyer and Pascal Perrineau. 63–80. Paris: Presses de la Fondation Nationale des Sciences Politiques.

———. 1996. "From Neo-Fascists to Post-Fascists? The Transformation of the MSI into the AN." *West European Politics* 19: 693–714.

———. 1997. "The Extreme Right in Europe: A Survey." In *The Revival of Right-Wing Extremism in the Nineties,* ed. Peter H. Merkl and Leonard Weinberg. 47–64. London: Frank Cass & Co.

Ignazi, Piero, and Colette Ysmal. 1992. "New and Old Extreme Right Parties: The French National Front and the Italian Movimento Sociale." *European Journal of Political Science* 22: 101–21.

Inglehart, Ronald. 1977. *The Silent Revolution: Changing Values and Political Styles among Western Publics.* Princeton, NJ: Princeton University Press.

Jackman, Robert W., and Karin Volpert. 1996. "Conditions Favouring Parties of the Extreme Right in Western Europe." *British Journal of Political Science* 26: 501–21.

Jaffré, Jérôme. 1985. "Les Fantassins de l'extrême droite." In *SOFRES Opinion Publique,* ed. Olivier Duhamel, Elisabeth Dupoirier, and Jérôme Jaffré, 186–192. Paris: Gallimard.

———. 1986. "Les élections législatives du 16 mars 1986." *Pouvoirs* 38: 145–57.

———. 1994. "Législatives 93: L'alternance inéluctable." In *SOFRES L'état de l'opinion 1994,* ed. Olivier Duhamel and Jérôme Jaffré. 141–58. Paris: Editions du Seuil.

———. 1995. "La victoire de Jacques Chirac et la transformation des clivages politiques." In *Le Vote de crise,* ed. Pascal Perrineau and Colette Ysmal. 159–78. Paris: Département d'Etudes Politique du Figaro/Presses de la Fondation Nationale des Sciences Politiques.

———. 1996. "Les changements de la France électorale." In SOFRES *L'état de l'opinion 1996,* ed. Olivier Duhamel et al. 129–50. Paris: Editions du Seuil.

———. 1997. "La décision électorale au second tour: Un scrutin très serré." *Revue française de science politique* 47: 426–37.

Janda, Kenneth, and Gillies, Robin. 1980. "Continuity and Change: 1950–1978." In *Political Parties: A Cross-National Survey,* ed. Kenneth Janda. 162–76. New York: The Free Press.

Jenkins, J. Craig. 1983. "Resource Mobilization Theory and the Study of Social Movements." *Annual Review of Sociology* 9: 527–53.

Kitschelt, Herbert. 1997. *The Radical Right in Western Europe: A Comparative Analysis.* Ann Arbor: University of Michigan Press.

Knapp, Andrew. 1987. "Proportional but Bipolar: France's Electoral System in 1986." *West European Politics* 10: 89–114.

Koopmans, Ruud. 1996. "Explaining the Rise of Racist and Extreme Right Violence in Western Europe: Grievances or Opportunities?" *European Journal of Political Research* 30: 185–216.

Laqueur, Walter. 1996. *Fascism: Past, Present, Future.* New York: Oxford University Press.

Laurent, Annie, and Christian-Marie Wallon-Leducq. 1992. "La double inconstance: Partis, électeurs et double vote." In *Le Vote éclaté,* ed. Philippe Habert et al. 231–46.

Lawson, Kay. 1978. "Constitutional Change and Party Development in France, Nigeria, and the United States." In *Political Parties: Development and Decay,* ed. Louis Maisel and Joseph Cooper. 145–77. Beverly Hills, CA: Sage Publication.

Le Bras, Hervé. 1986. *Les Trois France.* Paris: Editions Odile Jacob.

Lee, Martin A. 1997. *The Beast Reawakens.* Boston: Little, Brown and Company.

Le Gall, Gérard. 1989. "Un triple avertissement: Pour l'Europe, la démocratie et les socialistes." *Revue Politique et Parlementaire* 942: 11–20.

———. 1994. "Les Français et la sécurité." In SOFRES *L'état de l'opinion 1994,* ed. Olivier Duhamel and Jérôme Jaffré. 117–40. Paris: Editions du Seuil.

Le Gallou, Jean-Yves. 1984. *Les Racines du futur: Demain la France.* Paris: Editions Albatros.

Le Pen, Jean-Marie. 1984. *Les Français d'abord.* Paris: Editions Carrere-Michel Lafon.

———. 1985. *Pour la France: Programme du Front national.* Paris: Editions Albatros.

Levite, Ariel, and Sidney Tarrow. 1983. "The Legitimation of Excluded Parties in Dominant Party Systems." *Comparative Politics* 6: 295-327.

Lewis-Beck, Michael. 1984. "France: The Stalled Electorate." In *Electoral Change in Advanced Democracies,* ed. Russell Dalton et al. 425-46. Princeton, NJ: Princeton University Press.

Lipset, Seymour Martin, and Stein Rokkan. 1967. "Cleavage Structures, Party Systems and Voter Alignments." In *Party Systems and Voter Alignments,* ed. Seymour Martin Lipset and Stein Rokkan. 1-67. New York: The Free Press.

Maclean, Mairi. 1993. "Dirty Dealing: Business and Scandal in Contemporary France." *Modern & Contemporary France,* NS1 (2): 161-70.

Marcus, Jonathan. 1995. *The National Front and French Politics.* New York: New York University Press.

Marvick, Dwaine. 1976. "Continuities in Recruitment Theory and Research: Toward a New Model." In *Elite Recruitment in Democratic Politics,* ed. Heinz Eulau and Moshe Czudnowski. 29-44. New York: Sage.

Matas, David. "The Extreme Right in the United Kingdom and France." In *The Extreme Right: Freedom and Security at Risk,* ed. Aurel Braun and Stephen Scheinberg. 84-106. Boulder, CO: Westview Press.

Mayer, Nonna. 1987. "De Passy à Barbès: Deux visages du vote Le Pen à Paris." *Revue Française de Science Politique* 37: 891-906.

———. 1997. "Du vote lepéniste au vote frontiste." *Revue Française de Science Politique* 47: 438-53.

Mayer, Nonna and Pascal Perrineau, ed. 1989. Le Front national à découvert. Paris: Presses de la Fondation Nationale des Sciences Politiques.

Mayer, Nonna, and Pascal Perrineau. 1992. "Why Do They Vote for Le Pen?" *European Journal of Political Research* 22: 115-35.

———. 1993. "La puissance et le rejet ou le lepénisme dans l'opinion." In SOFRES *L'état de l'opinion 1993,* ed. Olivier Duhamel and Jérôme Jaffré. 63-78. Paris: Editions du Seuil.

Mayer, Nonna, and Henri Rey. 1993. "Avancée électorale, isolement politique du Front national." *Revue Politique et Parlementaire* 964: 42-48.

Mazzella, Frank. 1989. "Le Pen's Movement and the French Presidential-Legislative Elections of 1988." Paper presented at the 1989 Southern Political Science Association.

McCarthy, John D., and Mayer N. Zald. 1977. "Resource Mobilization and Social Movements: A Partial Theory." *American Review of Sociology* 82: 1212-41.

McMillan, James F. 1985. *Dreyfus to de Gaulle: Politics and Society in France, 1898-1969.* London: Edward Arnold.

Mégret, Bruno. 1986. *L'Impératif du renouveau.* Paris: Albatros.

———. 1990. *La Flamme: Les voies de la renaissance.* Paris: Editions Robert Laffont.

———. 1997. *L'Alternative nationale.* Text from National Front's home page on the World Wide Web.

Milza, Pierre. 1987. *Fascisme français: Passé et présent.* Paris: Flammarion.

Minkenberg, Michael. 1997. "The New Right in France and Germany: Nouvelle droite, Neue Rechte, and the New Right Radical Parties." In *The Revival of Right-Wing Extremism in the Nineties,* ed. Peter H. Merkl and Leonard Weinberg. 65–90. London: Frank Cass & Co.

Mitra, Subra. 1988. "The National Front in France: A Single-Issue Movement?" *West European Politics* 11: 48–64.

Nolte, Ernst. 1965. *Three Faces of Fascism.* New York: Holt, Rinehart and Winston.

Passeport pour la Victoire. 1988. Campaign document for the 1988 Le Pen presidential campaign.

Paxton, Robert O. 1972. *Vichy France: Old Guard and New Order, 1940–1944.* New York: Columbia University Press.

Pederson, Mogens. 1982. "Towards a New Typology of Party Lifespans and Minor Parties." *Scandinavian Political Studies* 5: 1–16.

Percheron, Annick. 1987. *La Région, An 1.* Paris: Presse Universitaire de France.

Perrineau, Pascal. 1985. "Le Front National: Un électoral autoritaire." *Revue Politique et Parlementaire* 918: 24–31.

———. 1989. "Les étapes d'une implantation électorale (1972–1988)." In *Le Front national à découvert,* ed. Nonna Meyer and Pascal Perrineau. 37–62. Paris: Presses de la Fondation Nationale des Sciences Politiques.

———. 1993a. "Le Front national: 1972–1992." In *Histoire de l'extrême droite en France,* ed. Michel Winock. 243–98. Paris: Editions du Seuil.

———. 1993b. "Le Front national, la force solitaire." In *Le Vote sanction,* ed. Philippe Habert, Pascal Perrineau, and Colette Ysmal. 137–60. Paris: Département d'Etudes Politique du Figaro/Presses de la Fondation Nationale des Sciences Politiques.

———. 1995. "La dynamique du vote Le Pen: le poids du gaucho-lepénisme." In *Le Vote de crise,* ed. Pascal Perrineau and Colette Ysmal. 243–62. Paris: Département d'Etudes Politique du Figaro/Presses de la Fondation Nationale des Sciences Politiques.

Perrineau, Pascal, and Colette Ysmal, eds. 1995. *Le Vote de crise.* Paris: Département d'Etudes Politique du Figaro/Presses de la Fondation Nationale des Sciences Politiques.

Petermann, Simon. 1986. "Le phénomène Le Pen en France." *Res Publica* 28: 75–93.

Petitfils, Jean-Christian. 1983. *L'extrême-droite en France.* Paris: Presses Universitaires de France.

Piat, Yann. 1991. *Seule, tout en haut à droite.* Paris: Editions Fixot.

Plenel, Edwy. 1984. "Les droites et les dynamises sociaux." *Nouvelle revue socialiste* 49–58.

Plenel, Edwy, and Alain Rollat. 1984. *L'Effet Le Pen.* Paris: LaDécouverte/Le-Monde.

Ponceyri, Robert. 1997. "L'étrange défaite de la droite." *Revue Politique et Parlementaire* 989: 26–48.

Pons, Gregory. 1977. *Les Rats Noirs.* Jean-Claude Simoën.

Pour la France. 1985. Paris: Editions Albatros.

Pour un Ordre nouveau. 1973. Campaign document.

Pour une vraie économie libérale. [1988?]. National Front publication.

Putnam, Robert. 1976. *The Comparative Study of Political Elites.* Englewood Cliffs, NJ: Prentice-Hall.

Reif, Karlhienz. 1985. *Ten European Elections.* Brookfield, VT: Gower Publishing Company.

Rémond, René. 1982. *Les droites en France.* Paris: Editions Aubier Montaigne.

———. 1993. *La Politique n'est plus ce qu'elle était.* Paris: Calmann-Lévy.

Revue Française de Science Politique. 1997. Appendix 47: 462–68.

Rollat, Alain. 1985. *Les hommes de l'extrême droite.* Paris: Editions Calmann-Lévy.

Rose, Richard, and Thomas T. Mackie. 1988. "Do Parties Persist or Fail? The Big Trade-Off Facing Organizations." In *When Parties Fail: Emerging Alternative Organizations,* ed. Kay Lawson and Peter Merkl. 533–58. Princeton, NJ: Princeton University Press.

Roussel, Eric. 1985. *Le cas Le Pen.* Paris: J. Clattès.

Safran, William. 1993. "The National Front in France: From Lunatic Fringe to Limited Respectability." In *Encounters with the Contemporary Radical Right,* ed. Peter H. Merkl and Leonard Weisberg. 19–49. Boulder, CO: Westview.

Schain, Martin. 1987. "The National Front and the Construction of Political Legitimacy." *West European Politics* 10: 229–52.

Schweisguth, Etienne. 1994. "L'Affaiblissement du clivage gauche-droite." In *L'Engagement Politique: Déclin ou mutation?,* ed. Pascal Perrineau. 215–38. Paris: Presses de la Fondation Nationale des Sciences Politiques.

Seligman, Lester. 1971. *Recruiting Political Elites.* New York: General Learning Press.

Seligman, Lester G., Michael R. King, and Chong Lim Kim. 1974. *Patterns of Recruitment.* Chicago: Rand McNally.

Shields, James G. 1995. "Le Pen and the Progression of the Far-Right Vote in France." *French Politics & Society* 13: 21–39.

Simmons, Harvey G. 1996. *The French National Front: The Extremist Challenge to Democracy.* Boulder, CO: Westview Press.

Smith, Anthony D. 1995. "The Dark Side of Nationalism: The Revival of Nationalism in Late Twentieth-Century Europe." In *The Far Right in Western &*

Eastern Europe, 2d ed., ed. Luciano Cheles, Ronnie Ferguson, and Michalina Vaughn. 13–19. Harlow, England: Longman.

Soucy, Robert. 1986. *French Fascism: The First Wave, 1924–1933.* New Haven, CT: Yale University Press.

Soudais, Michel. 1996. *Le Front national en face.* Paris: Flammarion.

Stirbois, Jean-Pierre. 1988. *Tonnerre de Dreux: L'Avenir nous appartient.* Paris: Editions National Hebdo.

Subileau, Françoise. 1996. "Le vote des Français à Maastricht: Le référendum comme procédure et l'Europe comme enjeu." *Modern & Contemporary France* NS4 (2): 145–60.

Szarka, Joseph. 1996. "The Winning of the 1995 French Presidential Election." *West European Politics* 19: 151–67.

Taggart, Paul. 1995. "New Populist Parties in Western Europe." *West European Politics* 18: 34–51.

Théolleyre, Jean-Marc. 1982. *Les Neo-nazis.* Paris: Messidor/Temps Actuels.

Tristan, Anne. 1987. *Au Front.* Paris: Gallimard.

Wagstaffe, Margaret, and George Moyser. 1987. "The Threatened Elite: Studying Leaders in an Urban Community." In *Research Methods for Elite Studies,* ed. George Moyser and Margaret Wagstaffe. 183–201. London: Allen and Unwin.

Weinberg, Leonard. 1997. "Conclusions." In *The Revival of Right-Wing Extremism in the Nineties,* ed. Peter H. Merkl and Leonard Weinberg. 271–82. London: Frank Cass & Co.

Weissberg, Robert. 1978. "Collective versus Dyadic Representation in Congress." *American Political Science Review* 72: 535–47.

Wieviorka, Michel. 1993. "Tendencies to Racism in Europe: Does France Represent a Unique Case, or Is It Representative of a Trend?" In *Racism and Migration in Western Europe,* ed. John Solomos and John Wrench. 55–66. Oxford: Berg Publishers.

Wilson, Frank L. 1994. *European Politics Today: The Democratic Experience,* 2d ed. Englewood Cliffs, NJ: Prentice Hall.

Wolfreys, Jim. 1993. "The Programme of the Front National." *Parliamentary Affairs* 46, no. 3: 415–29.

Ysmal, Colette. 1989a. *Les partis politiques sous la Ve République.* Paris: Editions Montchrestien.

———. 1989b. "Sociologie des Elites du FN (1979–1986)." In *Le Front National à Découvert,* ed. Nonna Mayer and Pascal Perrineau. 107–118. Paris: Presses de la Fondation Nationale des Sciences Politiques.

———. 1991. "Les cadres du Front national: Les habits neufs de l'extrême droite." In *L'état de l'opinion 1991,* ed. Oliver Duhamel and Jérôme Jaffré. 181–98. Paris: Edition du Seuil.

―――. 1994. "Transformations du militantisme et déclin des partis." In *L'Engagement politique: Déclin ou mutation?*, ed. Pascal Perrineau. 41–66. Paris: Presse de la Fondation National des Sciences Politiques.

―――. 1995. "La droite modérée sous la pression du Front national." *French Politics & Society* 13: 1–9.

Zelig, Yves M. 1985. *Retour du Front.* Paris: Bernard Barrault.

Action Française, 8, 11, 13–17, 19, 148
Algeria, 13, 21
Algerian War, 13, 21–25, 149–50
Alliance Populaire, 182
Alliance Républicaine pour la Liberté et le Progrès, 27, 150
Almirante, Giorgio, 193, 200
Antiparliamentarianism, 12, 18–20
Anti-Semitism, 13–14, 19–20, 28, 46, 89–90, 102, 221
Antony, Bernard, 164
Arrighi, Pascal, 64, 86, 90, 158, 216

Bachelot, François, 6, 64, 67, 90, 129, 158, 166, 216
Baeckeroot, Christian, 23, 27
Bardèche, Maurice, 57–58
Barre, Raymond, 70, 94
Bastien-Thiry, Jean-Marie, 25–26
Baur, Charles, 220
Bérégovoy, Pierre, 92
Berlusconi, Silvio, 200–201
Bild, Martial, 164, 167
Birenbaum, Guy, 7, 138
Bompard, Jacques, 121, 175
Briant, Yvon, 7, 64, 82, 158
Brigneau, François, 37, 41, 57

Catholicism and the French far right, 13–14, 18
Centre National des Indépendants, 153, 213

Cercle National des Combattants, 17, 161, 169
Cercle National des Femmes d'Europe, 161, 205
Ceyrac, Pierre, 86
Chaboche, Dominique, 159–60
Chapon, Jean-Luc, 219
Charzat, Michel, 60
Chauvierre, Bruno, 7, 82
Chevènement, Jean-Pierre, 96–97, 105
Chirac, Jacques, 3, 5, 58, 93, 219; 1995 Presidential Campaign and, 98–100; 1997 National Assembly elections and, 100–101, 103
Club de l'Horloge, 28, 163
Club du Panthéon, 27
Cohabitation, 80, 92
Comités d'Action Républicaine, 68, 163
Comite Tixier-Vignancour, 25–27, 33–34, 150
Communist Party, 3, 34–35, 47, 63, 67, 70, 74, 81, 95–96, 183
Corruption, 97–98, 189, 208–9
Cresson, Edith, 92–93
Croix de Feu, 13, 16–17

de Benoist, Alain, 27
de Chambrun, Charles, 64, 85
Defensive nationalism: defined, 204; reasons for, 204–8

de Gaulle, Charles, 28, 34; Algerian
  war and, 21–22, 24–25
de Macmahon, Marguerite, 152
Demarquet, Jean, 20, 42
de Rostolan, Michel, 6, 28, 64, 120
Descaves, Pierre, 64, 129, 220
Deutsche Volksunion, 199, 201
de Villiers, Philippe, 96–98
Dewinter, Filip, 197–98
Dien Bien Phu, 21
Dimitriadis, Chrysanthos, 192
Dreux: 1983 municipal elections, 3,
  60–61
Dreyfus, Captain Alfred, 13
Dubois, Jean-Michel, 168
Dufraisse, André, 161, 166, 168
Duhamel, Alain, 1
Dumas, Roland, 94
Duprat, François, 29, 37, 44, 57
Durafour, Michel, 89–90, 216

Ecole Normale d'Administration, 153
Elections: European 1979, 44; European 1984, 3, 59, 61–64; European
  1989, 4, 90–92; European 1994,
  94–97; Legislative 1956, 20–21;
  Legislative 1973, 39; Legislative
  1978, 43–44; Legislative 1986, 3,
  64–68; Legislative 1988, 3–4, 80–
  89; Legislative 1993, 4, 92–95;
  Legislative 1997, 5, 100–106, 217–
  19; Municipal 1971, 36; Municipal
  1983, 60; Municipal 1989, 4; Municipal 1995, 4–5, 100; Presidential
  1974, 43; Presidential 1981, 3, 44;
  Presidential 1988, 3, 68–71, 81;
  Presidential 1995, 4, 97–100; Regional 1986, 92; Regional 1992, 4,
  92–93, 140; Regional 1998, 221–22
Electoral system: influence on Front's
  success, 71–73; 1986 switch to proportional representation, 64–65;

two round system, 84–85, 94–95,
  111–12
Electorate, National Front: geographic concentration of, 84–89,
  125, 176–81; growth of, 183–85;
  loyalty of, 63, 181–83; sociodemo-
  graphics of, 184–92, 209; vote
  transfers of, 100
Entreprise Moderne et Libertés,
  168–69
Europe-Action, 26, 28
European Parliament, 4, 193
European Union: declining public
  support, 95, 206–8

Fabius, Laurent, 192
Faisceau, 16
Fatna, Hugette, 165
Fini, Gianfranco, 200–201, 210
Fraternité Française, 169
Frédéric-Dupont, Edouard, 64, 82,
  158
Freedom Party Austria, 195–96,
  209–10
Freulet, Gérard, 221
Front Anti-Chômage, 169
Front National de la Jeunesse (FNJ),
  167
Front National des Combattants, 24,
  147, 162

Gaucher, Roland, 164
Gauchon, Pascal, 44
Gaudin, Jean-Claude, 85, 88, 105
Gaullism, 22, 33–34, 58
Giscard d'Estaing, Valéry, 85, 93
Gollnisch, Bruno, 104, 159, 162–63,
  170
Gonnot, François-Michel, 220
Green Party, 81, 92, 183
Groupe d'Union et de Défense (GUD),
  30–31

Groupement de Commandos Parachutistes de Réserve Générale (GCP), 22
Groupement de Recherches et d'Etudes pour la Civilisation Européenne (GRECE), 28

Haider, Jörg, 195–96, 201, 210
Handlos, Franz, 198–99
Heure de Verité, 76
Holeindre, Roger, 6, 17, 23, 65, 159–61
Husbands, Christopher, 1, 41, 202

Italian Socialist Movement, 31, 36–37, 193–94

Jaffré, Jérôme, 45, 61
Jalkh, Jean-François, 103, 164
Jeunnesses Patriotes, 16–17
Jospin, Lionel, 5, 94, 99–100, 207, 222
Juppé, Alain, 99, 218–19

Kitschelt, Herbert, 71, 131, 202
Kohl, Helmut, 198, 202, 204

Lajoinie, André, 70
Lambert, Hubert, 42
Lambert, Philippe, 42
Lang, Carl, 99, 110, 159, 160, 164, 167
Laval, Pierre, 17–19
Lebfevre, Marcel, 146
Lecanuet, Jean, 26
Le Chevallier, Jean-Marie, 105, 175
Le Gallou, Jean-Yves, 64, 129, 161, 164
Lehideux, Martine, 120, 145, 161, 205
Le Jouaen, Hervé, 7, 82
Léotard, François, 219–20
Le Pen, Jean-Marie, 2–6, 13, 15, 20, 23, 24, 33, 35–36, 42–44, 47–48, 57–58, 62–63, 76–77, 94–95; anti-Semitism of, 19, 89–90, 221; as campaign manager for Tixier-Vignancour, 25–27; leadership role of, 212–16; legislative campaign of, 1997 and, 102–5; maurrassian influences, 15; National Front creation and, 52–53; National Front durability and, 106–8; presidential campaign of 1988, 68–71; presidential campaign of 1995, 97–100; role in elite recruitment, 64–67, 151–55; selected as Front leader, 38–39
Le Pen, Marie-Caroline, 104
Lepénisme, 117, 159, 213
Ligue des Patriotes, 16
Longuet, Gérard, 30

Maastricht Treaty, 95–98
Mainstream right: electoral deals with Front, 3, 47–48, 60–61, 85–89, 104, 221–22; reworking immigration laws and, 101–2, 124; usurping Front's agenda, 48, 93
Marchais, Georges, 63, 175
Maréchal, Samuel, 162
Martinez, Jean-Claude, 64, 67
Mauroy, Pierre, 73
Maurras, Charles, 14–15, 213–14
Mégret, Bruno, 6, 64, 67, 81, 88, 99, 110, 159, 161–64, 170, 175; as 1988 presidential campaign director, 68–71; on European Union, 130–31; on free trade and liberalism, 129–31
Mégret, Catherine, 5, 101, 175
Militer au Front, 110
Milza, Pierre, 38
Mitterrand, François, 3, 41, 44, 66–67, 73, 81, 92, 96
Mouvement Poujade, 11, 13, 19–21, 33, 149
MSI. *See* Italian Socialist Movement

National Alliance, 194, 200–201, 210

National Front: ancien combattant image of, 17, 22–24, 187; anti-Communism and, 29–30; Catholicism and, 13, 145–46; censorship and, 121; Comité Tixier-Vignancour and, 150; creation of, 11–13, 32–39; defined as a fringe movement, 40; democracy and, 203–4, 210–11; durability of, 106–14; economic agenda of, 122, 128–32; electoral breakthrough and, 71–78; European far right movement and, 193–94, 210; European Union and, 130–32, 189–90; homosexuality and, 121; immigration and, 46, 118, 124–27, 134–36; insécurité and, 46, 119–20, 126–27; Islam and, 124–25; leadership succession, 170–71; media and, 54–57, 74–76, 113–14; morality and, 120, 132; nationalism and, 120–21, 132–33; OAS and, 22–25, 150; populist character of, 190–92; pronatalist and anti-abortion position, 18, 120, 127–28, 135; royalists and, 15–16; technology and, 210; United States and, 130, 137; violence and, 203; women and, 145, 165, 187–89; youth and, 145, 182–83, 189–90

New Right, 27–28

Nolte, Ernst, 14

OAS. *See* Organisation de l'Armée Secrète

Occident, 26–31

Olivier, Philippe, 164

Ordre Nouveau, 8, 28, 30–31; creation of the National Front and, 36–41

Organisation de l'Armée Secrete (OAS), 11, 21–24, 150

d'Ormesson, Olivier, 82, 152

Parti des Forces Nouvelles (PFN), 41, 43–44, 156, 182

Party Organization, 107–10; Central Committee, 141, 166; Executive Bureau, 9, 141, 159–64; General Secretariat, 164–64; National Council, 166; National Secretariat, 164–65; Political Bureau, 157–58, 165–67

Pasqua, Charles, 80, 93, 97, 105, 219

Perdomo, Ronald, 88

Perrineau, Pascal, 190

Pétain, Philippe, 17–18

Petitfils, Jean-Christian, 1, 45, 223

Peulvast-Bergeal, Annette, 104

Peyrat, Jacques, 85, 158

Peyron, Albert, 85

Piat, Yann, 6, 81, 84, 87–90, 145, 166

pieds noirs, 21, 26

Pini, Giorgio, 200

Political party development: institutional facilitators, 46–47; life-cycle model, 49–50; political facilitators, 47–49

Political recruitment, 64–67, 142–44

Pompidou, Georges, 42

Porteu de la Morandière, François, 64

Poujade, Pierre, 19–21

Protest voting, 5, 173–74

Pujo, Maurice, 14

Rally for the Republic (RPR), 3, 62, 94, 174

Reagan, Ronald, 129–30, 137

Rémond, René, 17, 20, 205

Renouvin, Bertrand, 43

Republikaner, 193, 198–99

Restauration Nationale, 15–16

Reveau, Jean-Pierre, 159, 161–62

Robert, Alain, 30, 38, 41, 57

Rocard, Michel, 85, 92–94

Roussel, Jean, 64, 87–88

Royer, Jean, 43
RPR. *See* Rally for the Republic

Saenz de Ynestrillas, Ricardo, 194
Salan, General Raoul, 25–26
Schodruch, Hans-Gunter, 194
Schonhüber, Franz, 198
Séguin, Philippe, 219–20
Sergent, Pierre, 23, 166
Sidos, Pierre, 27, 43
Simonpieri, Daniel, 175
Socialist Party, 9, 34–35, 41, 66–67, 74, 81, 92, 94, 96–97, 174, 183
Stirbois, Jean-Pierre, 2, 6, 27, 42, 59–62, 65, 77, 84, 90, 110, 166; European Union and, 131
Stirbois, Marie-France, 60, 90, 95, 145, 170

Thatcher, Margaret, 130, 156
Timmermans, Franck, 164
Tixier-Vignancour, Jean-Louis, 25–28, 69, 150, 176
Touze, Jean-François, 28
Trautmann, Catherine, 105

UDF. *See* Union for French Democracy
Union de Défense des Commerçants et Artisans. *See* Mouvement Poujade
Union du Rassemblement et du Centre (URC), 81, 85, 87–89
Union for French Democracy, 3, 94, 174
Union pour la France, 94

Valois, Georges, 16, 214
Vanhecke, Frank, 194, 197
Vaugeois, Henri, 14
Veil, Simone, 1, 45, 74, 85, 89
Viarengo, Guy, 61
Vichy, 11, 17–19
Vietnam, 21, 23
Vitrolles, 101–2
Vlaams Blok, 197–98, 205, 209
Voigt, Ekkehard, 198–99
vote utile phenomenon, 63, 71–72

Waechter, Antoine, 92
Wagner, Georges-Paul, 6

Ysmal, Colette, 139, 184

Edward G. DeClair is associate professor in the Department of
Political Science, Lynchburg College.

Library of Congress Cataloging-in-Publication Data
DeClair, Edward G.
Politics on the fringe : the people, policies, and organization
of the French National Front / Edward G. DeClair.
p.   cm.
Includes bibliographical references and index.
ISBN 0-8223-2237-4 (hardcover : alk. paper). — ISBN
0-8223-2139-4 (pbk. : alk. paper)
1. Front national (France : 1972–   ) 2. Right-wing
extremists.   I. Title.
JN3007.F68D43   1999
320.944—dc21   98-25265